SOLDIERS OF THE VIRGIN

SOLDIERS OF THE VIRGIN

THE MORAL ECONOMY
OF A COLONIAL MAYA
REBELLION

✝

KEVIN GOSNER

THE UNIVERSITY OF ARIZONA PRESS

TUCSON & LONDON

The University of Arizona Press
Copyright © 1992
The Arizona Board of Regents
All rights reserved

97 96 95 94 93 92   6 5 4 3 2 1

Library of Congress Cataloging-in-Publication Data

Gosner, Kevin, 1951–
    Soldiers of the virgin : the moral economy of a colonial Maya
rebellion / Kevin Gosner.
      p.   cm.
    Includes bibliographical references and index.
    ISBN 0-8165-1293-0 (cloth : acid-free paper)
    1. Tzeltal Indians—Wars. 2. Tzotzil Indians—Wars. 3. Chol
Indians—Wars. 4. Chiapas (Mexico)—History. I. Title.
F1221.T8G67 1992
972'.75—dc20   91-42775
                                                  CIP

British Cataloguing-in-Publication Data
A catalogue record for this book is available from the British Library.

Publication of this book is made possible in part by grants from the
University of Arizona Columbus Quincentenary Program and the
University of Arizona Foundation, and the Provost's Support Fund of
the University of Arizona.

For my father

And there was an even older world beyond the ridges—the ground sloped up again to where a grove of tall black crosses stood at all angles like wind-blown trees against the blackened sky. This was the Indian religion—a dark tormented magic cult. The old ladies might swing back and forth in the rocking chairs of Villahermosa, the Catholics might be dying out "like dogs," but here, in the mountainous strange world of Father Las Casas, Christianity went on its own frightening way. Magic, yes, but we are too apt to minimize the magic element in Christianity— the man raised from the dead, the devils cast out, the water turned into wine. The great crosses leaned there in their black and windy solitude, safe from the pistoleros and the politicians, and one thought of the spittle mixed with the clay to heal the blind man, the resurrection of the body, the religion of the earth.

Graham Greene,
Another Mexico

CONTENTS

TABLES

MAPS

ACKNOWLEDGMENTS

On countless afternoons as an undergraduate at the University of Pennsylvania, I would walk over to the university museum to study in the museum library. To get there I had to pass through the galleries devoted to Andean and Mesoamerican archaeology and meander through the Potlatch restaurant, where groups of graduate students and professors were invariably gathered around cups of coffee, exchanging stories about fieldwork, plotting grant applications, or probing each other for opinions about the work of one scholar or another. They were animated folk, enthusiastic about their discipline, and they seemed like a community worth joining. In the library I often worked in the Daniel Brinton Collection of manuscripts on Native American peoples and browsed among the oversized volumes of old field reports on digs in Guatemala and Mexico. Ultimately I stayed at Penn for my doctoral studies in history and spent many more hours in the university museum. This book is a product of the sensibility nurtured there among the yellowed journals and the coffee drinkers in the Potlatch.

Many teachers, colleagues, and friends have helped me along the way. My biggest debt is to Nancy Farriss, from whom I first learned about colonial Mexico and the Maya. With enormous generosity, enthusiasm, and patience, she shared her own work and guided mine. Her contributions to this study are immeasurable, and its completion is a small return for the many years of support and encouragement she has given me. I also learned a great deal from Anthony F. C. Wallace, whose research seminar in ethnohistory got me started on the Tzeltal and whose gentle advice and criticism shaped my dissertation in important ways. The ethnohistory workshop at Penn proved a steady source of stimulation too. Still thriving, it remains the very model of scholarly collegiality.

The directors and staff of the Archivo General de Centroamérica, the Archivo de las Indias, and the Archivo Histórico Diocesano de San Cristóbal de las Casas enabled me to undertake the research necessary for this study, and grants from the College of Social and Behavioral Sciences of the University of Arizona provided funds for foreign travel and release time from teaching to write. Murdo MacLeod and Jan de Vos gave me good advice when I began my research, and I greatly appreciate their continuing interest in my work. I owe special thanks to Michael C. Meyer and to Richard Welsh, David Weber, Donald Weinstein, and Michael Schaller, all of whom have helped me make and sustain an academic career. Susan Deeds and Hermann Rebel offered valuable critical readings of several chapters, and Rebecca Orozco assisted me in obtaining photocopies of several documents in Guatemala City. Mary Sue Passé-Smith taught me how to use a word processor and prepared the final manuscript. In the last five years, my colleagues in the history department at the University of Arizona have extended steady moral support and warm friendship, especially Donna Guy, Karen Anderson, and (as they are known collectively around our house) "los profesores que bailan." Sincere thanks are due as well to Lee Cassanelli, Christopher Lutz, Leonel Sarazua, Gregório Concha Chet, Jan Rus, Robert Wasserstrom, Susan Schroeder, Matt Micka, and Michael Coleman.

No one has given more to this project than my wife, Margaret, who has been a party to it since the very beginning. For her strength and understanding, I owe a debt that can never be repaid, only forgiven. I am also grateful to the rest of my family—to Linda and Will, to Pamela Gosner, and to the Regans, especially my brother-in-law, Michael, who for some inexplicable reason read my entire dissertation.

This book is dedicated to my father, Kenneth Lynn Gosner. I grew up around books and typewriters, in libraries and museums, and amidst file cabinets of field notes and bottles of "pickled" toads and snakes he had collected for his work as a herpetologist. His stories of expeditions to Venezuela and Guatemala were my introduction to Latin America, and working the seine with him in the marshes of New Jersey at age five was my initiation to serious scholarship. He has taken me to many places to spark my curiosity and to encourage my independence. I have learned more from him than I can say.

SOLDIERS OF THE VIRGIN

I

INTRODUCTION

In August 1712, twenty-one pueblos among the Tzeltal, Tzotzil, and Chol Maya of highland Chiapas gathered in the village of Cancuc and proclaimed, "Ya no hay Dios ni Rey"—"Now there is neither God nor king!" They came together to defend a cult dedicated to the Virgin Mary. Since that June, Spanish authorities had been trying to suppress the cult by harassing its leaders and threatening to burn its chapel. During the next three months the rebels sacked churches and Spanish estates, ordained their own priests, and began to organize a regional government. They killed five Dominican curates, martyred Spanish and mestizo settlers in Chilón and Ocosingo, and successfully held off the provincial militia. When troops were sent from Guatemala, headed by the president of the audiencia himself, 5,000 to 6,000 "soldiers of the Virgin" fought as a single army to defend their religion and their new society. Cancuc finally fell to the Spanish in mid-November, but the revolt was not completely pacified until February of the following year, when the last rebel captains were taken.[1]

For more than a decade, no conference of Latin American historians has been complete without at least one session on Indian revolts or peasant rebellions. The old notion that native peoples were a docile, conservative population, traumatized into political impotency by the shock of the conquest and lulled into passivity by the paternalistic regime of the hacienda has fallen by the wayside. We now recognize that Indians often responded in kind to the violence and brutality of colonial life. Assaults against provincial governors and parish curates, and rioting in small country towns and villages, occurred periodically wherever indigenous peoples survived in significant numbers.

Nonetheless, for its scale and longevity, and for its violence and the self-conscious radicalism of its leaders, the Tzeltal Revolt of 1712 contrasts sharply with other incidents of its kind in colonial Mexico. William Taylor found that in New Spain the more typical forms of agrarian protest were "spontaneous, short-lived outbursts by members of a single community in reaction to threats from the outside; they were 'popular' uprisings in which virtually the entire community acted collectively and usually without identifiable leadership. . . . The rebellious behavior was controlled in the sense that there were few examples of general destruction and pillaging."[2] On all counts, the Cancuc rebellion departs from this archetype. The revolt is also distinctive because it took place well before the upsurge in rural violence that, throughout Spanish America, punctuated the last half century before Independence. After 1750 the spread of commercial agriculture, the bureaucratic reforms of the Bourbons, and cycles of crop failure caused by frost, drought, and locusts combined to erode the political autonomy of indigenous villages, threaten their lands, and increase the demands for their labor. In the Andes, native resistance in this period was marked by dramatic regional insurrections led by Juan Santos Atahualpa in 1742, Tomás Katari in 1777, José Gabriel Condorcanqui in 1780, and Julián Apasa in 1781. However, in New Spain, although the number of incidents of local rioting and assaults on Spanish officials and clergymen increased dramatically after 1760, regional rebellions like the Tzeltal Revolt still were exceedingly rare, and none were on the scale of the neo-Inca movements of Peru.

Among Mexicanists and Andeanists alike, the recent historiography of colonial Indian rebellions reflects the broader research agenda that has dominated colonial Latin American history since the mid-1960s.[3] In one way or another, implicitly and explicitly, social and economic historians have been preoccupied with questions about the emergence of capitalism. They have reexamined the concept of feudalism and its applicability to social, economic, and political structures in the sixteenth century; they have studied the links between local economies in the Indies and the trans-Atlantic trade with western Europe; they have debated whether economic systems are defined by the structure of markets or the organization of production; and they have tested the utility of class as an organizing principle in social relations against the criteria of race, ethnicity, and caste, which an earlier generation argued were more significant.

With these issues in mind, most historians who have studied agrarian protest have taken a materialist perspective and have concentrated on the economic conditions that promoted discontent among indigenous peasants and other rural laborers, and the political circumstances that frustrated Spanish efforts to end episodes of violence quickly. Their temporal focus has been almost exclusively on the late eighteenth century. In the current periodization, the year 1750 marks the beginning of a distinct new phase in the evolution of politics and the economy, a phase that culminated a century later in the emergence of repressive liberal regimes like that of Porfirio Díaz in Mexico and Justo Rufino Barrios in Guatemala and, throughout the hemisphere, the consolidation of export-oriented economies designed to meet market demands created by the Industrial Revolution in Europe and North America. In this context, late colonial Indian revolts and peasant rebellions have generally been seen as early responses to the social and political tensions generated by these new efforts to centralize the state and commercialize the rural economy, foreshadowings of the class struggles that have overwhelmed the region since the late nineteenth century.

For scholars who study Native Americans, this literature reflects a shift of interest away from the cultural characteristics that defined indigenous peoples as distinctive ethnic groups. The new emphasis is instead on the structural arrangements of work, property holding, and market participation that defined their place in the larger economy. Since Charles Gibson's pioneering study *The Aztecs Under Spanish Rule*, new research has focused on local land tenure patterns, changes in village agriculture and craft production, the organization of Indian wage labor, the material impact of the tribute system and the *repartimientos de mercancías*, and the entrepreneurial activities of the native nobility and commoners.[4] We have learned a lot about the intricacies of regional variation and the subtleties of periodization, and we have gained a more sophisticated understanding of how race and ethnic consciousness articulated with early glimmerings of class consciousness. In the process, however, we have risked stereotyping indigenous societies as generic peasantries and have often overlooked the distinctive features of their cultures that often shaped local and regional responses to colonial rule.

In his introduction to the edited volume *Resistance, Rebellion, and Consciousness in the Andean Peasant World*, Steve Stern cautions readers that "studies of peasant rebellion should treat peasant consciousness as problematic rather than predictable, should pay particular attention to the 'culture history' of the area under study, and should discard notions of the inherent parochialism and defensiveness of peasants."[5] The Tzeltal Revolt invites just such an effort. The Cancuc rebels articulated a radical vision of a new society. They chose new leaders, constructed new institutions, elaborated new rituals, and created new myths. While they wanted to be rid of Spanish authority, they also hoped to revitalize social and political relations within and among their own communities. Along the way, they confronted disagreements and conflicts among themselves that reveal a good deal about the social experience of village life, and the symbols they invoked tell us much about the ideas and values that framed their understanding of that experience. Only by linking a study of the material causes of the rebellion to the culture history of the highland Maya can we begin to understand these complexities.

The concept of moral economy offers a useful framework for exploring this link. E. P. Thompson fixed the term in the lexicon of social science in an essay on food riots in eighteenth-century England, "The Moral Economy of the English Crowd in the Eighteenth Century." In it he wrote:

> It is of course true that riots were triggered off by soaring prices, by malpractices among dealers, or by hunger. But these grievances operated within a popular consensus as to what were legitimate and what were illegitimate practices in marketing, milling, baking, etc. This in its turn was grounded upon a consistent traditional view of social norms and obligations, of the proper economic functions of several parties within the community, which, taken together, can be said to constitute the moral economy of the poor. An outrage to these moral assumptions, quite as much as actual deprivation, was the usual occasion for direct action.[6]

Thompson argued that rioters took action to protest not simply high prices for bread but more fundamentally the loss of a paternalist model of the market that in the past had enabled the government, by custom and law, to regulate grain sales and prices during periods of shortage. At stake were traditional assumptions about the moral obligations of government toward the poor, assumptions that were disappearing with the emergence of a new political economy at the end of the eighteenth century.

The concept of moral economy achieved wider currency with the publication of James Scott's *The Moral Economy of the Peasant: Rebellion and Subsistence in Southeast Asia.* One of Scott's purposes was to explain why peasants, not proletarians, most often provided the "shock troops of rebellion and revolu-tion" in former colonial territories.[7] Toward that end, Scott insisted that the focus of research had to shift away from causation and toward the cultural construction of peasant consciousness. He argued this especially forcefully in his essay "Protest and Profanation: Agrarian Revolt and the Little Tradition":

> First, far too much scholarly labor has been expended on the precipitants of peasant rebellion and far too little on the shared values and goals which find expression through rebellion. We need to know more about why peasants rebel than we can learn from statistics of taxes, harvests, and hunger. Sec-ond, it seems clear that compared with, say, the proletariat, the political culture of the peasantry is strongly influenced by factors which are not purely a consequence of its relationship to the means of production. To put it somewhat differently, the proletariat has to create its class subculture in a new environment while the peasantry, like traditional artisans, inherits a greater residue of custom, community, and values, which influences its behavior.[8]

This perspective drove the conceptual framework of Scott's book, and from his study of early-twentieth-century peasant rebellions in Burma and Viet-nam he concluded:

> Woven into the tissue of peasant behavior, then, whether in normal local routines or in the violence of an uprising, is the structure of a shared moral universe, a common notion of what is just. It is this moral heritage that, in peasant revolts, selects certain targets rather than others, certain forms rather than others, and that makes possible a collective (though rarely coor-dinated) action born of moral outrage. . . .
>
> How, then, can we understand the moral passion that is so obviously an integral part of the peasant revolts we have described? How can we grasp the peasant's sense of social justice? We can begin, I believe, with two moral principles that seem firmly embedded in both the social patterns and injunc-tions of peasant life: the *norm of reciprocity* and the *right to subsistence* (Italics in original).[9]

Scott's analysis derived from a broad reading of the comparative literature on peasantries and owed something to the social anthropology of Mexico and Guatemala. Though none of them actually used the term *moral economy*, Robert Redfield, George Foster, and Eric Wolf had all articulated views of peasant values and social relations that also emphasized the social imperative of reciprocity and the economic charge to secure subsistence.[10]

Among anthropologists and historians, Wolf's model of the closed corporate peasant community has been the driving paradigm of most studies of Mesoamerican native societies for three decades. In recent years the paradigm has been revised and refocused as consensual models of culture and social relations—functionalism's legacy in American anthropology—have given way to conflict models influenced by world-system and dependency theory, and by other materialist approaches in social science. Wolf's own later work, especially *Europe and the People Without History*, has contributed significantly to this process. In 1986, in an essay entitled "The Vicissitudes of the Closed Corporate Peasant Community," he acknowledged the model's "most patent shortcomings" and discussed how the original formulation had been misread by some. Among his comments were these:

> It was still a history that relied primarily on Spanish sources—written from the top down, as it were—and not enough on accounts representing the point of view of the conquered or written in the native languages. This led to a disregard of territorial entities and kinship structures intermediate between household and community, as well as to a disregard of connective networks among people in communities, networks other than those of the market. . . . Beyond these shortcomings, however, lies a more serious problem, the fact and nature of conflicts internal to the corporate communities. . . . Finally, much new material has accumulated on systems of symbolic action in such communities. The boundary between "Indians" and non-Indians has never been static, but rather an arena contested by people on both sides of the labor reserve and internal colony. . . . What we have not yet done systematically is to look at the multiplicity of symbolic actions as ideology, as expressions of different interests and aspirations embodied in cultural forms.[11]

While it is directed to the debate on closed corporate peasant communities, Wolf's self-critique also speaks to a revisionist perspective on the peasant moral economy. Like Wolf's paradigm, Scott's conceptualization of peasant values has been criticized for idealizing rural social and cultural life, for understating the degree of contention and conflict among peasants of unequal rank or status, and for underestimating the willingness of individuals to pursue their own self-interest. As a result, much recent work on the moral economy of peasantries in colonial Latin America has emphasized how the articulation of social norms, the principle of reciprocity, and the symbolic expression of community values mediated not only relations between Indians and Spaniards but also inequalities among Indians themselves. Steve Stern, for example, has cast the social and cultural dynamics of highland communities, in both Mesoamerica and the Andes, as a "struggle for solidarity."[12] He outlines how political alliances between indigenous elites and colonial administrators, and the gradual commercialization of the rural economy, sharpened rank divisions within native societies and contributed to incipient class formation. To counterbalance these developments, he argues, communities created mechanisms like the civil-religious cargo system to promote social integration and to articulate an ethos that valued cooperation and local solidarity. In the same vein, Eric Van Young has written of "conflict and solidarity" in Indian villages in the hinterland around Guadalajara, Mexico, during the late eighteenth century.[13] Citing Lewis Coser and Max Gluckman, among others, on the integrating function of conflict, Van Young argues that the native elites' efforts to arbitrate relations with outsiders, particularly with Spanish *hacendados* in disputes over land, offset growing community resentment about their wealth and political privileges.[14]

The settings for both Stern's and Van Young's work—Huamanga and Guadalajara—were highly commercialized zones where local *kurakas* and *caciques* had become substantially Hispanicized by the eighteenth century. By comparison, in the decades before and immediately after the rebellion, Chiapas was a poor, undercommercialized province in which caciques had disappeared from all but a few prosperous towns in the Grijalva Valley. Nonetheless, the Tzeltal, Tzotzil, and Chol Maya, as well as the Zoque and Chiapaneco, all confronted sharp divisions based on unequal rank and status within their local populations, divisions that, as elsewhere, were exacerbated by the political and economic consequences of colonization. Their moral economy, too, functioned to mediate inequalities that existed both among themselves and in their relations with Spanish authorities. It, too, defined community norms about reciprocity between village authorities and townspeople, about the minimum requirements for subsistence, and about acceptable levels of outside demands for tribute and labor.

The construction of these values was a dialectical process that set native custom against constraints imposed by colonial administrators and outside economic forces. In this context, norms of reciprocity were constantly being renegotiated between the two sides as conditions changed. Given social inequalities among the Maya themselves, these norms also were often contested by groups and individuals within communities who held competing interests. Because of both these factors, the effort to sustain the moral economy always held the potential for conflict and often set in motion strategies of resistance. Consequently, the Maya moral economy revealed as strong a preoccupation with local political autonomy and legitimacy as with the security of subsistence. Further, because community values and codes of conduct were articulated through myth and ritual, a defense of the moral economy often took the form of a defense of community religious practice. For the Maya, moral economy was embedded in beliefs about the supernatural—about the interdependence of humankind and the gods, about the omnipresence of spirits, about the sacred character of the natural world, about the potency of visions, and about the efficacy of ritual. In other words, the Maya moral economy extended beyond their concerns as peasants to encompass the cultural and spiritual preoccupations that defined their identity as a distinctive ethnic group. This premise is fundamental to an understanding of the religious idioms invoked by the rebels in Cancuc, and it speaks to a dimension of peasant political culture in colonial Mexico that has not been well studied. It also extends the concept of moral economy beyond the secular contexts emphasized by E. P. Thompson and James Scott.

Since native elites played such key roles in the dynamic between community solidarity and community conflict, they are a major focus of this book. Their legitimacy depended not only on how effectively they managed contact with colonial authorities but also on how capably they fulfilled their ritual obligations and how convincingly they tapped traditional ideas about the supernatural origins of secular power. The Tzeltal Revolt began as a conspiracy among dissident Maya *principales*, who mobilized to redefine and revitalize the moral economy by endorsing a new religious cult. Their goals were both to offer a better defense of the material interests of their communities and to preserve their own rank and privileges during a period when the economic demands of colonialism were intensifying and when new initiatives by Spanish authorities threatened various forms of community worship.

As anyone who has studied agrarian revolt can attest, peasants and other rural poor have rarely lacked cause for taking up arms. Often the puzzle is not why peasants rebel but why they do not. In 1712, native peoples throughout Chiapas were subject to similar economic pressures and similar forms of outside intrusion, yet only a relatively small proportion of them mobilized to support the rebels in Cancuc. To explore why this was true, the present study takes a long view of the history of the province and emphasizes regional contrasts in economic and political development that were rooted in the commercial and subsistence potential of local ecologies. These contrasts, as chapter 2 outlines, appeared early in the history of Chiapas, centuries before the arrival of Europeans. A long view also promotes a better understanding of the construction of a postconquest moral economy. This was a gradual process marked by interesting periods of experimentation, adaptation, and resistance. To place the Tzeltal Revolt in this larger context of postconquest Maya culture history, the story must begin, as it does in chapters 3 and 4, with the sixteenth century.

Readers familiar with work on the Tzeltal Revolt by Herbert Klein, Robert Wasserstrom, Victoria Reifler Bricker, Severo Martínez Peláez, André Saint-Lu, and Antonio García de Leon may wonder what the present study has to contribute. This is the first book-length treatment of the rebellion, and the first to lend equal weight to the history of the revolt and its political, economic, and cultural causes. To that end, it is the first to draw widely and comprehensively from all three of the principal archives with holdings on colonial Chiapas: the Archivo General de Centroamérica in Guatemala, the Archivo Histórico Diocesano in San Cristóbal de las Casas, Mexico, and the Archivo de las Indias in Seville. Beyond the scale of the work, its account of regional mobilization, the structure of political authority at Cancuc, and the role of local elites during the rebellion differs in important ways from the renderings of Klein, Wasserstrom, and Bricker. I have reevaluated the role of the rebel bishop, Sebastián Gómez de la Gloria, identified for the first time the original circle of conspirators, and examined more closely the social origins of rebel captains. I argue that the extent of regional participation has been exaggerated and that the consolidation of authority by Cancuc's leaders has been overstated, The view presented here of the economic conditions that provoked the rebellion departs from the world-systems perspectives offered by Wasserstrom, Martínez Peláez, and García de Leon. A focus on contrasts in regional development within the province, and on contrasts between seventeenth- and eighteenth-century economic history, suggests that the material forces that pushed the Tzeltal toward insurrection derived more from the weak commercial potential of the highlands and from the depressed condition of the market in and around Ciudad Real than from the integration of the *altiplano* into an Atlantic system linked to markets in Europe. As outlined above, the following chapters also extend the analysis of causation beyond strict material factors to include cultural contexts and religious beliefs. While Edward Calnek touched upon these topics in his thesis some thirty years ago, among recent scholars only Wasserstrom has explored them in any depth.

Fortunately, the volume and variety of material available to scholars concerning the rebellion, and the Maya generally, make a detailed study of its complexities possible and positively invite competing interpretations. Along with more than a hundred pages in the important contemporary chronicle *Historia de la provincia de San Vicente de Chiapa y Guatemala*, completed by Fray Francisco Ximénez in 1720, four long *legajos*, comprising some 6,000 pages, can be found in the Archivo de las Indias. The legajos include letters from Dominican friars, provincial bishops, and Crown officials, trial testimony and confessions from hundreds of the participants themselves, and reports to the Royal Council that give precise accounts of the uprising and the campaign to end it. In addition, a lengthy syllabus of ethnography on the highland Maya of Chiapas makes studying the cultural context of the rebellion all the more compelling. Perhaps no indigenous people anywhere in the New World has been so scrutinized by outsiders as the Tzotzil of Zinacantán and Chamula. Since the 1950s, first with the University of Chicago's Man-in-Nature Project, and later with the Harvard Chiapas Project, anthropologists have produced a steady stream of monographs on everything from Maya curing ceremonies and the persistence of the 260-day calendar to the changing ecology of *milpa* agriculture and the politics of civil and religious officeholding.[15] This literature provides a rich source of descriptive information and a variety of provocative hypotheses about continuities and changes in Maya culture and social life. Any attempt to reconstruct the moral economy of the colonial Maya would be impossible without it.

To conclude this introduction, let me offer a final caveat. In thinking and writing about the culture history of a native people, especially the Maya, the historian must be wary of certain hazards. The temptation to romanticize and to attribute a kind of timelessness to Maya culture is almost irresistible, but to talk of cultural survivals or continuities with the distant past is to risk putting a happy face on a history characterized by violence, disease, hunger, and killing poverty. Today nearly a million Maya live in Chiapas and four million in neighboring Guatemala. Most still speak their own native tongue, and many are *costumbristas* who consult village shamans and continue to worship their ancestors or their old gods at household and community shrines. For many visitors to Chiapas, their first look at the Maya is of zinacanteco farmers along the highway to San Cristóbal, whose iridescent tunics and beribboned straw hats sparkle in the gray fog that often envelops their fields. From a distance, their settlements, especially the smaller ones, seem bucolic, nestled in the quiet pine forests, with smoke rising from cooking fires and sheep grazing on the hillsides nearby. Tzotzil and Tzeltal women still wear finely embroidered *huipiles*, and until ten years ago, men from the outlying villages could still be seen in the city market bare-legged and in distinctive wrapped drawers of white cotton. These images of pastoral serenity are unreal, of course. The highland Maya are starved for land and food. They suffer from endemic hepatitis and tuberculosis. Their men are forced to work for meager wages on the commercial farms around Tuxtla. When they have tried to colonize vacant lands nearer the valley, they have been evicted by the Mexican army as squatters. Today political affairs in rural Chiapas are under the jurisdiction of the military, and relations between the Maya and the federal government bear little resemblance to the progressive corporatism envisioned by postrevolutionary *agraristas* and proponents of *indigenismo*.[16] Even these conditions are far better than those in neighboring Guatemala, but as peasant militancy intensifies among the Tzotzil and Tzeltal, and fears of an active insurgency grow in Mexico City, violence on both sides seems likely to escalate.[17]

The highland Maya nearly vanished after the Spanish conquest and have lived with political repression and poverty ever since. Their material culture and their values and ideas about the world reflect that experience. Among them, tradition (*costumbre*) is not an immutable artifact from the past but something that has been reshaped and altered as the people of each generation have reexamined their own history, struggled to construct their own identity, and fought to defend their way of life. The Tzeltal Revolt offers a dramatic and vivid manifestation of this extraordinarily complex process.

ENVIRONMENT AND EARLY HISTORY

At half past five, after a toilsome ascent, we reached the
top of the mountain, and rode along the borders of a
table of land several thousand feet high, looking down
into an immense valley, and turning to the left, around
the corner of the forest, entered the outskirts of
Tumbala. The huts were distributed among high,
rugged, and picturesque rocks, which had the
appearance of having once formed the center of a
volcano. . . . Altogether it was the wildest and most
extraordinary place we had yet seen.
— John Lloyd Stephens[1]

Right behind Sivacá the trail stands up on end to climb
the first of a series of ramparts that lie like a defense
about the highland country. It was very much like
trying to ride up a gutter on the side of a house. . . .
We pushed and pulled and tugged. There was the usual
repetition of fallen horses and packs to be put on again.
Thus for two hours, slipping and scrambling, until at
last we came to a level place where an old wooden cross,
decorated with offerings of flowers marked the top of
the pass— 1,660 meters, 600 meters (about 1,900 feet)
above Ocosingo.
— Frans Blom and Oliver LaFarge[2]

Geologists describe the central highlands of Chiapas prosaically as a plateau
of cretaceous limestone fractured by fault-line scarps into a rough terrain of
steep ridges and upland valleys. The plateau covers some 7,000 square
kilometers of pine and oak forest extending northeast from the Grijalva
River to the borders of Tabasco to the north and the Petén to the east. San
Cristóbal de las Casas, the current name of the old colonial capital of Ciudad

Real, lies in the highest zone on the plateau. Just north of the city are the summits of Cerro Zontehuitz, at 2,858 meters, and El Huitepec, at 2,660 meters. Heights diminish to between 1,000 and 1,500 meters to the northeast near Ocosingo and to the southeast toward Comitán. This is *tierra fría*, cold country. During the dry season—roughly from November through April—a crisp, clear winter night can bring freezing temperatures. In the summer and early fall, rainfall is heavy (especially in June and September), the upper reaches of the mountains are engulfed in fog banks, and the air is often damp and chilly. The climate supports only one harvest a year.

THE CENTRAL HIGHLANDS BEFORE THE CONQUEST

The archaeological record of the plateau shows that it has always been a poor, underpopulated region on the margins of larger, more complex societies that have developed in the adjacent lowlands.[3] Humans first came to the highlands around 14,000 B.C. They were nomadic hunters and gatherers who camped near small lakes in the lower valleys. José Luis Lorenzo and Arturo Guevara Sánchez have studied several of these sites near Teopisca and Aquacatenango.[4] The transition to agriculture, larger settled communities, and higher forms of political organization was long, slow, and undramatic. Ceramic and architectural remains for the Preclassic period (1500–200 B.C.) are remarkably scarce. The earliest ceremonial centers, of which only thirteen have been found, date from 600 B.C. Their earthen terraces and stone foundations are situated near the rivers and arroyos of the valleys southwest of San Cristóbal and Comitán. The largest is Solferín on the eastern edge of the plateau.[5] None compares with sites like Kaminaljuyú in highland Guatemala, El Mirador in the Petén, and Cerros on the Caribbean coast of Belize, which all feature massive pyramids and elaborate stone carvings.

After 200 B.C. the pace of change began to quicken in the highlands, leavened by the florescence of Maya civilization in the lowlands to the east. Migrants from the Petén, motivated by population growth, commercial expansion, and warfare, moved into Chiapas during the Early Classic period. They built fortified settlements on hillsides above the valley floors, close to sinkholes that assured water in the dry season and high up so that they could be defended more easily against aggressive neighbors.[6] Most of their sites, including Chincultic, El Cerrito, Yerbabuena, Cerro Campanatón, and Rancho

Map 2.1. Southern Mesoamerica

San Nicolás, were to the southeast. They consisted of a single pyramid surrounded by smaller buildings with masonry walls, and terraced fields for intensive agriculture. The number of sites was still relatively small, and few featured the architectural details associated with public ritual at the larger lowland centers. Only one date marker has been found in the highlands proper for this period, in the small ballcourt at La Esperanza.[7] T. Patrick Culbert has reported that examples of trade goods from outside the highlands rarely appear in the Kan-phase ceramics of this period and that Maya polychrome styles developed elsewhere at this time are not found here.[8] All of this suggests that these were rustic frontier settlements, still very much on the margins of the Maya world.

But local populations grew, and after A.D. 400 new waves of Maya immigrants arrived from the Río Nentón area of the Cuchumatanes and from the Petén just west of the Usumacinta River. The Tojolabal moved into the valley east of Comitán, while the Tzeltal spread throughout the highlands from the higher reaches west of Ocosingo to the valley southeast of San Cristóbal.[9] During this dispersal the Tzotzil language emerged among the inhabitants of the central zone of the plateau as a language distinct from Tzeltal.

By the Late Classic period, between A.D. 700 and 1000, the highlands achieved its widest occupation as older sites were rebuilt and expanded and new settlements were created. More than fifty urban centers date from this period, including Moxviquil, Ecatepec, Tenam Puente, and Chincultic. The largest was Yerbabuena, near Aquacatenango. Like their Preclassic antecedents, their locations afforded protection in time of war. Virtually all were built on steep promontories overlooking valleys well suited to agriculture and with stone walls or terraced platforms added to enhance their defenses. Site patterns were in the style of Maya ceremonial centers elsewhere. A series of raised level platforms supported complexes of masonry buildings, with open plazas dominated by one or more pyramids. All of the sites included an I-shaped ballcourt. Dated monuments were now common. They were grander than anything that had preceded them but still small and simple by lowland standards. In contrast to the impressive stone and masonry craftsmanship found at lowland centers like Palenque and Tikal, the buildings themselves had very little decorative detailing, and public sculptures and monuments were in low relief.

To Robert M. Adams, the relatively small impact of artistic stylings from the core area of Maya civilization suggested that the central highlands remained on the periphery of major Late Classic trade routes and were beyond the political ambitions of powerful Maya kings in the lowlands.[10] The rarity of Fine Orange pottery, common among Maya peoples almost everywhere else at this time, reinforces his conclusion. This is not to say that the plateau was entirely isolated. Obsidian, amber, quetzal feathers, and salt from Chiapas found their way to markets outside the region, since the sources of supply for these goods were limited in southern Mesoamerica.[11] But the volume of this trade was apparently not great enough truly to integrate the highlands into broader regional networks.

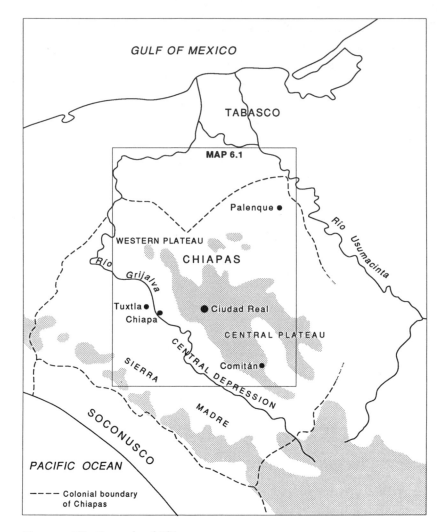

Map 2.2. The Geography of Chiapas

The history of the Early Postclassic period in highland Chiapas also points to its relative isolation. By about A.D. 900 the great metropolises of the Classic Maya—Tikal, Copán, Palenque, Quirigúa, Yaxchilán, Piedras Negras, and Bonampak—had all been abandoned, climaxing more than a century of gradual decline.[12] The Terminal Classic, as the period is so aptly named, was a time of warfare and revolt, economic collapse, and enormous loss of life. But the Maya in Chiapas escaped this apocalypse. In fact, the vitality of the Late Classic period continued until well after A.D. 1000, especially in the southwest, and little in the archaeological record of the plateau distinguishes the Late Classic from the Early Postclassic. However, by the mid thirteenth century, decline had set in here as well. The reasons for it are no more clear than they are for the lowland centers, but the symptoms were similar. At first, cruder, less finely crafted ceramics replaced earlier, more sophisticated forms, and dated stone monuments were no longer erected. Then smaller sites were gradually depopulated. Finally, the large urban settlements in the southeastern valleys near Teopisca and Aquacatenango, like Yerbabuena and Cerro Chavín, were abandoned. After A.D. 1250, very few new centers thrived. Two that did were at San Gregorio in the Río Tzaconeja Valley east of San Cristóbal, and at Copanaguastla along the Río San Vicente near the southeastern limits of the plateau.[13] The size and location of these sites suggested to Adams that populations were moving out of the smaller valleys into the larger basins and coming under the political domination of incipient native states, which were often at war with one another. The ceramic inventory of the period is marked by the emergence of distinctive local styles, a change that Culbert views as consistent with Adams's theory and indicative of the hardening of political boundaries.[14]

On the borders of highland Chiapas, the war-ridden character of Postclassic times has been attributed not only to the breakdown of the old Classic-period kingdoms but also to the expansionist ambitions of Toltec peoples from central Mexico and various groups of "Mexicanized" Mayas from the river deltas of the Grijalva and Usumacinta in Tabasco, known collectively as the Putun.[15] Beginning in the late tenth century, architectural styles and iconographic motifs throughout southern Mesoamerica reflected strong influence from central Mexico. Images of foreign warriors became commonplace, and the symbols of new religious cults, especially the feathered serpent associated with Quetzalcóatl, proliferated. Toltec expansion was also associated with the widespread distribution of a new ceramic style, plumbate ware, a glazed monochrome pottery that often incorporated effigies of humans or animals. Cultural influences did not flow in a single direction, however, and some of the finest achievements of Toltec-era art and architecture in central Mexico reveal the lessons of Maya craftsmen, especially the stelae at Tula carved in high relief.[16]

Among the Maya, the most famous site associated with this period is Chichén Itzá in northern Yucatán. A Late Classic Puuc site, Chichén was conquered by a Putun group known as the Itzá early in the tenth century, and it became the capital of a new kingdom that extended across the peninsula. Because Yucatec Maya chronicles of this period in the *Books of the Chilam Balam* record the arrival of Toltec warriors here in A.D. 987 (a date that coincides with the expulsion of the great king and culture hero Topíltzin-Quetzalcóatl from Tula), archaeologists once accepted that the florescence of Chichén Itzá was the consequence of an alliance between the Itzá and these foreign invaders. That view has been substantially altered in the last decade, however.[17] Doubters have not been entirely won over, but many scholars now believe that Chichén Itzá was developed solely by the Itzá themselves and that its history is representative of a cyclical process of emigration, conquest, and assimilation carried out by Putun Mayas from Tabasco and southern Campeche (a region then known as Chontalpa) that began in the last years of the Classic period.

The earliest evidence for this process dates from around A.D. 800, first at the Altar de Sacrificios and then at Seibal, sites on the Río Pasión, a tributary of the Usumacinta in the Petén. New ceramic and architectural styles, and carved images of Mexican deities and rulers with unmistakably foreign faces, testify to military conquest. Two remarkable sites from the same period in central Mexico itself, Xochicalco and Cacaxtla, reveal that the Putun Maya even made forays outside the Maya zone.[18] Xochicalco has carved images of Maya figures, a ballcourt like the one at Copán, and niche stelae like those of Piedras Negras. Cacaxtla features a stucco mural, worked in a Maya style, that depicts both Maya and Mexican warriors.

As the history of Chichén reveals, the rise of the Toltecs later in the tenth century did not deter Putun ambitions. The Itzá and other Maya groups in Tabasco were able to parlay their trade contacts with central Mexico and their conversion to the cult of Quetzalcóatl into a political alliance with Tula that furthered their expansion into the Maya lowlands. While the Itzá built their kingdom at Chichén, other Putun groups moved up into the headwaters of the Usumacinta and Motagua rivers.[19] A number of sites in this region are modeled after settlement patterns at Chichén Itzá and feature Fine

Orange ceramic ware of Gulf Coast manufacture. Some Putun settled in the highlands themselves, most notably at Chuitinamit on the shores of Lake Atitlán.[20]

After the overthrow of the Itzá lord at Chichén Itzá in A.D. 1221, a new series of Putun initiatives was undertaken in the Maya highlands. The *Popol Vuh*, the *Annales of the Cakchiquel*, and the *Memorial de Tecpán Atitlán*, as well as other native chronicles, all tell of the arrival of small bands of warriors around A.D. 1250.[21] They were said to have been commissioned to carry out their conquests by the rulers of Tulan, the legendary seat of Toltec power (the historical Tula), and to have come to the highlands after a long, arduous journey from the Gulf Coast. They conquered local peoples, built fortified settlements in a central Mexican style, and introduced new forms of political organization and public ritual. But theirs was not an army of occupation. The sources say they came in small numbers and without women. They built on their initial military victories by forming alliances with native highlanders and by intermarrying with the local nobility to form new ruling lineages. In the process, they assimilated much of indigenous highland culture, including Maya languages native to the region, like Quiché, Cakchiquel, and Tzutujil. By the fourteenth century these interlopers had established four kingdoms, which corresponded to the principal language groups—Quiché, Cakchiquel, Rabinal, and Tzutujil—and were loosely confederated under the most powerful of them, the Quiché. Around A.D. 1400 the Quiché moved their capital to Utatlán and, through military conquest, established their supremacy within the old confederation. By midcentury the Quiché controlled virtually all of the western highlands, but a successful revolt by the Cakchiquel in 1470 ended their hegemony.

As Adams outlined, native peoples in highland Chiapas also were moving into newly fortified settlements during the Late Postclassic, and statelike systems of political organization may have been emerging at the very time that similar changes were taking place in nearby Guatemala. But the extent to which these developments were a consequence of Putun expeditions into Chiapas remains uncertain. Writing in the early 1960s, before the impact of Mexicanized Mayas during the Postclassic period was widely recognized, both Adams and Culbert emphasized that central Mexican influence was notably absent in the architectural and ceramic record of the period, and both concluded that, as in earlier eras, the plateau remained marginal to political developments in neighboring regions. Little archaeological work has been done since then in the highlands proper that challenges this view.

But a year after Adams published the results of his reconnaissance, Edward Calnek, an archaeologist and ethnohistorian from the University of Chicago, offered an alternative view of Postclassic history in which a Putun group figured very prominently.[22] Calnek based his reconstruction on a careful comparison of details included in a seventeenth-century Maya genealogy from highland Chiapas, the *Probranza de Votán*, with additional information from ethnohistorical sources on Yucatán and the Usumacinta basin.[23] The *Probranza* recorded the origins of a noble lineage, the Votán, whose founder Calnek identified as having been born on Cozumel, an island off the coast of Yucatán known to have been a base of Putun operations since Late Classic times. The lineage's namesake was said to have circumnavigated the peninsula and to have journeyed into Chiapas by way of the Laguna de Términos and the Usumacinta River. He established a capital, known as Nachan, in the lowlands just below Tumbalá and from there extended his authority into the plateau and even as far as Soconusco. The *Probranza* also tells of the arrival of a second group, identified in Tzeltal as the Tzequil, who spoke a central Mexican language. Votán was said to have ceded control of a portion of the highlands to the Tzequil in return for their recognition of his ultimate authority. On the basis of linguistic comparisons, Calnek surmised that these events were roughly contemporaneous with the founding of the Acalán state on the borders of Chiapas in Tabasco, which would place them in the mid fourteenth century.

For the Tzeltal and Tzotzil, the legacy of Votán's conquest, as Calnek discusses it, was similar to that of the Putun invasions among the Quiché and Cakchiquel. Various central Mexican rituals and symbols were integrated into the iconography and religious practices of the highlands; political authority came to be legitimated by association with one of the founding Putun lineages; Nahuat loan words entered the local lexicon; and Nahuat place names were substituted for indigenous Maya ones. The question, of course, is why this incursion, which seems to have had such a wide-ranging political and cultural impact, did not leave a greater impression on the archaeological record. This has troubled Mayanists working on the Quiché as well, though a richer trove of ethnohistorical sources for Guatemala has enabled them to corroborate information from different texts and thus to put together a more detailed and convincing scenario.[24] Recent studies by John Fox, Dwight Wallace, and others also have begun to reconcile seeming contradictions between the archaeology and the ethnohistory.[25] Unfortunately, comparable work has not been undertaken for Chiapas, and the conclusions of Adams and Culbert remain at odds with those of Calnek.

Nevertheless, the new scholarship on the Putun diaspora, as it has come to be called, has thrown the weight of evidence in Calnek's favor. The parallels with events in neighboring regions are simply inescapable, although the work on the Quiché suggests ways in which Calnek's historical reconstruction is likely to be revised. Toltec-inspired origin accounts are notorious for telescoping chronology, and genealogies often obscure local history by invoking archetypal links to the mythic rulers of Tulan. In Guatemala, archaeological discoveries over the last decade have shown that the Putun migrations and conquests were carried out over a longer period than once was thought and that the political consolidation of the Quiché state was a more gradual and complex process. In light of this, Calnek may have read the *Probranza de Votán* too literally, and he seems likely to have attributed too much to a single incursion. Future archaeological studies may well show that the Putun influenced the history of the Chiapas highlands as early as the Late Classic period. It is also true that they may not have done so, of course, and the possibility cannot yet be ruled out that developments in the southern zone of the plateau during the Postclassic were, as Adams and Culbert concluded, largely independent of both the Toltecs and their Putun allies.

The history of the last century before the Spanish conquest can be told with somewhat more certainty. At contact the highland Maya were organized into small chiefdoms, or *cacicazgos*, ruled by hereditary nobles.[26] Chamula, one of the more prominent of the chiefdoms, was said by Bernal Díaz del Castillo to have consisted of about 800 houses.[27] These communities traded among themselves, but their relations were often less than amicable. Warfare was common, and a few of the towns periodically tried to exert control over their neighbors. The most prosperous of them was Zinacantán, a Tzotzil settlement on the southwestern corner of the plateau. Zinacantecos controlled salt beds near Ixtapa and were active in local commerce between the highlands and the Grijalva Valley.[28] The Florentine Codex reveals that the Mexica or Aztecs sent traders there to acquire amber, skins, and bird feathers, especially those of the quetzal,[29] and Moctezuma Xocoyótzin briefly stationed a garrison in Zinacantán to secure a highland route to Soconusco, a Mexica tributary state and an important supplier of cacao. But the highlands were never conquered by Tenochtitlán, and Mexica texts characterize the region as a dangerous, hostile frontier.

NEIGHBORS TO THE WEST

While the Mayas of the central plateau were poor, politically fragmented, and marginal to major Mesoamerican systems of trade during most of their early history, their neighbors in the lowlands just to the west were not. They too would be included in the Spanish province of San Vicente de Chiapa, but their early history was quite different.

The Central Depression is a deep valley that separates the highlands from the Sierra Madre, an imposing chain of very tall mountains, some over 4,000 meters high, that formed the southern border of Chiapas during the colonial period. The Grijalva River drains this basin, flowing from its headwaters in Guatemala to the Gulf coast of Tabasco. The colonial town of Chiapa de Indios (now Chiapa de Corzo) is located where the river breaks through the western corner of the central plateau. One of the longest ceramic sequences in all of Mesoamerica, with debris dating from about 6700 B.C., is found here.[30] That record reveals commercial links, beginning in Preclassic times, that extended to Oaxaca, the Gulf Coast, Campeche, and eastward to the highlands of Guatemala and the Petén. By the Classic period, the settlement at Chiapa de Indios was part of a trade network that stretched all the way to El Salvador, and the variety of ceramic styles found there is truly remarkable.

The origins of the early inhabitants of Chiapa de Indios and the western end of the Grijalva Valley are unknown, but sometime after A.D. 500 the Chiapaneco settled here. They are thought to have come from central Mexico by way of Soconusco. The region was most densely populated during the Late Classic period and then shared in the general decline of the Postclassic, when most sites were abandoned. Even during the nadir of the Postclassic, however, trade with southern Oaxaca and the Gulf Coast apparently continued.

By the late fifteenth century, Chiapa de Indios was once again a regional power as trade along the Grijalva River revived during the growth and expansion of the Mexica empire. The fertile valley could support a rich, diverse agriculture, but the vitality of the Chiapaneco state derived from its military control of the commercial artery through the valley and its subjugation of nearby Zoque towns. Bernal Díaz del Castillo reported that the chiapanecos "robbed passengers and travelling merchants, and brought off the inhabitants of these districts to colonize and till their ground."[31] When the Spanish arrived, the chiapanecos were making a bid to extend their jurisdiction into the highlands, especially over the salt beds controlled by Zinacantán. The orientation of fortifications there, and at Chamula and Huistán, suggests that they were built to resist Chiapaneco raids.

Northwest of Chiapaneco territory, the Zoque occupied the Middle Grijalva river basin below the Sumidero canyon, as well as the western edge of the central highlands, which is sometimes identified separately as the western plateau. Zoque is a linguistic cousin of Mixe, spoken in Oaxaca, and Zoque peoples apparently moved into western Chiapas from the Gulf Coast during the Classic period. Archaeological research has been impeded by the Netzahualcoyotl Dam, which flooded many Zoque sites, but the ceramic sequence that has been reconstructed is long, rich, and varied.[32] This portion of the Grijalva is more easily navigable than the upper segment in the Central Depression, and it provided a thoroughfare for trade with southern Veracruz and Tabasco. Ceramics from the Early Preclassic period, around 1350 B.C., show a close association with the important Olmec sites of La Venta and San Lorenzo. By 300 B.C., trade existed with Oaxaca and the Petén, and in the Classic period the region was an integral part of the wide network that included the Chiapaneco and reached throughout southern Mesoamerica.

Little is known about the Zoque in the Postclassic period apart from the fact that they apparently also suffered a decline. On the eve of the Spanish conquest, however, they were thriving again, with large towns at Tuxtla northwest of Chiapa de Indios, Quechula, Copainalá, and Tecpatlán despite the torments inflicted upon them by the Chiapaneco.[33] The Zoque were major producers of cacao and cochineal, and theirs was the most prosperous district in indigenous Chiapas.

THE ECOLOGY OF COLONIZATION

Throughout Spanish America the commercial potential of the physical environment and the size and complexity of indigenous societies largely determined regional patterns of social and economic development after the conquest. In New Spain the valleys of central Mexico attracted the largest numbers of immigrants because densely settled Indian populations provided a ready source of labor and tribute, and the climate suited European food crops and cattle ranching. In 1547, Spanish frontiersmen found gold and silver deposits near Zacatecas to the north, luring European and Indian settlers from the central basins. These fortune hunters and their workers created large towns and a hinterland of settled villages in a region where native peoples had been nomadic. Mexico City, like Tenochtitlán before it, became the hub of a complex regional commercial network that linked populations from Zacatecas to Veracruz and that included secondary centers like Puebla and Querétaro. Ultimately the links extended across the Atlantic to Cádiz and Seville, and even to Antwerp and Vienna. The social history of central Mexico, as a result, must be set against the early history of European capitalism.

Southern Mesoamerica—Oaxaca, Yucatán, Chiapas, and Guatemala—attracted far fewer Spanish settlers because little gold or silver was found here. After a boom in cacao exports at the end of the sixteenth century, the economy of Central America, in particular, stagnated. In many parts of the region, the European population, which was relatively small to begin with, declined after 1620 and did not recover until more than a century later. Consequently, southern Mesoamerica would remain much more "Indian" in character than Central Mexico. Spanish populations were confined more or less to provincial administrative centers like Mérida, Antequera, Santiago, and Ciudad Real. The urban markets in these cities were large enough to support at least some commercial agriculture, small business, and local artisanry. But these economies were poor by central Mexican standards and would remain so until well into the eighteenth century. Spaniards here largely depended on the tribute system to provision their cities and acquire trade goods, and the social transformations associated with the early transition to capitalism, especially wage labor and private landholding, developed comparatively late.

Chiapas was a political creation of the conquest, with no real foundation in the systems of economic and ethnic relationships that had prevailed earlier. In the sixteenth century the Spanish would attempt to create a regional economy in the highlands, with its nexus at Ciudad Real, by forcing Tzotzil and Tzeltal laborers to migrate seasonally to plantations in the Grijalva Valley and even, for a time, to Soconusco. They would also divert cacao from Soconusco through the colonial capital that otherwise would have gone straight to Mexico City. By the end of the seventeenth century, these efforts had failed, and most Spaniards abandoned hopes of building a new economy in the highlands in favor of opportunities in the Upper and Middle Grijalva basins. In the long run, their choice, and its impact on development in the nineteenth century, had profound consequences for the native peoples of Chiapas. By the early nineteenth century, the Chiapaneco had ceased to exist, and the Zoque had been pushed out of the western plateau and confined to a small area on the Gulf Coast. But the Tzeltal and Tzotzil survived, in place, in the central highlands.

3

SPANISH RULE IN THE HIGHLANDS

Though Chiapa in the opinion of the Spaniards be held
to be one of the poorest countries of America, because
in it as yet there have been no mines discovered, nor
golden sands found in the rivers, nor any haven upon
the South Sea, whereby commodities are brought in and
carried out, as to Mexico, Oaxaca, and Guatemala, yet
I may say it exceedeth most provinces and yieldeth to
none except it be to Guatemala in the greatness and
beauty of fair towns.

— Thomas Gage[1]

In 1524, Luis Marín, a captain in the service of Hernán Cortés, led a small
expedition of Spanish and central Mexican soldiers into the Upper Grijalva
river basin.[2] After moving through Zoque country unmolested, they confronted a great army near Chiapa de Indios. Bernal Díaz del Castillo, who
fought with Marín, described the scene: "We found the whole force of Chiapa
drawn up to receive us. Their troops were adorned with plumage, and well
armed offensively and defensively, and the hills resounded with their shouts
on our appearance. It was dreadful to behold the fury with which they threw
themselves upon us like enraged lions. . . . The enemy attacked us here so
desperately that hardly one of our soldiers escaped without a wound."[3]

In the evening after the first battle, Marín was approached by ten *caciques*
who were enemies of the Chiapaneco and who offered to make an alliance.
With their help the Spaniards defeated Chiapa and carried their *entrada* up
into the central plateau against the Tzotzil Maya at Chamula and Huistán.
Again, with aid from other Indians, including the people of Zinacantán, the
Spanish were victorious. But soon after this, Chamula rebelled when a
Spanish soldier seized a cacique to extort gold from the town. Marín was
forced to withdraw his troops and return to his base at Coatzacoalcos on the
Gulf Coast in Tehuantepec.

A second, larger entrada was begun soon afterward under Diego de Mazariegos. After some initial success, Indian resistance at Chiapa compelled another retreat. Then, early in 1528, Mazariegos returned with a still larger force and finally conquered Chiapa, Chamula, and Zinacantán, and established a Spanish presence in the Grijalva Valley and on the edge of the *altiplano*. Villa Real, the first provincial capital, was founded in March 1528 at Chiapa de Indios. Then, in April, Mazariegos moved the settlement of fifty-seven citizens (*vecinos*) to a healthier location in the highlands, a broad valley that native peoples called Hueyzacatlán.[4] In 1536 the small town was incorporated as a proper city, Ciudad Real.

Until 1544, political control over Chiapas was contested by representatives of competing Spanish factions in Mexico and Guatemala, a reflection of the wider struggles for power that took place throughout New Spain following the conquest of Mexico and Central America.[5] Mazariegos, who claimed authority from Alonso de Estrada, governor in Mexico City, was displaced in 1529 by Juan Enríquez de Guzmán when Nuño de Guzmán asserted control over Mexico as president of the newly constituted Audiencia de México. A year later Pedro de Alvarado won jurisdiction over Chiapas under his patent as governor of Guatemala. Then in 1535 Alvarado ceded the governorship of Chiapas to Francisco Montejo in exchange for that of Honduras. Montejo served for four years until the new Audiencia de los Confines was established in Guatemala. For the rest of the colonial period, Chiapas remained part of Central America.

While these disputes were being argued before the Crown, colonial rule was extended over Maya communities in the interior of the highlands as Spanish settlers pacified rebellious towns and claimed *encomiendas*, the private grants that entitled them to a share of tribute and personal service. The first encomiendas had been given out by Marín even before the conquest was secured.[6] These were superseded and new grants were distributed when Mazariegos arrived. Then, during the 1530s, as local political authority changed hands, so too did many encomiendas. Alvarado and Montejo each transferred titles to their own favorites.

Though the Chiapaneco launched large-scale rebellions in 1532 and 1534, the Tzeltal and Tzotzil peoples in the highlands accepted Spanish control with little resistance after the initial conquest.[7] Conditions along the frontier with Tabasco and the Petén, however, remained unsettled.

Unconquered lacandones from the rain forest constantly raided Chol villages in the district around Tila and Tumbalá, disrupting Spanish efforts to control the province and protect the communication routes that linked Chiapas with Tabasco, Campeche, and Yucatán. In response, between 1530 and 1586 the conquerors organized a series of pacification campaigns to break the Lacandón.[8]

One such entrada, in 1535, provided a pretext for further depredations among the highland Maya. Francisco Gil Zapata was authorized by Pedro de Alvarado to move against the Lacandón and establish a Spanish town on the Usumacinta River near Tenosique.[9] When that effort failed, Gil and his lieutenant, Lorenzo de Godoy, turned to slave raiding among Tzeltal and Chol peoples at Bachajón, Tila, and Petalsingo, peaceful towns already parceled out to *encomenderos* in Villa Real. The incident is one of the more notorious episodes in the history of the conquest of Chiapas. To intimidate local chiefs into handing over people to be enslaved, Gil burned one *principal* alive, cut a hand off another, and the noses off two others. The *cabildo* in the provincial capital condemned his activities and, during the proceedings that followed, found that Gil had signed a contract with a Spanish merchant to deliver some two hundred slaves to Mexico City.

Though encomenderos in Villa Real were quick to denounce Gil for his cruelty, their own conduct was hardly a model of compassion, and many committed atrocities themselves. Until the arrival of Fray Bartolomé de las Casas as bishop in 1545 and the reforming *visitas* of Juan Rogel (1546–48) and Gonzalo Hidalgo Montemayor (1549), encomenderos in Chiapas held free rein within their entitlements.[10] Their levies of tribute and labor were unregulated, and their control of these commodities, either for their own use or for sale to other entrepreneurs, enabled them to dominate early economic development and to become major landowners and regional merchants.

In Chiapas, encomienda labor, or *servicio personal*, was used in a variety of contexts. Some tributaries really did perform personal service for the encomendero—doing household domestic work, constructing town and country residences, and transporting tribute goods from the villages to the city. But the most abusive tributary labor was in plantation agriculture. After early experiments with gold panning, Spaniards turned to sugar cultivation in the Grijalva Valley. By the late 1540s, audiencia president Alonso López de Cerrato reported a "tyranny" of such planters.[11] Many mills were owned and operated by encomenderos themselves, using tributary laborers who lived under conditions of virtual slavery. But even those run by Spaniards without grants used encomienda workers, leasing them from those who held titles. In either case, for Indians the work was hard and often fatal. One plantation, Cerrato wrote, suffered 2,000 deaths a year.

Encomenderos in Ciudad Real also leased their tributaries as porters, or *tamemes*, to officials and merchants journeying through the highlands.[12] While the route through the Grijalva Valley and along the altiplano was by no means easy, it was an active thoroughfare for travelers between Santiago, the capital of the audiencia in Guatemala, and Mexico City or Veracruz. In addition, cacao growers in Soconusco, on the Pacific coast, sometimes shipped their produce through Ciudad Real to avoid customs duties.[13] Porterage, too, was difficult and dangerous work for native peoples, especially when highlanders like the Tzeltal and Tzotzil were forced to carry loads to the coasts or the river basin near Chiapa de Indios, which were hot, insect-ridden regions where disease spread more easily and exhaustion came more quickly than in the highlands.

Tribute was also demanded of native communities, of course. We know few of the finer points of the tribute system prior to 1550, but the burden was clearly a heavy one.[14] Montejo heard repeated complaints about excessive demands during his general visita of the province in 1541, as did Las Casas in 1545. Those encomenderos who invested in sugar may have required mostly labor from their tributaries, but others, especially those with grants nearer Chiapa de Indios or among the Zoque to the northwest, where cacao was grown, seem likely to have required tribute in this and other marketable commodities. In the highlands, Zinacantán paid tribute in cacao during this early period but stopped doing so sometime in the seventeenth century. Fray Antonio de Remesal claims the town was required to turn over nearly 120 *cargas* (about 360 bushels), an extraordinary amount by later standards.[15] Some scholars have suggested that other Tzotzil and Tzeltal towns were required to pay in cacao and were consequently forced to travel to Soconusco to work or trade for it, but just how extensive this practice was cannot be documented.[16] Most Maya communities in the highlands seem more likely to have contributed a mix of labor as tamemes and sugar workers and tribute in the form of cotton cloth (*mantas*), maize, chiles, beans, and other foodstuffs. Though not cash crops in the same sense as cacao or cochineal, these staples were nonetheless of considerable commercial value in Ciudad Real and Guatemala, where Spanish populations depended on Indian production for their food supply.

This first generation of European settlement, which was dominated by the political and military ambitions of the *conquistadores* and the economic initiatives of local encomenderos, came to an end in the 1540s with the incorporation of Chiapas into the Audiencia of Guatemala. Government and patronage began to be more systematic and less arbitrary. Encomenderos and vecinos in Ciudad Real found themselves subject to new legislation and new restrictions imposed by outside authorities, the Dominicans arrived to compete for political and economic control of Indian towns and villages, and the effects of the enormous decline in the size of the native population began to be felt.

The creation of the Audiencia de los Confines coincided with the passage of the New Laws in 1542 and 1543, legislation designed to end Indian slavery, withdraw rights to personal service from encomienda grants, and forbid the assignment of new encomiendas.[17] Like most administrators in New Spain, Alonso de Maldonado, the first president of the Audiencia de los Confines, avoided enforcing the edicts. Instead, he cautioned the Crown that if rights to tributary labor were curtailed, Spaniards who depended on such workers to operate their estates and plantations would go under. In 1546, however, he sent an audiencia lawyer, Juan Rogel, to Ciudad Real to review conditions there.[18] Much to the outrage of local citizens, Rogel went ahead with cuts in tribute rates and prohibitions on certain uses of native labor. Indians were no longer to be permitted to work inside sugar mills or to carry burdens more than twenty leagues from their homes.

Then in 1548, with Fray Bartolomé de las Casas in Spain lobbying for more vigorous enforcement of the New Laws, a new audiencia president, Alonso López de Cerrato, encouraged his *oidores* to legislate stricter controls in the provinces.[19] When the *visitador* Diego Ramírez reported that conditions in Chiapas had changed little since Rogel's visit, Gonzalo Hidalgo de Montemayor was dispatched in the spring of 1549 to enact further reforms. With the authority of a royal judge, he announced the abolition of Indian slavery and reductions in tribute. Seventeen encomenderos had their tributaries taken from them. Four held encomiendas in the highland towns of Cancuc, Tenango, Chamula, and Zinacantán. All were found guilty of abusing personal-service obligations. Later in the same year, a royal decree outlawed the substitution of personal service for tribute, and in Chiapas the encomendero's right to the labor of his tributaries ended.[20]

Of course, new legislation did not by itself bring an end to the more exploitive practices of the first generation. Though the bureaucracy was expanding, enforcement was beyond its means, and, equally important, the Crown still treated offenders with leniency. All seventeen encomenderos whom Montemayor deprived of their titles won back their grants on appeal. Still, conditions in the highlands were changing by the end of the 1540s. Las Casas was appointed the first bishop of the province in 1545. (Ciudad Real was the seat of a separate bishopric as early as 1539; after 1596, the jurisdiction included Chiapas and Soconusco.) Although he pursued his crusade outside the province, other Dominicans came to stay. The friars challenged the conduct of encomenderos on several fronts, initiating court proceedings against them and encouraging native leaders to resist demands for excessive tribute and labor. In the long run, their direct intervention, and their own draw on native resources, had a much greater impact on Spanish rule than the oratory of their bishop.

Although Marín had brought a Mercedarian friar, and Mazariegos two priests who founded the first parish at Villa Real, the Church played a minor role in the early colony until the Dominicans arrived in 1545.[21] The city maintained a cathedral, with a dean and canon, and a Mercedarian monastery, but only three priests—Gil Quintana, Juan de Perera, and Nicolás Galiano—were pursuing missionary activities in the pueblos. The Dominicans moved quickly to take the lead. Soon after their arrival they founded convents at Chiapa de Indios and Zinacantán. Later that same year they began their campaign to resettle dispersed Indian settlements in larger communities (congregaciones).[22] In subsequent decades, as new friars arrived from Europe and elsewhere, more convents were built: in 1555 at Copanaguastla, a Tzeltal town in the valley south of the capital; in 1570 at Tecpatlán among the Zoque; and in 1579 at Comitán, a Tzeltal town southwest of Ciudad Real.

When the Dominicans moved into Indian towns, they challenged the status quo head on. Local civil officials were reluctant or unwilling to enforce recent reforms, but the friars were not. In Chiapa de Indios, the cacique, Juan Notí, was beaten by the parish priest for supplying laborers for the encomendero's sugar mill.[23] Throughout the province the friars instructed Indians to pay only the lower, revised tribute assessments. Encomenderos fought back, of course, urging native officials to withhold food and services from the clergy. It was a battle that, in a province with limited resources, would never end.

In 1550 the cabildo in Ciudad Real reported that the seven sugar mills that had been the most profitable enterprises in the province were in ruins and their owners in debt.[24] The problem, officials explained, was a lack of workers, and for this they blamed the Dominicans. With the intrusion of the friars into the villages, encomenderos were no longer free to recruit labor as they pleased, but the real cause of the labor shortage in Chiapas was not Dominican interference but the precipitous decline of the native population.[25] Epidemics had swept through the province even before the conquerors arrived, the earliest between 1519 and 1520. Then during 1529–1531, 1532–1543, and 1545–1548 successive waves of pox and fever, sometimes coinciding with drought and locust inundations, struck again. Peter Gerhard has estimated that the population decline in Chiapa de Indios and Chamula between 1524 and 1595 was at least 57 percent.[26] Half of the remaining population of Zinacantán perished in a single year of plague in 1565.

Murdo MacLeod has described the late 1550s as "a turning point, a pause in the growth of the economy of the sixteenth century."[27] Having played out the most easily extracted resources and facing the end of their abundant labor supply, Spanish settlers were forced to turn to less labor-intensive and more carefully regimented enterprises. Throughout Central America they experimented with new crops, at once consolidating and diversifying local industries. Izalcos had some success with cacao, and Honduras with mining. In Nicaragua and Guatemala, indigo production was expanded, providing a steady source of income even though producers were disappointed that the industry never took off on a scale comparable to the cacao boom that had preceded it.

In Chiapas, while cochineal and indigo were tried in the lowlands near Chiapa de Indios and on the Pacific plain, Spaniards in the highlands shifted their investments to schemes that did not depend on a large work force. In the Grijalva Valley, some built lucrative businesses raising horses for markets in Mexico, and in the larger highland valleys near Comitán and Ocosingo, cattle ranching began. But many encomenderos simply had to rely on selling goods they collected as tribute, their livelihood dependent on the strength of urban markets within the province.

Despite the downturn in the economic fortunes of Chiapas, those urban markets remained active. Between 1550 and 1611, the number of Spanish vecinos in Ciudad Real grew, albeit slowly and unevenly. No one struck it rich, but the local economy had not yet collapsed either. During this period the distribution of wealth and political power within Spanish society gradually shifted. The descendants of the conquerors, who had been the richest encomenderos, lost their dominance. Some of the more productive encomiendas reverted to the Crown, including Chiapa de Indios in 1552, and receipts from others declined as the number of tributaries fell.[28] Some grants were given to well-connected individuals in Guatemala. Then in 1569 management of the province was transferred from the cabildo in Ciudad Real to an *alcalde mayor* appointed from outside, at first by the audiencia and later by the Crown.

The sons and daughters of the province's founding families complained bitterly as they saw their political power curtailed and their fortunes disappear. They sent letters to the Crown pleading for the restoration of encomiendas and requested funds from the royal treasury to pay for civic projects that in other provinces were supported with local funds. In 1583, for example, the cabildo wrote to the audiencia asking for money to build a nunnery, or *casa de monjas*.[29] The structure was necessary, they said, because the destitute daughters of the conquerors were without marriage prospects. In 1619 a letter from the bishop explained: "This city was once populated by rich and noble people of great quality because its founders were men of spirit, as shown in their person and houses, or by their great haciendas, so profitable to Your Majesty. . . . [Now] because so many people have died, those that remain, although they hold to the noble obligation of serving Your Majesty, are lacking the rents and encomiendas to do so."[30]

The "age of the encomienda" ended in Chiapas during the early decades of the seventeenth century as the Indian population continued to diminish. Two epidemics hit, in 1600–1601 and 1607–1608. Gerhard reports that losses were highest in the Grijalva Valley, but in Comitán a third of the remaining population died.[31]

THE SEVENTEENTH CENTURY

In 1951, Woodrow Borah wrote a short monograph, *New Spain's Century of Depression*, in which he suggested that the combined effect of the decline of the Indian labor supply and curtailed silver production (as evidenced by falling silver receipts) was a protracted economic depression that began in 1576 and continued for more than a century. In response, Borah wrote, Spaniards moved from the cities to vacated Indian lands, formed large landed estates, or *latifundias*, to provide foodstuffs for local markets, and recruited labor through debt peonage. Subsequent publications by the French historians Huguette and Pierre Chaunu, who studied fluctuations in the transAtlantic trade, and François Chevalier, who examined the origins of the Mexican hacienda, supported Borah's hypothesis.[32]

Since this formative work, the economic history of the seventeenth century has been reexamined by successive generations of historians.[33] By the late 1960s an alternative view had begun to emerge that suggested that the decline in silver imports from Mexico and the overall shrinkage of the transAtlantic trade between Seville and Veracruz reflected not economic contraction but economic reorganization. Mexico had begun to hold onto its resources and to develop local enterprises and local markets as urban populations in the colony expanded and as peninsular industries failed to meet colonial demand. This was the interpretation put forward by John Lynch in the second volume of *Spain Under the Habsburgs* (1969) and it was supported in a series of regional studies that turned away from macroeconomic analysis to focus on smaller-scale local patterns of development. John Super, William Taylor, and Marta Espejo-Hunt showed how some regions in seventeenth-century New Spain—Puebla, Querétaro, Oaxaca, and Yucatán, respectively—saw more commercialized regional economies develop as local urban markets grew and export markets within the colonies opened up.[34] In addition, Peter Bakewell, John TePaske, and Herbert Klein have shown that overall silver production held steady for the century as increases at some mines compensated for declines at others.[35]

Later research has also confirmed, however, that other areas did experience a sustained depression in the seventeenth century, and Central America was one of them. As Murdo MacLeod has outlined, the region's isolation from major markets and its shortages of capital and labor were disadvantages that local plantation owners could not overcome.[36] After 1620 the cacao and co-chineal industries were in decline, indigo was stagnating, and food shortages were chronic in cities and towns. Spaniards were moving to the country to live on small estates or turning to the civil and especially the ecclesiastical bureaucracy for their livelihood. Though signs of recovery began to appear after 1680, the depression was not clearly over until the 1730s.

In Chiapas the course of seventeenth-century economic change mirrored that of Guatemala. Economic decline set in after 1620, as reflected in a fall in the number of Spanish citizens in Ciudad Real from 280 in 1620 to only 50 by 1657–59.[37] Even for Central America, where many towns lost population during the seventeenth century, this was a large drop. Some Spaniards owned plantations in Soconusco, and they went there to carry on a diminished cacao trade. Others left for Guatemala or Mexico. Still others moved onto ranches and small farms near Chiapa de Indios and among the Zoque, and southward toward Copanaguastla—areas closer to markets in other provinces, where economic conditions were worsening more slowly. A similar shift had taken place in the 1540s, though at that time Spaniards experimenting with new enterprises maintained city residences; now, apparently, they did not. As the century wore on and the prospects for recovery seemed to dim still further, the sons of the elite left Chiapas altogether. By 1720 only thirty-four Spanish families resided in Ciudad Real, and twenty-four in other parts of the province. Nearly half of the adult sons of these families had gone to other regions in New Spain.[38]

The effect of hard times was to magnify the social and economic contrasts that had earlier emerged between the lowlands (*tierra caliente*) and the highlands (*tierra fría*). Towns in the valleys and along the Camino Real began to have significant Spanish and especially mestizo populations.[39] But very few *ladinos* went to live in or near pueblos in the highlands north and east of Ciudad Real. Until the eighteenth century, only Ocosingo and Chilón, where cattle ranching was established and the Dominicans maintained sugar estates, shared their town with non-Indians. Between 1701 and 1710 a few Spaniards received titles to land near Petalsingo, but there is no evidence of their having established settlements there by the time of the great rebellion.[40]

Differences in the social landscape within Chiapas were already evident in 1625, when the English Dominican Thomas Gage visited the province. Ciudad Real, he later wrote, "is one of the meanest cities in all America. . . .

[T]he Jesuits having got no footing there (who commonly live in the richest and wealthiest places and cities) is a sufficient argument of either the poverty of the city, or of the want of gallant parts, and prodigality in the gentry."[41] In contrast, Gage described Chiapa as "very rich, and many Indians in it that trade about the country as the Spanish do. They have learned trades befitting a commonwealth, and practice and teach them within their town. They want not any provision of fish or flesh, having for the one the great river joining unto their town, and for the other the many *estancias* (as they call them) or farms abounding with cattle."[42]

Sidney David Markman recently described how the poverty of the capital was reflected in its architecture. From around 1620 until the late 1670s, no major building projects were initiated, and when construction picked up at the end of the century, much of the work consisted of repairs on such important structures as the convent of Santo Domingo and the cathedral. In 1693 the original cathedral building, made of adobe and still in disrepair, was pulled down altogether and a new building begun from scratch, a project that took more than thirty years to complete. Until 1737, when a single fountain was built, there was no public water supply in the city, water having to be hauled from the Río Amarillo, and as late as 1748, 413 of the city's 534 permanent houses had thatched roofs.[43]

By 1696 almost as many ladinos, most of whom were mestizos, were living in Chiapa de Indios as in the capital, and large numbers of mestizos and *españoles pobres* were reported to be living in Tuxtla, Ocozocoautla, Comitán, and other towns.[44] If the Indian population is counted, Chiapa de Indios and Tecpatlán were larger settlements than Ciudad Real itself. MacLeod describes a similar shift in the regional distribution of the Spanish and mestizo population for Guatemala.[45] He contrasts the Cuchumatanes and Verapaz, where Maya pueblos were spared Spanish-speaking neighbors, with areas to the south and east, where rural ladino settlements were becoming common. But the experience of the upper highlands of Chiapas and Guatemala was not characteristic of all of New Spain. In many districts of the viceroyalty, including such "Indian" provinces as Yucatán and Michoacán, the movement of mestizos and Spaniards into the bigger villages and the spread of private estates large and small were placing Indians and ladinos in closer and closer proximity.

In these areas, the context of Spanish rule in the countryside was becoming more complex and diversified because economic relations were no longer tied mainly to the tribute system or labor drafts, and social relations were no longer quite so dominated by priest, encomendero, and royal tax collector. The growing number of haciendas offered seasonal labor opportunities or a complete escape from the heavy tax burden of the independent pueblo.[46] So, too, did the textile workshops (*obrajes*), though after midcentury these enterprises may have moved more quickly toward debt peonage and more coercive forms of labor exploitation.[47] Greater numbers of mestizo and mulatto peddlers plied their trade along back roads and highways and in native markets. The most profound changes occurred near those Spanish cities and towns whose populations were expanding—Antequera and Mérida, for example.[48] Nearby Indian communities shared in their growth as their populations were swelled by migrants from farther out in the hinterland and their economies came to be more closely integrated with that of the city. Some took advantage of opportunities for seasonal or daily wage labor. Others became independent producers and grew larger surpluses to meet local demand. Throughout New Spain the participation of rural Indian societies in the larger market economy, and the social and cultural adjustments that the transition compelled, had begun.

The impact of more intensive commercialization of peasant economies and the significance of market expansion in the seventeenth century for theoretical questions about the emergence of capitalism are questions that have engaged historians and political economists for several decades. The challenge for theorists is to wrestle the apparent contradictions of colonial development into a coherent and systematic conceptual framework. How does one reconcile the emergence of dynamic local and international markets in which sophisticated entrepreneurs participated, risking capital and calculating profit, with the persistence (indeed the reemergence after the demise of European serfdom) of archaic, feudal-like systems of coerced labor and land tenure in which these same entrepreneurs encouraged a paternalistic labor regime and squandered their fortunes in an elaborate but unproductive prestige economy?

An earlier generation argued that when Castile, dominated by an aristocracy that claimed seignorial rights to vast tracts of land for sheep pasturage, took control of the colonial enterprise and shunted aside Aragón, with its strong mercantilist history in the Mediterranean, the feudal character of political and economic relations in southern Spain was recreated in the New World.[49] Abundant supplies of cheap labor and vast reserves of silver made Spanish commercial interests complacent and conservative, saving them from the necessity of innovating and modernizing. Finally, European racism and Catholic cultural supremacy legitimated slavery and other forms of forced servitude and impeded experiments with free wage labor. This generation accepted the idea of a seventeenth-century depression and saw the *latifundias* as feudal refuges that enabled the landowning elite to shift their emphasis from production for the market to production for use.

An alternative paradigm began to be articulated in the 1960s, associated first with Andre Gunder Frank's *Capitalism and Underdevelopment* and later, and more fully, with the two volumes of Immanuel Wallerstein's *The Modern World-System*. Frank and Wallerstein argued that the structures that earlier scholars had identified with the legacy of Iberian feudalism—especially forced labor—were actually the products of a geographical division of labor within a global capitalist economy that originated from a core in Europe after 1450 and that had been extended to far-flung peripheries in Asia and Latin America by 1640. They contrast development in the European core, where production centered on capital-intensive, high-profit finished goods using competitive free wage labor, with development on the periphery, where production was concentrated in commercial agriculture, which used various systems of coerced labor. In Wallerstein's scheme, forced servitude in Spanish America was the product of several factors, including the inability of Caribbean sugar growers to attract European indentured workers and the ease with which preconquest labor drafts in Mexico and the Andes could be adapted to serve sixteenth-century colonial economies. More generally, Wallerstein attributes the division of labor to the "logic" of the world-system and suggests that when Indian population losses depleted the labor pool, capitalists on the periphery had no alternative but to enlist the state to help them recruit workers.

Frank, Wallerstein, and other scholars identified with dependency and world-system theories held center stage in the social sciences for much of the 1970s, with the result that there is now an equally important body of literature that is critical of their definitions of capitalism, the presumptions of their conceptual frameworks, and the evidence they have used to support their theoretical conclusions.[50] Some critics have quarreled with their emphasis on the market and have insisted that changes in the organization of labor should be at the center of any theory of capitalist development. For this group, what defines capitalism is not the rise of a global, Eurocentric marketplace in the sixteenth century but the full development of free wage labor during the Industrial Revolution in the nineteenth century. From this perspective, the colonial period in Latin America was a long period of pre-capitalist transitions.

Other critics have accused world-systems theorists of a kind of determinism that, on the one hand, exaggerates the uniformity of social and economic development within the system and, on the other, overlooks the ability of colonized peoples to impose constraints on their exploiters. Steve J. Stern, for example, citing the "diverse array" of labor relations and land tenure systems in colonial Latin America, has argued that local and regional market conditions, demographic patterns, and political cultural contexts often had a much stronger impact on the organization of production than did economic imperatives imposed from the core. This view is shared by the authors of the regional studies on seventeenth-century Mexico noted earlier as well as by scholars like Eric Van Young who have studied regional economic history in the eighteenth century. Carol A. Smith has suggested that regional development in colonial Guatemala was shaped as much by patterns of Maya resistance as by the economic potential of localities within the province.[51] Although some scholars may find her conclusion to have been overstated, it reflects a consensus among contemporary historians that the Spaniards' reliance on a system of indirect rule and the necessity of preserving semiautonomous peasant economies often enabled native peoples to resist encroachments on their land and to negotiate the terms under which their labor was utilized.

The economic history of seventeenth-century Chiapas supports this revisionist view of Wallerstein's model. Within the province, regional development was shaped almost entirely by the relative strength or weakness of local markets and the commercial value of locally consumed cash crops and manufactured goods rather than by economic factors imposed by business interests in Guatemala, Mexico City, and Europe. This marked a change from the early years of the colony, when the economy was driven by outside demand for sugar, cacao, cochineal, and Indian slaves, and when expansion of the urban market at Ciudad Real was fueled by a healthy flow of commercial traffic along the Camino Real. During this period Chiapas was very much part of an emerging world-system, though by the end of it, production was already geared more for local markets than from external ones.

This early commercialization of the provincial economy pushed a portion of the native population into new modes of production. Initially, in conformity with Wallerstein's model, Indians were drawn into the coercive labor systems of slavery and *servicio personal*. With the abolition of both in the 1540s, wage labor was introduced, and in theoretical terms the transition to capitalist production was underway, but only on a very small scale and for a short time. In 1611 the biggest employers of Indian wage labor were two Dominican-owned sugar mills (*trapiches*) near Copanaguastla and another outside of Ocosingo, none of which used more than twenty full-time laborers.[52]

The onset of the depression in the seventeenth century assured that the modest transformation then underway would remain confined to the small number of private estates in the Grijalva basin—some of which were owned by Chiapaneco and Zoque caciques—and in the highland valleys south of Ciudad Real. For the majority of native peoples in the province, their labor would continue to be organized under what social scientists define as the tributary mode of production.[53] Under this system, Indians retained control of their land and of the basic decisions about when and where to plant and how the fields would be worked. This is not to say that native peoples were no longer exploited, or even that they were less exploited. Tribute demands compelled them to produce surpluses, and the pressure to devote more energy to products that the Spanish valued than to their own needs could be very great indeed. These pressures intensified still more when alcaldes mayores consolidated a system of forced sales known as the *repartimiento de mercancías*, discussed below. The impact of the repartimiento on the mode of production defies easy categorization. The system did compel Indians to orient production still more closely to the demands of the Spanish marketplace, and as a result, peasant production was further commercialized. However, as Nancy Farriss has emphasized, these forced exchanges can hardly be defined as market transactions.[54] Moreover, the system did not alter either the Indians' control over the organization of labor or the use of land. In terms of theory, the repartimiento de mercancías left the tributary mode of production intact, and in the years leading up to the great rebellion in 1712, although highland Maya peoples suffered more bitter exploitation, they did not experience any fundamental transformation in the structure of their village economies.

STRAIN AND CHANGE ON THE EVE OF REBELLION

In his book *Spanish Central America*, Murdo MacLeod points to "signs of strain and change" in the region between 1685 and 1730:

> At first these new tensions were minor. The depression was a long one, and the social arrangements which it helped to produce became firmly rooted. By the end of the century, however, it was obvious that the society formed at mid-century was undergoing slow but radical changes. In most cases these tensions, strains, and signs of disequilibrium and change existed before. It is the intensity and frequency of occurrence, and the conjunction of these events in the same span of years which gives them their significance.[55]

A number of factors contributed to the uncertainty and increasing activity of this period. In Guatemala, after several decades of relatively healthful conditions, epidemic diseases struck again in 1683 and continued to plague the province through the 1720s.[56] They often coincided with locust infestations, and the result was a dramatic decrease in local Maya populations. Between 1680 and 1735, losses of 75 percent were reported in Amatitlán and Escuintla. But despite the new demographic crisis, there were signs that the depression was ending. With demand for Central American indigo rising in European markets and a revival of silver mining in Honduras, the export economy was healthier than it had been in years.[57] In turn, these industries stimulated local commerce throughout the region, including contraband trade with English smugglers along the Caribbean coast. But all of this took place against a backdrop of the collapse of Habsburg rule in Spain, and the unsettled politics of the metropolis would have an impact on political and economic conditions in the colonies.

John Lynch described the years from 1677 to 1687 as "Castile's tragic decade."[58] The period began with successive years of torrential rains together with an epidemic of plague. Tens of thousands died in Andalucía, and the rural economy was left a shambles. A dramatic rise in prices followed. Then, in 1680, debasement of the currency and the imposition of price controls led to deflation, large numbers of bankruptcies, and a deep depression. To combat this collapse, Charles II's ministers moved to streamline the bureaucracy and reform fiscal policy. Under Spain's first prime ministers, the Duke of Medinaceli (1680–1685) and the Count of Oropesa (1685–1691), the Crown attempted to reduce the number of officials who served on state councils, eliminate supernumerary positions, and centralize the bureaucratic chain-of-command by strengthening the authority of state ministers. Changes in fiscal policy were designed to cut spending and reduce the annuities paid out to the rich and privileged in the form of pensions and interest on state bonds. To ease the burden on the poor, proposals to eliminate the tax on foodstuffs and basic consumer goods were considered, though never implemented.

In Central America the late Habsburg reforms attacked the Guatemalan elite's control of conscripted labor and tax revenue. In 1683, administration of the repartimiento labor draft was shifted from the cabildo in Santiago to the audiencia.[59] The change could not have come at a worse time. That same year, an outbreak of plague had led to labor shortages near the capital, where haciendas were still dependent on conscripted workers, and local Spaniards were already coping with increased competition for Indian labor brought on by the revival of silver mining in Honduras, where mine operators sought to bring in repartimiento workers from the neighboring province. The transfer of the repartimiento promised to increase the costs of recruiting labor. With wider competition for a limited number of workers, the bribes demanded by labor-draft officials were sure to be larger.

Some thirty years earlier, collection of the *alcabala*, or sales tax, had also been transferred from the cabildo to the audiencia.[60] Now the creole elite's share of tax revenue was further reduced by an assault on encomienda entitlements. More grants were taken over by the Crown as they became vacant, and those that remained in private hands were heavily taxed. In 1685 the entire encomienda revenue for that year was claimed by the Crown to help cover military expenditures in the Caribbean.[61]

For Spaniards in Guatemala, these reforms posed new obstacles to economic recovery just when it seemed that the depression might be lifting. The taxes on encomienda receipts, coupled with the loss of control of sales-tax revenue, contributed to a new currency crisis as cash was siphoned off by the Crown. Local entrepreneurs were forced to assume larger debts and limit new investments. To lessen their escalating tax burden, they turned increasingly to the illicit trade in contraband. Creoles and peninsular officials, who in the past had found ways to cooperate, now found themselves more and more at odds. By the late 1680s the Guatemalan elite was ready for open rebellion. Their anger over transfer of the labor repartimiento and the threat of food shortages in the capital compelled the Crown to return its administration to the cabildo. In 1688, when an audiencia judge, Pedro Enríquez doubled the sales tax on indigo, growers refused to pay.[62] Enríquez then impounded the entire year's production pending receipt of a judgment on the dispute from Spain. He managed to survive an assassination attempt but lost his office when the Crown reversed his decision and jailed him for putting the peace of the kingdom at risk.

Another political crisis came to a head in 1690, when Joseph de Escals, an oidor on the audiencia, bitterly denounced its president, Jacinto de Barrios Leal, in proceedings brought before the Crown.[63] Escals, an ardent reformer, set out to challenge a variety of practices that had become routine in seventeenth-century Central America. Barrios Leal was accused of taking tens of thousands of pesos in bribes, of trading in the contraband market, of depriving the Crown of its *quinto*, or one-fifth share, of mining revenue, and of appointing close relatives to lucrative administrative positions throughout the kingdom. Escals also accused him of rape.

The confrontation set key factions in Central American politics against one another. Escals acted with the support of the bishop of Guatemala, Andrés de las Navas y Quevado, and the alcalde mayor of La Corpus, a mining district in Honduras, whose local authority was being threatened by appointments made by Barrios Leal. Escals also had the support of a sector of the merchant community that was not allied with the president. Barrios Leal had his own supporters among other oidores on the audiencia and the alcaldes mayores in San Salvador and Sonsonate.

The outcome of Escals's challenge was affected by a second campaign that he waged against the Dominicans. In 1690 he undertook a full-scale visita of their administration of Indian parishes in Guatemala and Chiapas, and at its conclusion he wrote a report that was highly critical of both the friars and the bishops who had condoned their practices. Among his recommendations was the abolition of *cofradías* (confraternities), an end to the payment of fees for celebrating the sacraments, and prohibitions against bishops' use of community funds to cover visita expenses. Church leaders were outraged, and they persuaded the Holy Office of the Inquisition in Mexico City to indict Escals for insulting the dignity of the episcopate.[64]

Escals had made too many enemies, and though he remained on the audiencia until 1698, his reform crusade failed. The Crown sided with the president in his dispute with the oidor, and when Escals could not get along with Gabriel Sánchez de Berrospe, Barrios Leal's successor, they called him back to Spain. For Miles Wortman, the episode reveals Habsburg power at its nadir: "The very moment that Central America's export economy was expanding the Habsburg bureaucracy was too impotent to gather fruits from it."[65]

In Chiapas, political tensions were also on the rise at the end of the seventeenth century, though here the prospects for economic recovery were less hopeful. The exodus of Spanish citizens from the provincial capital continued through the early 1720s, suggesting that local creoles remained dispirited and pessimistic about their future. Pestilence returned to the province in 1704, and though the extent of population losses is uncertain, in the highlands this marked the beginning of a prolonged decline that lasted, in the aftermath of the Tzeltal Revolt, through the 1730s.[66]

Despite stagnating economic conditions—or more likely, because of them—both the civil and ecclesiastical bureaucracies in Chiapas acted with renewed energy during this period. In the 1680s the alcaldes mayores reinstated yearly censuses of tributary populations, collected tributes more efficiently, and expanded their commercial activities more aggressively. The Jesuits arrived in 1678 to found the city's first grammar school,[67] and between 1658 and 1712 three activist bishops, Fray Mauro de Tobar y Valle, Fray Francisco Núñez de la Vega, and Fray Bauptista Alvarez de Toledo, promoted a variety of new projects designed to reform parish administration, renovate the physical resources of the Church, and bolster ecclesiastical finances. They also launched aggressive campaigns against native idolatry. These initiatives provide the backdrop for the 1712 revolt. They weighed heavily on native peoples throughout the province, but especially so on the Maya in the central highlands, the poorest region in Chiapas. Here, where simple subsistence was difficult to secure even in the best of times, the Tzeltal, Tzotzil, and Chol would find it impossible to shoulder the added burden.

GOVERNMENT AND COMMERCE

Since the early years of the colony, the control of regional trade and commercial production had been in the hands of high civil authorities who used their official powers to recruit labor and accumulate capital. Their offices gave them distinct advantages over their competitors, especially as the depression deepened during the course of the seventeenth century. As a result, they were often envied by local native sons. The Spanish community in Ciudad Real was a contentious lot in any case, and no one attracted more resentment than the alcalde mayor. With the notable exception of the bishop, each provincial governor was the most prosperous man in Chiapas during his brief tenure in the province.

The first alcalde mayor was selected by the audiencia in 1569, but a decade later the Royal Council took control of these appointments. The new arrangement periodically led to jurisdictional disputes because not all the provincial governors in Chiapas were close associates of the president of the audiencia, even though officially they served as his lieutenants.[68] In the 1580s, for example, the audiencia president named two *corregidores* to collect tribute in Crown towns around Chiapa de Indios and Ciudad Real, and early in the seventeenth century, three *jueces de milpa* were appointed to inspect agricultural production in the villages.[69] On these occasions, the alcalde mayor protested, and eventually the Crown upheld his authority. By the 1620s the offices of corregidor and juez de milpa were officially eliminated when the Royal Council became convinced that they were engaging in illegal commerce and neglecting their official duties. Nonetheless, some presidents continued to challenge the powers of provincial governors by naming their own agents to collect tribute.[70] The issue was settled once and for all in June 1691, when the Crown resolved a complaint by the alcalde mayor, Manuel de Maisterra y Atocha, in his favor.[71] The Royal Council confirmed the provincial governor's authority to collect and manage the public auction of tribute goods and henceforth barred the audiencia president from appointing his own agents to the task. This came at a time when the Habsburg court was determined to reassert its control of the bureaucracy and when a new royal appointee to the Audiencia, Joseph de Escals, was in the midst of a bitter struggle with its president, Jacinto de Barrios Leal.

Much was at stake, of course, in these periodic battles over the control of native tribute because wholesale markets in the province depended on the public sale of these goods and because by manipulating the tribute rates and the selling price of tribute commodities, the official in charge could make very sizable profits. In Chiapas the system worked much the same as everywhere else in the colonies.[72] Communities were assessed as one body, with the amount of tribute determined by the number of tributaries in various categories. A census, or *padrón*, of eligible tributaries was to be carried out every year to compute each town's next assessment, or *tasación*. Following the reforms of the mid sixteenth century, labor was no longer required, and payment was made twice yearly, on June 24, the day of San Juan Bauptista, and January 1, during Christmas. The payment was in kind—usually mantas, maize, chiles, beans (*frijoles*), chickens (*gallinas*), and, depending on the region, cacao, honey, fiber mats (*petates*), agave thread (*pita*), sweet gum (liquidambar), and cochineal. Native town officials (*justicias*) were responsible for the actual collection. Receipts were turned over to the alcalde mayor and sold at public auction in Ciudad Real before revenues were finally passed on to the Crown. By 1650, six tax jurisdictions, called *partidos*, had been established to improve accounting procedures. Table 3.1 shows the amount of tribute collected in these districts in a representative year, 1719. The statistics highlight the importance of maize and cotton cloth in the inventory of tribute goods, and the lesser place overall of cacao, which was grown principally among the Zoque on the western plateau and among lowland Tzeltal towns on the northern border with Tabasco.

Tribute revenue was ultimately bound for the royal treasury in Santiago but not before a considerable portion was deducted to serve other constituencies.[73] Ecclesiastical institutions—the office of the bishop, the convents, the nunnery, the hospital, and the seminary—received their measure. The secular clergy depended on such income, and the Dominicans also received a share of it. Local militia officers—*capitanes*, *alferezes*, and *sargentos mayores* recruited from among the Spanish citizenry—also received funds to maintain garrisons in Ciudad Real, Comitán, and Chiapa de Indios. Finally, some receipts went to encomienda titleholders, who still held rights to tribute from certain pueblos (or parts of them), though they no longer participated in its collection, exercised any responsibility for their tributaries, or could

TABLE 3.1   TRIBUTE REVENUES FOR 1719

	Tostones	Mantas	Mais	Chile y frijol	Cacao
Barrios	160		25 f.		
Chiapa	3,032	2,739	2,766 f.	214 a.	3 c. 29 z. 375 g.
Coronas y Hueytiupán	862	610	561 f.	43 a.	4 c. 57 z.
Los Llanos	4,222	2,833	2,792 f.	162 a.	1 c. 37 z. 299 g.
Zendales	3,602	3,046	2,938 f.	193 a.	17 c. 8 z.
Zoques	2,110	1,450	1,354 f.	80 a.	40 c. 29 z. 375 g.

SOURCE: AGI: AG, 312: Autos de la averiguación de los fraudes de los alcaldes
        mayores: Carta del maestro de campo don Francisco Rodríguez de Rival, April
        12, 1719.
ABBREVIATIONS: a. almudes   g. granos
                  c. cargos   z. zontes
                  f. fanegas

rely solely on such income for their livelihood.[74] Some titles were held by
prominent men and women in Ciudad Real, but many were also in the
hands of widows and gentlemen in Guatemala.

Charles Gibson reported that rates and procedures for collecting tribute
in the Valley of Mexico had begun to be standardized by the late 1570s.[75] In
Guatemala, however, MacLeod has indicated that practices varied throughout the seventeenth century, and as the jurisdictional disputes of the mid
seventeenth century reveal, the same was true of Chiapas.[76] Yearly *padrones*
were neglected in the province for more than half the century, leading to
inaccurate assessments and making it easier for tax collectors to manipulate
the system to their own advantage. For some twelve communities, the census of 1665 was the first in thirty years; for eighteen others, the first in
eighteen years.[77] In twenty-one towns, no more padrones were undertaken
until 1679 and eleven others lacked counts for periods ranging from three to

TABLE 3.2   TRIBUTE RATES FOR THE HIGHLANDS IN 1690

Full tributaries	one manta
	1 fanega of maize (116 lbs.)
	1 chicken
	½ almud of chiles (about 5 lbs.)
	¼ almud of beans
Males and females married in other towns	½ manta (2 piernas)
	½ fanega of maize
Widows, widowers, single adults, etc.	1⅓ piernas of manta
	1 chicken

SOURCE: AGCA: A1.30 20 (I): Autos de la visita general, 1690; AGCA: A3.16 (I): Tasaciones, 1693.

seven years.[78] In response to complaints from the clergy, annual censuses were made more frequently after 1678, and tribute rates were apparently fixed at that time, as shown in Table 3.2.

As noted earlier, some pueblos also included honey, liquidambar, pita, and cochineal in their tribute payments. With the exception of Palenque, Tila, and Moyos, Maya communities in the highlands no longer included cacao in their assessment, though Zinacantán, and perhaps others, had done so in the early years after the conquest.[79] With minor variations, rates in the rest of the province were the same as in the highlands, except for the Zoque, who regularly paid a higher proportion of their tribute in cacao—at two zontes, or 800 beans, per full tributary.[80]

Though rates were still fixed in kind, communities sometimes substituted currency for produce at an exchange rate determined, in theory, by the fair market value of the goods assessed as tribute.[81] In practice, exchange rates varied within the province and were almost always inflated by the alcalde mayor to increase the amount of cash collected. When cash receipts were eventually reported to the Crown, accounts were calculated according to the lower, official exchange rate, and the balance was kept by the alcalde mayor to finance his own enterprises. The audiencia struggled well into the eighteenth century to establish standard equivalences and enforce them—with little success.

By 1690 most Tzeltal towns in the highlands commonly paid their levy of corn, beans, chiles, and chickens (but not cotton cloth) in coin. The alcalde mayor argued that, because of distance and poor roads, transporting bulk loads of foodstuffs to the capital for auction was inconvenient. The *servicio de tostón*, a separate tax always paid in coin, was introduced in 1592. At two *reales* per full tributary, it was a comparatively small addition to the tax burden, though an increase nonetheless.

The public auction of produce collected as tribute also gave the alcalde mayor an opportunity to profit from his official role as tax collector. He simply increased the selling price of goods above the accepted market price, forwarded to the royal treasury the value of the receipts based on fair prices, and pocketed the difference, a counterpart of the practice of raising the exchange rate between cash and kind in the villages. By the 1670s these price-manipulations had become routine.[82] But what made them possible was the alcalde mayor's control of a large share of all the goods marketed in the province, not just those collected as tribute.

In Thomas Gage's time, the provincial governor was already recognized as a heavy trafficker in cacao and cochineal.[83] By midcentury, when much of the interregional commercial activity described in Gage's *A New Survey of the West Indies* had dried up, the alcalde mayor took over a still larger share of commerce as merchants from other provinces, and many of Ciudad Real's own merchants, departed for more lucrative markets. Then, as he consolidated his political position, he won competitive advantages over the trading community that remained. Lacking rivals, he could charge higher prices and force Indian communities to trade with him alone.

The foundation of the alcalde mayor's commercial activity was the repartimiento de mercancías, the forced sale of one commodity in exchange for payment in another. This was often combined with the *derrama*, whereby native communities were compelled to buy unprocessed materials and sell back a finished product at a price below what private traders would pay. Another device, which lacked any subtlety or subterfuge, was simply a prohibition on the trading of certain goods between Indians and private merchants, and the confiscation of an entire product at a price far below the fair market value. For example, in 1675 the cabildo in Ciudad Real complained to the audiencia that the alcalde mayor, Andrés Ochoa de Zarate, had appointed lieutenants in each of the six tax districts and had bought all the mantas woven that year.[84] They claimed that not only were the appointments illegal according to a royal decree of 1613 but also the monopoly deprived them of a commercial livelihood that in the past had also profited the Indians. Cabildo members, they argued, had paid fair prices for the cloth, but the alcalde mayor did not.

Native peoples were compelled to participate in these schemes for a number of reasons. One was the threat of force. Village justicias who refused to cooperate might be beaten, imprisoned, or deprived of their office. But the most compelling device was the demand that tribute payments be made in cash. In a local economy with little demand for wage labor and a shrinking urban market, the repartimiento de mercancías was the primary source of currency for most Indian communities in the province.

All of these schemes are well documented in testimony presented to the audiencia in 1708 by Clemente de Ochoa y Velasco and Manuel de Morales, respectively alférez and *alcalde ordinario* on the cabildo in Ciudad Real.[85] They claimed that since he had taken office as alcalde mayor two years earlier, Martín González de Vergara had systematically committed fraud in his administration of the royal treasury and had extended a monopoly (*estanco*) over most of the commerce in the province. His commercial activities angered the two men not only because they and others were deprived of business but also because, as consumers, they were forced to pay artificially high prices for essential foodstuffs. The case is of very special interest because Fray Francisco Ximénez would cite González's repartimientos as a major cause of the Tzeltal Revolt. González died on May 31, 1712, before the rebellion was underway, but the Crown launched a full-scale review of his administration in the aftermath of the revolt that tied up his estate in court for more than a decade.[86]

Ochoa y Velasco's and Morales's accounts of his activities reveal just how indistinguishable the alcalde mayor's official duties and private enterprises really could be. Apparently the tribute in mantas was accurately accounted for and, in a break from custom, was transported directly to the Office of the Royal Treasury in Santiago without first being offered for sale in Ciudad

Real. Other items, however, were put on the block in the provincial capital. The accepted market price of corn, said the complainants, was four reales per fanega. In his first year, González set a selling price of eight to ten reales per fanega and then added to the cost of carrying maize from the pueblos to the city, the farther the distance, the higher the surcharge. With that, the most expensive lots were selling for twelve reales, three times the recognized fair price. Chiles, beans, and chickens also were sold at higher rates, though no porterage fees were passed on. Pueblos that the alcalde mayor considered too far from the capital to make carrying produce convenient were compelled to pay all but the assessment in mantas in coin. Rates ranged from eight reales per fanega of corn in Chiapa de Indios to twelve among the Zoque and a peso among the Tzeltal.

According to the two men, González used some of the funds collected as tribute to finance a second marketing operation. Money taken from the Zoque bought corn in Los Llanos and the Guardianía de Hueytiupán at six reales per fanega. That maize was brought to Ciudad Real, the alcalde mayor offering three reales per fanega to porters, though the going rate for such a distance was twenty-two. By day, some of the corn was sold publicly from the *casas del cabildo* at twelve reales per fanega. Then, by night, from Vespers until 10:00 P.M. and from 4:00 A.M. until daybreak, it was sold by the almud in the alcalde mayor's own home or in the house of his lieutenants, Gaspar de Sierra (the *alcalde de primer voto*) and two others, Juan de Peña and Juan Ramírez Olandes. These sales were thought to be especially scandalous. It was bad enough that the alcalde mayor should peddle corn by the almud like a common trader, but he also hired Indian women from the *barrios* to make tortillas and sold them from his own home at a rate of thirty per real. To paint an even darker picture, Ochoa y Velasco and Morales reported that women and young girls, who presumably frequented the houses of González and his lieutenants to purchase goods, often returned home with their virtues "lamentably diminished."

To complement the sale of foodstuffs in Ciudad Real, González also traded finished goods and luxury produce with both Indians and Spaniards, using the repartimiento de mercancías and the derrama to acquire the desired commodities. The alcalde mayor procured raw cotton from pueblos in Los Llanos and la Guardianía de Hueytiupán at an undisclosed price. He sold portions of it to private merchants and to Indians who needed cotton for mantas to be paid as tribute. The rate for each was six to eight reales per *arroba* (twenty-five pounds), two to four reales above the fair price. The rest he redistributed in the partidos of the Tzeltales, Los Llanos, the Zoque, and la Guardianía de Hueytiupán, to be sold to Indian justicias for the low price of only two reales per arroba and woven into mantas that González sold for his own profit. He paid one real per pierna for a finished manta of three piernas, four reales below the accepted fair price. Fiber for cord was apparently distributed without charge in lots of five *libras*, yielding a libra of string (*hilo*), for which the maker was paid one real. González also saved on transport costs for both raw cotton and the finished cloth. He paid half a real per twelve arrobas of fiber hauled from pueblo to pueblo, distances of ten to twelve leagues, and nothing at all for the porterage of mantas to Ciudad Real.

The alcalde mayor purchased unprocessed agave fiber in Tabasco and had it transported without pay by Zoque Indians from Quechula and Chicuacán to their pueblos, where it was made into thread. With the justicias acting as middlemen, as they did in the repartimiento of cotton, the Indians were paid three reales each to turn two pounds, four ounces of raw fiber into finished thread that sold for one peso.

González acquired cacao, cochineal, and tobacco simply by compelling native producers to sell only to his lieutenants or him and forbidding them to sell to other merchants. He bought most of the cacao from native justicias in the Zoque province at eight to ten pesos per *cargo* of seventy pounds. It was carried to the alcalde mayor's home in Ciudad Real by porters, who received no pay for their labor. The resale price of the cacao was, unfortunately, not recorded. He also purchased cochineal from the Zoque—nearly a thousand arrobas at three pesos per arroba. The fair price was from four to six pesos. Tobacco he purchased in the Tzotzil town of Simojovel. In 1707, González acquired 21,000 *manojos*, or "handfuls," paying one real per three manojos. While most of the foodstuffs marketed by the alcalde mayor seems to have been sold locally, much of the cacao and cochineal were exported to Mexico. One year, for example, the alcalde mayor of Tehuantepec bought cochineal, exchanging clothing made in Puebla and salt for it. These González then sold in Ciudad Real.

Along with the evening selling of tortillas and almudes of corn, González was reported to have dealt in small quantities of other items: pigs, bacon, cheese, wax, and small Chamula-made boxes that were sold to the clergy.

But, while his control of high-volume or wholesale commerce was described as a monopoly, he shared retail markets with other merchants. Other sources report a steady coming and going of small traders along the Camino Real and in the larger villages to the north.[87] Any town with some local ladino settlers probably featured a resident group of petty merchants, and much of the retail trade within the province and between Chiapas and neighboring provinces was carried on by small-scale peddlers, working alone and trading in modest quantities of regional specialties.

Despite the protests of Clemente de Ochoa y Velasco and Manuel de Morales, Martín González de Vergara held his post until his death in late May 1712. Other sources suggest that neither his methods nor the scale of his activities was particularly unusual. Robert Wasserstrom has shown how, in the mid to late eighteenth century, alcaldes mayores created an even more extensive commercial network using similar practices.[88]

Not all of the means available to a provincial governor to profit from his office were so complex. The great range of his responsibilities required periodic visits to the pueblos, and these occasions provide some of the earliest examples of official exploitation. Visits would sometimes last a month or more, during which the community was expected to provide food and services for the alcalde mayor and his entire retinue. Indians were supposed to be paid for this, but they rarely were. Such was the case in 1642 when the alcalde mayor, Diego Ordóñez de Villa, entered Ocosingo to open a new road. He was accompanied by five hundred Chiapaneco auxiliaries and a hundred mestizos.[89] For two months they pilfered corn and pigs, occupied houses, demanded labor, and confiscated mules, *machetes*, and grinding stones. They paid for none of it and threatened the lives of those who resisted. In 1690, community officials in Chilón reported that the last visit by the alcalde mayor had cost them 450 *tostones* in "salaries and costs" and that another 120 tostones had been removed from the town treasury. The total sum was more than the yearly income of the parish priest and nearly equaled the value of the pueblo's annual tribute assessment.[90] Most visits were probably not as costly as these, but late in the seventeenth century, royal officials were visiting the pueblos much more frequently, as were ecclesiastical functionaries, and resentment among the Maya at having to bear the costs of feeding these uninvited guests was increasing. After the rebellion, the audiencia enacted new legislation that stipulated that any visitors to an Indian pueblo, whether a Church or Crown official or a simple traveler, had to pay the proper price for the services they received.[91] It seems very unlikely that such ordinances were obeyed, but their passage shows that the Spanish at least recognized the severity of the problem.

THE CHURCH

In Chiapas the division of labor among different branches of the Church was established by 1600. From their six convents at Ciudad Real, Chiapa de Indios, Tecpatlán, Copanaguastla, Comitán, and Ocosingo, the Dominicans administered some eighty-three towns and villages, nearly the entire province. The Franciscans, who came late to Ciudad Real (1577) and who never challenged their Dominican brothers, maintained a single convent in the capital. From there they tended two adjacent Indian barrios, San Diego and San Antonio, and two Tzotzil parishes: San Felipe Acatepeque, south of the city, and Asunción Hueytiupán, to the north, which included Simojovel and the Tzeltal pueblo of Moyos. The Mercedarians, the first of the three mendicant orders to come to Chiapas, abandoned the province after the 1540s. Finally, the secular clergy held four benefices. Two, Ciudad Real and Xiquipilas, in the Zoque province, were for the most part ladino towns. The others, Tila and Tumbalá, were Chol pueblos that the Dominicans had forfeited in 1595. These parishes included the Tzeltal towns of Petalsingo and Palenque, respectively.[92]

Neither the regular nor the secular priests in Chiapas lived full-time in the Indian parishes to which they were assigned. They resided instead in the convents and visited their parishes to say mass on designated Sundays or to attend feast-day celebrations sponsored by the native religious cofradías. Early in the seventeenth century this system made for frequent and sometimes long absences between visits. But in the middle of the century the Dominicans took steps to improve their administration by designating several more pueblos (along with the towns where the convents were located) as *cabeceras*, or parish seats. By 1654 there were fifteen Indian parishes in the province. More were established in the highlands during the 1660s when a new bishop, Fray Mauro de Tovar y Valle, attempted to install secular priests in several Dominican benefices. Seven cabeceras were named among the

Tzeltal (Cancuc, Bachajón, Guaguitepeque, Oxchuc, Yajalón, Tenejapa, and Ocosingo) and two among the Tzotzil (Chamula and Zinacantán).[93]

Though the friars still did not live in the Indian communities full-time, these measures were designed to assure that they spent more time outside of their convents. During the seventeenth century, the number of holy-day celebrations sponsored in each pueblo also expanded, and this too reduced the time between a *cura*'s visits. By the 1690s, mass was regularly celebrated at least twice a month in five of the seven Tzeltal cabeceras.[94] In Cancuc twenty-five cofradía-sponsored fiestas and eight festivals were supported by individual alferezes, as well as celebrations for Holy Week and el Día de San Juan, the town's patron saint's day. In sum, there were at least forty-seven occasions that called for a priest to be present.

Despite these efforts to establish a stronger presence among the native peoples of Chiapas, the Dominicans still were overextended. Royal guidelines called for one priest for every four hundred tributaries, a ratio the order could not maintain in Chiapas for lack of priests.[95] In 1617 the Dominican community in the province numbered forty-three, seven of whom were lay brothers; in 1650 it numbered forty-five, and in 1664, fifty-two. Not all of these friars were available for parochial tasks. A good number were old and infirm, and others were occupied as teachers. As a consequence, the relatively few qualified parish priests were asked to administer rather large jurisdictions—large in both geographic and demographic terms. The curate of Chamula, for example, administered nine separate pueblos. In the highlands the residential pattern of dispersed settlement made the job still more difficult, and increases in the population of many Indian pueblos after the middle of the century extended the friars even further. As Table 3.3 shows, the shortage of priests was most severe in the central highlands.

The size of the benefices undermined the friars' effectiveness as teachers of Christianity, as spiritual advisors, and as overseers of native religious practices. Even after the reforms of the late seventeenth century, some highland pueblos still celebrated mass only five or six times a year.[96] There were also complaints that even when priests visited the pueblos they often refused to be inconvenienced by their native parishioners. It was said, for example, that they refused to go out to the milpas to attend the sick or to give the last rites.[97] Direct contact between priests and most Indian men and women

TABLE 3.3   RATIO OF PRIESTS TO FULL TRIBUTARIES
IN 1684

Priory of Chiapa	1:487
Priory of Ciudad Real	1:722
Priory of Comitán	1:608
Priory of Ocosingo	1:735
Priory of Socoltenango	1:423
Priory of Tecpatlán	1:577

SOURCE: AGCA: A3.2 (I) 15,207 825: Padrón de los indios
tributarios que estaban bajo la administración de religiosos
de la provincia de San Vicente de Chiapa y Guatemala,
1684.

must have been limited and infrequent. Under such circumstances, the friars depended on native assistants called *fiscales* and *maestros de coro* to tend to tasks they could not, or would not, do themselves. These officials were selected in every pueblo to assure attendance at the Mass, to lead liturgical singing and chanting, and to help maintain the registries of baptisms, marriages, and burials.

The Crown would have preferred to replace the Dominicans with secular clergy. The mendicant orders had been assigned to parochial work in the Indies only because of the unusual circumstances of the conquest. Empowered by the papacy under the *patronato real* in 1493, the Crown had enlisted the regular orders in 1522 to introduce the faith to pagan peoples in the New World.[98] By the end of the sixteenth century, with the mission of conversion theoretically completed, the Crown supported, in principle, the transfer of parish administration to the secular wing of the Church. In 1574, Philip II upheld the authority of bishops over regular clerics assigned to serve parishes. The bishops, in turn, began to replace the regulars with secular clergymen. In Peru the transition took place during the next half-century. But in New Spain the regular orders resisted until after the mid eighteenth century, when Bourbon reformers insisted that the secularization of Indian parishes be completed.

The first serious attempt to oust the Dominicans in Chiapas began in 1654, when Fray Mauro Tobar y Valle, a Benedictine, became bishop.[99] The issue was raised again in 1680, 1686, 1721, 1746, and 1763.[100] Each time the Dominicans managed to hold on to their benefices. Finally, in the 1770s, during the most intensive phase of the Bourbon reforms, the Crown ruled against them.

The longevity of Dominican rule in Chiapas was in large measure a reflection of the deterioration of local Spanish society during the prolonged economic decline between 1620 and 1740. By 1721 the two communities were roughly equal in size, and the seculars could rightly claim to match the manpower of the friars. The secular clergy totaled forty-eight, forty of whom were natives of the province. However, an extensive review carried out by the alcalde mayor on behalf of the Crown concluded that the seculars were ill-equipped to replace the Dominicans in the villages. Twelve commissioners reported that the secular clergy lacked the necessary language and literary skills, even though since 1678 Ciudad Real had had its own seminary. Only sixteen of the forty-eight were judged functionally literate, and only twelve of them knew local native tongues. One evaluator, who disagreed with the commissioners' report, argued that not one of the seculars had the skills to preach in an Indian language, and another evaluator passed only three on combined linguistic and literacy ability. The failures were blamed in part on neglect for letters in the curriculum of the seminary, but the commission also attributed the seculars' lack of intellectual sophistication to the cultural environment in the homes of Ciudad Real's Spanish families, where the children grew up speaking a mix of Nahuatl and Castilian learned from Indian servants from the city's barrios.[101]

Most Dominicans, on the other hand, were native Guatemalans, who, as adolescents, had been educated in Santiago at either the Jesuit Colegio de San Lucas or the Universidad de San Carlos. The handful of young men from Ciudad Real who did join the order were also educated in the Guatemalan capital. However, the commission attributed the Dominicans' skill in native languages to the training they had received in the convents in Chiapas prior to their assignments as curates.

At stake in the secularization controversy, of course, was not only the quality of the priests who would tend Indian parishes but also access to the material resources of native communities. While each new bishop lamented the diocese's poverty and dependence on royal pensions and stipends, the Dominicans received a reliable income from gratuities and fees collected in each pueblo. Local Spaniards whose sons were leaving the province for lack of economic prospects must have looked longingly at this potential source of income. In 1690 a justice from the audiencia, Joseph de Escals, carried out a lengthy visita in Chiapas, part of an investigation into the activities of both the alcalde mayor and the Dominicans.[102] The following account offers a good example of the revenue collected in each town.

Fray Mateo García administered Chilón, a Tzeltal pueblo in the parish of Bachajón. Each year, according to native witnesses, the pueblo gave him two hundred tostones in coin and seventy fanegas of corn. During his periodic visits he also received ten to twelve eggs each day and the labor of four men who cared for his horses, a *mayordomo* who supervised his household, and at least three female servants, who made his tortillas and cooked his meals. For baptisms he was paid two reales; for marriages, nine tostones and two reales; for burials, from one to six tostones; and for requiem masses, or *misas del cuerpo*, four tostones. He said mass once a month, for which he was given three tostones. In addition, the town's six cofradías together sponsored thirty fiestas a year, paying from three to six tostones for masses said on these occasions. Finally, nine more fiestas were funded by different alferezes, each of whom offered twelve tostones for the priest's attendance. Fray Mateo's total yearly income in Chilón was valued at more than four hundred pesos. He also served Bachajón, a slightly larger pueblo, and received a comparable income there.

Table 3.4 lists the total value of the revenue the Dominicans received in each pueblo. The figures vary because the cabeceras and more populous towns were expected to contribute more toward the priests' "sustenance," in coin and produce, than smaller pueblos less frequently visited. Fees collected "para sustento" were really a kind of tax, for they greatly exceeded even the hungriest friar's appetite, though they were not a head tax like the tithe exacted from Spaniards, mestizos, and mulattos. Parish seats and larger centers sometimes celebrated more fiestas, and this also accounts for part of the variation.

Two sources of parish revenue were particularly criticized. The audiencia repeatedly chastised the friars for demanding fees for administering the sacraments. According to Justice Escals, one result of the practice was that

TABLE 3.4   ECCLESIASTICAL FEES COLLECTED IN DOMINICAN
PUEBLOS IN 1690

Pueblo	Pesos	Reales
PRIORATTO DE CHIAPA DE INDIOS		
Acalán	522	
Chiapa	3,030	4
Chiapilla	104	
Osuta	228	4
Pochuta	73	
Suchiapa	452	6
Tuxtla	2,011	6
PRIORATTO DE CIUDAD REAL		
Amatenango	573	7
Aquacatenango	311	4
Chamula	758	4
Huistán	87	2
San Andrés	117	
San Miguel Mitontic	60	2
San Pablo	112	2
San Pedro Chenaló	121	6
Santa Caterina	84	4
Santa María Magdalena	105	6
Santa Marta	85	2

SOURCE: AGI: AG, 215: Autos de la visita general, 1690.

NOTE: The amounts shown in the table represent the total payments
given to the parish priest for presiding at baptisms, marriages, and
burials and for celebrating Mass on various saints' days and during
Holy Week. The amounts do not include payments made "por
sustento," that is, payments made to the priest to cover the cost of
food and domestic service during his visits.

Pueblo	Pesos	Reales
Santiago	114	2
Tenejapa	111	
Teopisca	666	
Teultepeque	513	3
PRIORATTO DE COMITÁN		
Comitán	636	7
Zapaluta	455	5
PRIORATTO DE OCOSINGO		
Bachajón	300	
Cancuc	442	3
Chilón	400	5
Guaguitepeque	270	
Ocosingo	458	
Sibacá	302	4
Sitalá	240	4
Tenango	227	4
Yajalón	501	7
PRIORATTO DE SOCOLTENANGO		
Istapilla	56	
Pinula	72	
San Bartolomé de los Llanos	611	1
Socoltenango	646	
Soyatitlán	497	1
PRIORATTO DE TECPATLÁN		
Chalpultenango	1,101	2
Chicoacán	178	4

Pueblo	Pesos	Reales
Coalpitán	112	3
Coapilla	87	
Copainalá	830	1
Isguatán	306	6
Ixtacomitán	775	6
Jitotol	878	2
Ocotepeque	149	2
Ostuacán	180	3
Pantepeque	108	
Pueblo Nuevo	356	6
Quechula	106	
Sayula	216	4
Silocuchiapa	136	7
Tapalapa	705	1
Tecpatlán	1,009	4
Usumacinta	226	4

Indians passed up the rites rather than pay for them. Children were left unbaptized until the age of three, he claimed, and single adults often postponed official marriages.[103] Some observers thought it extremely callous that priests not only charged for the last rites but also refused to travel to where the sick lay dying.

Civil authorities and bishops who were not Dominicans also disapproved of the cofradías and suggested that the Indians had been encouraged to establish such organizations simply to provide the priests with additional income.[104] Moreover, critics claimed, the fiestas sponsored by cofradías led to public drunkenness, attracted unsavory peddlers who sold gunpowder and other forbidden goods, and encouraged the kind of dancing, music, and ritual that came very close to pagan idolatry. But despite official condemnation, the Dominicans refused to alter their practices. Fees, they argued, were necessary to maintain the friars in such a poor province, and the cofradía celebrations had proved to be an essential and productive part of the evangelical enterprise.[105]

Though it was the most important, parish revenue was not the only source of income for the order. By the mid seventeenth century, the Dominicans had accumulated extensive landholdings in the Grijalva Valley and in the western and central highlands. These included two sugar estates, one near Chiapa de Indios, the other near Ocosingo, as well as more than a dozen estancias in the hinterlands around Ixtapa and Soyaló to the northwest and around Comitán and Socoltenango to the southeast.[106]

A detailed account of how the Dominican community used its revenue will not be attempted here. A portion, of course, went to feed and clothe the friars, pay for servants, and otherwise maintain the convents. Money also went to buy statuary, candles, incense, chalices, patens, vestments, and even the organs that were used in every parish church. Though church buildings in most pueblos were fairly modest on the outside, they were endowed with an impressive array of ceremonial paraphernalia on the inside. Some funds were passed on to other offices within the order, and sums not earmarked for church purposes provided capital for loans made to private citizens.[107]

Nearly all of the revenue collected in Indian parishes went to the Dominicans, but provincial bishops were also able to tap native resources directly by charging fees and soliciting alms during their periodic visitas, or tours of inspection.[108] Like the visits of the alcaldes mayores, these tours were undertaken more regularly late in the seventeenth century. Fray Marcos Bravo de la Serna completed three between 1677 and 1680, while his successor, Fray Francisco Núñez de la Vega, carried out seven between 1686 and 1709. They both collected *derechos por la visita*, fees to underwrite their tours, exacting fourteen tostones from cofradías in each pueblo. They also required alms for requiem masses devoted to deceased members of the cofradías. Presumably they also received food and services during their stays, though the value of these is unknown.

Thanks to the account of Fray Ximénez, the most notorious visita carried out by a bishop was that of the Franciscan friar Bauptista Alvarez de Toledo in 1709. Ximénez denounced Alvarez de Toledo for his "desmedida codicia," his "limitless greed," and described the tour in remarkably scathing language, particularly the "business" (*renglón*) of forcing Indians to have their children confirmed:

> at three reales for each child, bringing such scandal and ruin upon the Indians that those who could not pay were put in jail, and afterward the jails in all the pueblos that he visited were full. Where they had mantas, the confirmation was made for cloth, where cacao, for cacao; where they had chocolate cakes, in chocolate cakes. With this strategy, the value was very great, a peso for each confirmation, and when all these fruits were collected, and given to his agents to be sold, the value was much greater.

He continued, "whereas earlier bishops had visited every three years, this one visited after a year and a half, taking from each Cofradía seven pesos de visita and twelve or more pesos for masses . . . taking all the *fábricas* and *sustentos* of the communities. The first inspection had left them exhausted and they could not tolerate the second."[109]

Actually, Bishop Alvarez de Toledo was neither the first to charge the cofradías for derechos por la visita nor the first to carry out additional inspections within three years. Ximénez's sainted Fray Núñez de la Vega had collected fees, and he had also inspected the bishopric every two years. However, Alvarez de Toledo's immediate predecessors apparently had not imprisoned Indians who were unable to pay, and Núñez de la Vega had forgiven the debts of bankrupt cofradías without penalty. Cofradía ledgers, which are discussed in the next chapter, show that Alvarez de Toledo's administration was indeed ruinous.[110] The principal carried by cofradía treasuries typically diminished by half after his visita in 1709, though the decline cannot be entirely accounted for by fees and alms he required during the inspection. Among those fees was a new charge of eight reales imposed on each cofradía to support a new Hospital de la Caridad in Ciudad Real. Ximénez is undoubtedly right in blaming the bishop for contributing to the conditions that led to the Tzeltal Revolt. Among those imprisoned for refusing to have his child confirmed was Lucas Pérez, a fiscal in Chilón who later held a key ceremonial position among the Cancuc rebels.[111]

Not all of the burdens placed on the Maya by the Church at the end of the seventeenth century were economic. In 1687, Bishop Núñez de la Vega began a new campaign against idolatry and witchcraft, the most aggressive campaign in more than a century. His *Constituciones diocesanas* exhorted parish curates to be more vigilant, and to aid their efforts, it included detailed descriptions of curing ceremonies and Maya shamanism. In Oxchuc, the bishop conducted an *auto da fé*, burning the painted images of two indigenous deities, Poxlon and Hicalahau, that he had discovered—much to his horror—nailed to a beam in the village church.[112] There, and in other towns as well, he confiscated the ritual almanacs, or calendar boards, used by Maya shamans. Then, during the visita of Joseph de Escals in 1690, cofradía rituals came under attack. These initiatives upset the uneasy truce that native practitioners and the parish clergy had agreed upon as the zealotry of the early friars gave way to the pragmatic tolerance of their successors. Núñez de la Vega's denunciation of postconquest syncretism threatened the Maya's cultural accommodation to the new spiritual order in a fundamental way. His actions were one of a number of factors that assured that when the Maya responded to the crisis of the early eighteenth century, they would call upon supernatural forces.

CONCLUSION

Drawing on Eric Wolf's early work on peasants and James Scott's studies of the moral economy of village life in Southeast Asia, John Tutino recently offered a conceptual framework for understanding agrarian violence in Mexico.[113] Rural peoples rebel, he argued, when they believe their subsistence base is in jeopardy. Threats to that base are a function of four variables: material conditions, autonomy, security, and mobility. Do people have access to the basic goods necessary for subsistence? Can they produce those goods independently? Can they produce them consistently? And can they choose other alternatives when one source of subsistence fails? Noting that peasants, small farmers, wage workers, and tenants rarely enjoy high levels of all four variables, Tutino suggested that violence is provoked when a decline in one or more areas is not compensated by an improvement in another. For example, "Peasants accustomed to subsistence autonomy become outraged when that independence is threatened or undermined by visible elite or state actors—and when that loss of autonomy is not compensated by access to ways of life that are dependent yet secure."[114] In a literature often preoccupied with the abstract analysis of "big structures and large processes"[115] and cluttered with social science jargon, Tutino provides a remarkably lucid and useful model for understanding the material causes of the Cancuc rebellion.

For most of the seventeenth century, with the Spanish economy in decline, the Tzeltal and their neighbors were free of the kinds of threats to their subsistence base that elsewhere pushed Indians toward violence, especially later in the eighteenth century. The population ratio of Spaniard and mestizo to Maya was low, especially in the highlands, and there was little danger that village lands would be overrun by ladinos eager to own or rent property. There was no large-scale labor draft, nor was there much demand for Indian labor on Spanish haciendas and estancias. Though village alcaldes in Ocosingo complained that they were losing tributaries to nearby estates, nothing in the record suggests that local production suffered for it. Declines in the Maya population itself, even when reversed sometime around midcentury, assured that community holdings were more than adequate for local subsistence and diminished the likelihood of boundary disputes with neighboring settlements. Until the 1670s, at least some communities produced enough food to trade in the market in Ciudad Real.

Still, by all accounts the Maya of the plateau were poor. Climate limited them to one harvest a year, and yields were lower in the highlands than in the lower valleys. Further, while the contraction of the provincial economy freed them from certain kinds of intrusions, the limited need for day or seasonal laborers left highlanders with few opportunities to supplement subsistence agriculture with other forms of income. The margin between adequate food supplies and scarcity, then, was narrow even in the best of times.

The principal economic threats to subsistence in Chiapas during this period were the repartimientos de mercancías and the visitas of alcaldes mayores and provincial bishops. We know too little about the details of village agricultural productivity and food consumption to measure the impact of these demands with precision—too little, for example, to confirm Robert Wasserstrom's assertion that the repartimientos by themselves left native peoples chronically on the edge of starvation.[116] But there can be no doubt that together they significantly reduced whatever "surpluses" the Mayas may have produced. The visitas in particular laid waste to stores of corn, frijoles, fowl, and eggs, leaving everyone in the community hungry for weeks or months afterward. In Tutino's terms, their impact was to erode the security of subsistence by creating periodic shortages of essential staples.

In an average year, villages in the highlands seem to have been able to absorb the loss. But the draining off of community food reserves left them more vulnerable to famine in years of bad harvest or crop failure. Fray Francisco Ximénez, in fact, blamed the repartimientos of the alcalde mayor, Martín González de Vergara, for worsening the effects of a locust plague soon after he took office in 1706. The entire province, he wrote, was "aniquilada," almost completely destroyed by the resulting famine and the disease epidemic that followed.[117] Though Ximénez described the event in the most dire terms, it was not widely reported or commented upon by other sources, so one hesitates to make too much of it. But tribute accounts from several of the towns that would figure prominently in the 1712 uprising—Ocosingo, Bachajón, Tumbalá, and Tila—do show sharp drops in revenue between 1690 and 1710 that likely were linked to the crop failure. One might wish for more evidence, but at least for these pueblos it seems safe to conclude that the famine contributed significantly to participation in the rebellion.

Tutino's model points to the root cause of the 1712 uprising: the erosion of the highland Maya's security of subsistence by the escalating demands of civil and ecclesiastical authorities. Fray Francisco Ximénez recognized this at the time, and there is no reason to question his conclusion. Ultimately, subsistence was a function of ecology. This fact helps to explain why communities in the Grijalva basin and the lower valleys, such as Los Llanos, did not join the rebels. There, the same conditions that supported the production of cash crops like cacao and cotton also sustained two corn harvests a year. Even though these towns also were forced into intensely exploitive commercial exchanges, their subsistence was more secure than that of their brethren at higher elevations.

Identifying the material causes of the rebellion, however, offers only a partial explanation of the rebels' motives. To understand why their movement began as a religious cult, to account for their politics and the social origins of their leaders, and to clarify local and regional patterns of mobilization, we have to look beyond material causes.

NATIVE SOCIETIES AFTER THE CONQUEST

> Certain Indians, regardless of their guilt, were accused
> of crimes and imprisoned in the jail in Ciudad Real,
> even though they were rich and substantial men. These
> Indians were left exhausted and so poor they were
> reduced to beggary. In this state, for which there was no
> resolution, and having been respected leaders in their
> pueblos, they became angry and vengeful. They incited
> their people to rise up.
>
> —Fray Francisco Ximénez[1]

The first century of Spanish rule devastated Indian societies and cultures in Chiapas. They were overwhelmed by an enormous population loss, the extinction or forced relocation of whole towns and villages, the end of their control over regional trade, the subversion of local political autonomy, the introduction of a European Christian worldview, and the imposition of Roman Catholic ritual and practice. Yet native peoples endured. Those who survived reconstructed much of their social organization, kept up (more often than not) with subsistence needs and tribute demands, and held on to many of the forms, beliefs, and values of their cultural traditions.

In recent years, new work in demographic history has given scholars a clearer idea of the factors that promoted the biological and cultural survival of Indian populations in the New World. Linda Newsom has suggested that native groups in Spanish America can be divided into three types.[2] One experienced a sharp decline following contact but gradually recovered population later in the colonial period. This pattern was common in central and southern Mexico, highland Central America, and the Andes. The second faced a steady decline with no recovery. This was typical of the native experience in the temperate zones of the viceroyalties of New Granada (Venezuela, Colombia, and Ecuador) and the Río de la Plata (Argentina and Uruguay).

The third type, characteristic of the Caribbean islands and coastal Venezuela, was comprised of groups that disappeared entirely within two generations.

In general, mortality rates were somewhat lower and recovery came sooner in regions where complex urban societies had developed in the centuries before the European invasion. In these areas, larger populations assured that, despite catastrophic losses, significant numbers remained to reproduce themselves. The material conditions that promoted the rise of civilizations in the first place—ecological diversity, fertile soils, and adequate rainfall, among others—also contributed to the recovery of traditional economies that provided subsistence and sometimes marketable surpluses. Some scholars argue, in fact, that the indigenous peasants who survived, especially those in central Mexico and highland Guatemala, were better fed after the conquest than before.[3] Lower population densities, the reversion of cropland to game-rich woodland, and the collapse of highly exploitive native states may well have allowed them to produce and retain larger amounts and more varied types of foods.

As Table 4.1 shows, in comparable terms the native peoples of Chiapas survived the conquest and subsequent colonization in larger numbers than many of their counterparts elsewhere in the hemisphere. By 1611, according to Peter Gerhard, 62.5 percent had perished, an appalling depopulation ratio of 5.1:1—five dead for each survivor.[4] Yet this was significantly less than estimated ratios for a comparable period in other regions. In Chiapas, with the notable exception of Chiapa de Indios, the precipitous decline seems to have bottomed out by the middle of the seventeenth century. In many Zoque pueblos on the western plateau, the pace of decline slowed and populations remained viable even though losses continued until the end of the colonial period. In the central highlands and the region known as los Llanos, Tzeltal and Tzotzil populations actually began to recover.

Why they recovered is difficult to say. Gerhard suggests that native peoples may have acquired immunities to some European diseases, yet disease epidemics swept through the province again in the eighteenth century.[5] To test the hypothesis, more work needs to be done on distinguishing disease types. An alternative explanation may be found in the consequences of the provincial economic decline between 1620 and 1680. The easing of demands on their labor and the relaxation of Spanish administrative controls may have

TABLE 4.1   COMPARATIVE RATIOS OF POPULATION
DECLINE

Chiapas	1524–1611	5.1:1
Central Mexico		
Plateau	1532–1608	13.2:1
Coast	1532–1608	26:1
Peru		
Sierra	1520–1630	3.9:1
Coast	1520–1630	16.7:1

SOURCES: Linda Newsom, "Indian Population Patterns in Colonial
Spanish America," 42–46; Peter Gerhard, *The Southeast
Frontier of New Spain*, 160; Sherburne F. Cook and Woodrow
Borah, *The Indian Population of Central Mexico, 1531–1610*;
Noble David Cook, *Demographic Collapse: Indian Peru, 1520–
1620*.

left highland populations better able to meet their subsistence needs and
therefore more resistant to illness. But this, too, remains only an hypothesis.

Murdo MacLeod has emphasized that the demographic recovery was temporary.[6] In the early eighteenth century, the combined effect of new
epidemics and crop failures brought on by locusts brought renewed devastation
in the province.[7] Disruption of the agricultural cycle during the 1712 revolt,
and Spanish repression afterward, worsened conditions still more for several
Tzeltal communities. Yet without the increase in their numbers during the
seventeenth century, the consequences of the crisis in the eighteenth would
have been even more dire for the highland Maya, and though many people
perished between 1705 and 1735, their numbers had begun to increase
again by midcentury (see Appendix A).

Biological survival did not, of course, assure cultural survival. The preservation of distinctive ethnic identities depended on the vitality of social,
political, and economic arrangements centered in autonomous indigenous

communities. If native settlements were overrun by Spaniards or mestizos and if communal lands were lost to hacendados or *estancieros*, these arrangements were undermined and the communities were endangered. If Indians left their towns to live on private estates or in Spanish cities, the incidence of intermarriage with mestizos or mulattos increased and the pace of acculturation accelerated. Consequently, native cultural survival was more likely in regions where Europeans settled in smaller numbers or where local conditions helped to preserve the social and economic integrity of the community. No indigenous cultures survived unchanged, however. This was as true of "primitive" Lacandón populations in the rain forest of the southern Petén as it was for the Tlaxcalans of central Mexico. Cultural survival under Spanish rule was achieved through the successful adaptation of older institutions and beliefs, and the creation and integration of new ones, which reinforced ties of community and ethnic identity even though they often failed to keep the forces of exploitation entirely at bay.

Three institutions introduced by the Spanish played important roles in the preservation of native communities: the municipal council, or *cabildo*; the parish offices of *fiscal, maestro de coro*, and *sacristán*; and the parishioners' association, or *cofradía*. Each was established to meet the needs of the colonial civil and ecclesiastical bureaucracy and functioned to structure and mediate contact between the community and the outside. But each would also contribute to the internal dynamics of native life, providing contexts for acting out local politics and mechanisms for mobilizing social interaction, allocating material resources, and articulating basic values.

In the period from roughly 1580 to 1680, the three institutions took on a life of their own in the native communities of Chiapas. As outlined in the previous chapter, for much of the seventeenth century the highland Maya were relatively neglected. The worst violations of the conquest generation were well past, and a depressed economy turned the attention of many enterprising Spaniards elsewhere. Murdo MacLeod has suggested that these conditions, which also prevailed in western Guatemala, gave the Maya a chance to achieve a "new equilibrium."[8] At the end of the century, however, civil and ecclesiastical administrators gradually built up their control in the pueblos, and these institutions were subject to new constraints. When their stability was undermined, the incidence of community violence increased and the potential for rebellion was raised.

THE NATIVE NOBILITY

The Spanish institutions of local government were grafted onto earlier forms of community political organization controlled by the indigenous nobility, the caciques and principales. In Chiapas during the first twenty years of the colony, civil officials, *encomenderos*, and Dominicans led a sustained attack against this hereditary elite. Their actions were not intended to destroy the native hierarchy but rather to assure that it would serve their own, often competing interests. They either removed legitimate elites and filled posts with individuals who were ineligible according to traditional rules of succession or they so compromised native leaders whose tenure was sanctioned by their peers that their people turned against them. By 1582 the audiencia reported that no cacique in Chiapas could trace his lineage back to a preconquest patrimony, or *señorío*.[9]

The structure of the native hierarchy also was altered by population losses and by the *reducciones* of the 1560s and 1570s. High mortality reduced the pool of eligible marriage partners among the noble lineages and sometimes forced caciques and principales to violate the traditional rules of endogamy. The merging of dispersed settlements could involve the joining of two distinct cacicazgos or force lesser lineages to forfeit their privileges to families of higher rank.

Three episodes in particular illustrate the kinds of pressure that Indian elites fell prey to. In 1535, Francisco Gil, a lieutenant governor appointed by Francisco de Montejo, led an *entrada de guerra* into the central highlands.[10] Though accounts vary, in Tila, a Chol town not far from Tabasco, Gil burned perhaps fourteen caciques and principales to death. They had been reluctant to supply porters and had resisted demands for slaves. Two other principales were publicly disfigured and left behind to serve as reminders of the dangers of opposing Spanish rule.

Another well-documented scandal took place in the 1540s in Chiapa de Indios.[11] There the encomendero, Balthasar Guerra, imprisoned the cacique, Pedro Notí, for cooperating with the friars and deprived him of his cacicazgo. Guerra installed a kinsman of Don Pedro in his place, Juan Notí, who then suffered constant harassment from the Dominicans, who beat him for supplying labor and materials to Guerra's sugar mill.

The third case occurred during the same period in Zinacantán.[12] A principal, Bartolomé Tzun, was named *alguacil* by the Dominicans and lent his enthusiasm to the friars' efforts to promote baptism and deprive other principales of their concubines. His acts of violence and physical abuse, however, prompted an outcry. Led by principales loyal to town interests, the pueblo protested to civil authorities in Ciudad Real, and eventually Tzun was removed from office and exiled from the province.

By the end of the sixteenth century, native political life had been reshaped to serve the colonizers. In some towns the introduction of Indian governorships completed and institutionalized the transformation of the cacique from a figure who governed according to indigenous rules and sanctions to one whose power and authority were legitimized by Spanish courts and often exercised in an Hispanic style. The office was a reward for loyalty, piety, and rectitude—their *títulos* used just those words.[13] In contrast to central Mexico—where, early in the seventeenth century, caciques yielded control over local government—in Chiapas, Indian governors retained their authority.[14] Their titles explicitly confirmed their superiority over the native cabildos and commanded alcaldes and *regidores* to obey their wishes and respect their privileges.[15] Included in these "honras, grácias, y mercedes" were free labor on a milpa set aside for their use, free household service, and exemption from tribute obligations.

The preservation of cacicazgos, however, was not assured by administrative fiat. Throughout Spanish America, if the economic circumstances of traditional elites deteriorated, their political authority usually diminished. Though their customary rights may have given them easier access to land and labor, unless caciques and principales developed entrepreneurial expertise in the new colonial marketplace, they were likely to descend into poverty and lose their privileges.

The field has long recognized that elites in the Andes were skilled social climbers who parlayed their traditional rights into large private landholdings and lucrative trading networks.[16] These *kurakas*, as they were called, also made good use of the Spanish courts and entered into strategic marriages with prominent European families to protect their political prerogatives. For Mesoamericanists, one of the revelations of the last fifteen years of scholarship has been that Indian elites in Mexico and Central America also were often remarkably successful merchants and landholders whose business acumen helped them to preserve their place in the native social hierarchy.[17]

In Chiapas, caciques remained particularly strong among the Zoque, where governors were appointed in Tuxtla and Quechula throughout the colonial period. Their control of cacao production made them valuable to Spanish civil officials and provided them with a lucrative cash crop well into the eighteenth century. These caciques diversified their economic activities and became landholders, with investments in horses and cattle. In addition, they were partners to the alcaldes mayores' commercial schemes.[18] Caciques also were named governors in each of the Indian barrios in Ciudad Real, where, presumably, they were active in the commerce of the city.[19] The richest and most powerful native lord in the province was the governor of Chiapa de Indios, whom Thomas Gage described this way: "This Governor may wear a rapier and dagger, and enjoyeth many other liberties denied the rest of the Indians. No town hath so many dons in it of Indian blood as this. Don Felipe de Guzmán was governor in my time, a very rich Indian, who commonly kept in his stable a dozen of as good horses for show and ostentation as the best Spaniard in the country."[20]

Time and again, Indian governors proved to be important allies of the colonial government. The cacique of Chiapa de Indios regularly supplied the alcalde mayor with horses, porters, and foot soldiers,[21] and during the 1712 rebellion his counterpart in Tuxtla and he provided horses, men, and other supplies to the audiencia forces that marched against the rebels.[22]

In most native communities in the province, however, by the end of the sixteenth century the office of cacique had fallen vacant, and governors were not appointed. The weakness of cacicazgos reflected the relative poverty of the region and the low level of political consolidation at the time of initial contact. In the highlands, only Ixtapa, a Tzotzil town west of Ciudad Real, seems to have retained a cacique into the eighteenth century without interruption.[23] His cacicazgo, which also included Zinacantán, San Gabriel, and Soyaló, was confirmed in 1701, but colonial records reveal nothing else about him. Ixtapa and Zinacantán controlled the province's only source of salt, and this likely provided the material base that enabled the cacique to preserve his position. Heirs to cacicazgos in Chamula and Bachajón petitioned the Crown for confirmation of their fathers' privileges in 1601 and 1640 respectively, but no other reference to caciques in these towns has been found for later periods.[24]

To reestablish order and good government following the Tzeltal Revolt, governors were reintroduced in Yajalón, Sibacá, Tenejapa, Oxchuc, Moyos, Tila, Tumbalá, and Ocosingo.[25] In Yajalón the appointee apparently claimed ancestral cacique status, but the origins of the other governors are unknown. By the 1740s, except in Ocosingo, these offices had again fallen vacant.[26]

The disappearance of cacicazgos, however, did not signal the extinction of the lineage hierarchy altogether, for the status of lower-ranking nobles, or principales, survived the cataclysms of the sixteenth century. Remesal and Ximénez each take for granted the fundamental division between noble and commoner in their accounts of highland communities after the Conquest,[27] and a Tzeltal dictionary compiled around 1560 by Fray Domingo de Ara, the former parish priest of Copanaguastla, documents the persistence of the distinction.[28]

Other evidence suggests that the lineage hierarchy survived at least into the eighteenth century. In 1695, Bishop Núñez de la Vega reported the preservation of calendar almanacs that included the origin myths of prominent lineages.[29] Just where these almanacs were found, and whether principales as well as caciques kept them, is unknown, but Núñez de la Vega makes it clear that the texts were not kept as relics. They were still being used in religious ceremonies, proof that recitations of the myths still had social significance as an element of religious belief that legitimated the status hierarchy.

Under Spanish law, principales did not enjoy the same rights and privileges as caciques. They were not exempt from tribute payments, nor were they allowed to claim customary rights to labor or land. In Chiapas they were not even entitled to use the honorary *don* before their names. Under these circumstances, their claims to noble status might well have become meaningless, an historical anachronism. But they did not, because principales adapted to the realities of colonial rule and reclaimed their political power by asserting control of the key civil and religious offices introduced by the Spanish.

THE CABILDO

For most of the seventeenth and eighteenth centuries, native government in the central highlands was exercised by officeholders in cabildos without supervision from an Indian governor. Every community with pueblo status had its own cabildo, with two alcaldes, four regidores, and two alguaciles. The alcaldes and regidores were ranked (*de primer voto*, *de segundo voto*). They served one-year terms, and during their tenure they were exempt from paying tribute and were entitled to free labor on their milpas, though the Crown disapproved of the latter practice.[30]

In the sixteenth century, when the system was introduced, local encomenderos, parish priests, and Indian governors filled cabildo offices with their own favorites, with the highest positions often going to kinsmen of the cacique.[31] Spanish law, however, provided for the election of native justicias by the communities themselves, and elections were customary by the early seventeenth century. In Chiapas they were usually held in the village church on New Year's Day, with the outgoing alcaldes and regidores serving as electors.[32] A public ceremony followed the vote, and the wooden staffs, or *varas*, the symbols of officeholding, were given over to members of the new council. They were required to present themselves within a week or two before the alcalde mayor in Ciudad Real for confirmation of their election.

The principal responsibility of the justicias was to uphold public order. They were required to make sure that the land was worked industriously and that tributes were paid on time. They maintained the jail and supervised the housing of travelers in the village *casa de húespedes*, or inn. It was their job to keep suspicious vagrants out of the pueblo and to prohibit itinerant peddlers from hawking their wares door-to-door, and they were supposed to suppress the illegal manufacture of liquor and punish public drunkenness. They were also charged with ensuring that their townspeople led lives of Christian virtue. They were instructed to see that children always attended mass, that no unmarried couples lived under the same roof, and that men and women were properly married. Among their most important duties was sponsorship of the celebrations that marked Holy Week and All Saints' Day.[33] They also contributed to the fiesta honoring the town's patron saint, which was primarily supported by one of the village cofradías. The prominent role of civil officeholders in community religious life has not always been recognized by scholars, but as the next chapter shows, it was a fundamental source of their legitimacy and an important element in the broader construction of Maya ideas and values concerning power, authority, and hierarchy.

The expenses of the justicias' administration were paid out of the town's treasury, the *caja de comunidad*. These funds were established when the cabildos themselves were founded in the late 1540s and 1550s. They were supported by a separate tax and by the profits from the sale of crops raised on a special plot of land, the *milpa de comunidad*. The tax rate in the late seventeenth century was two reales or one pierna of cotton cloth per full tributary. Those in other categories paid a rate of half that.[34] Cultivation of the milpas de comunidad was briefly suspended by the highland Tzeltal around 1690, when the alcalde mayor imposed a tax of four reales on those who worked them.[35] The visitador Joseph de Escals, whose activities are discussed in the previous chapter, lifted the surcharge, and the practice resumed.

The colonial system of government placed native officeholders in a precarious position. They had to maintain a delicate balance between protecting the interests of their pueblo and facilitating the activities of Spanish civil and ecclesiastical administrators. To fulfill this complex role and exercise power effectively, candidates for office needed the consent both of those they governed and those who wielded greater authority. For this reason, throughout Mexico and Guatemala the native cabildos had first been filled by male kindred of the caciques and Indian governors, or by principales. This system allowed the Spanish to introduce an essentially Iberian administrative structure into the Indian community without completely disrupting its traditional political culture. Designed to promote effective local control and to institutionalize the dependence of Indian leaders, it nonetheless reinforced older indigenous relations of hierarchy and authority, and provided a measure of continuity between the preconquest and postconquest political structure. Though Spanish encomenderos, parish priests, and provincial governors sometimes imposed their own choice for an office, normally the hereditary elites elected officeholders. The system allowed a measure of autonomy that, though subject to strong outside influence, was nonetheless real.

Over time, in some parts of the viceroyalty the principales did lose their monopoly over cabildo officeholding as the lineage hierarchy eroded and became less of an index of wealth, status, and power.[36] In part this reflected the same conditions that promoted the decay of cacicazgos. Severe mortality in a community could diminish the integrity of lesser elite lineages, with the result that Spanish courts would no longer recognize the validity of claims to noble status. The impoverishment of principales also weakened their authority. In some cases, the decline of the political power of the principales was a consequence of the rise of commoners, or *macehuales*. In

Oaxaca, for example, the economic revival of the mid eighteenth century stimulated local markets and created opportunities for Indians to expand their participation in commerce and specialized crafts.[37] As a result, principales, who had preserved their control of the cabildos until then, were forced to allow commoners to hold office.

Where macehuales moved into civil officeholding, the meaning of the term *principal* was altered, and the process that gave village leaders legitimacy was changed. The term no longer applied solely to members of the Indian nobility but instead included all those who had served in offices on the cabildo and had acquired the requisite status. For this reason, some scholars translate *principales* as *elders*.[38] The practice is especially common in historical writing by anthropologists, whose ethnographic experience leads them to look for continuities in the past. In contemporary Maya communities, the term *principales* does indeed refer to a group of older men and former officeholders, whose age and political experience confer high status and influence.[39]

This definition of *principal* follows from a more fundamental view of how the political and social dynamics of native communities changed after the conquest. It derives from Eric Wolf's classic interpretation of the origins of contemporary rural villages, and it presupposes that the transformation of highly stratified autochthonous cities into small-scale peasant communities resulted in a general leveling of economic and status differences and the emergence of more egalitarian societies.[40] From this perspective, the legitimacy of cabildo officeholders no longer derived from traditional ideas about the privileges and obligations of the noble lineages. Preconquest political culture, which had reinforced the primacy of vertical social hierarchies and upheld the authority of a small elite, gave way to a system that promoted horizontal social integration and broadened the base of political participation.[41]

Among the Tzeltal, Tzotzil, and Chol, colonial records indicate that political authority in each pueblo remained in the hands of a small elite throughout the colonial period, and there is no evidence to suggest that the system for selecting civil officeholders was altered to distribute power more widely or more equitably. As noted above, in tribute accounts, visita reports, and trial testimony the distinction between principal and macehual persists, evidence that the Spanish recognized the continued significance of some differences in rank within native communities. By design, the system of cabildo elections, whereby incumbents elected their own successors, made it easier for elites to maintain their monopoly over community governance and more difficult for nonelites to challenge their authority. As discussed below, the system for filling the parish offices of fiscal and maestro de coro also perpetuated the position of a privileged minority, and the cofradía offices of *prioste* and *mayordomo* were almost certainly controlled by elites as well. Taken together, their control of the three officeholding structures enabled elites to dominate the political affairs of their communities.

The elites' dominant position was tempered by other factors, however. One was the existence of factions among the principales, who often challenged the legitimacy of rival candidates for office or opposed the conduct of incumbents and sought their ouster. In fact, much of what is known about the dynamics of civil officeholding is found in court proceedings initiated by representatives of these factions who were seeking to overturn election results or remove individuals from office. A second factor was the link between the principales and their broader constituencies among commoners, who expected village leaders to conform to standards of reciprocity and political obligation defined by the community at large.

Both of these factors were at work in an election dispute in the Tzeltal town of Guaguitepeque that was brought before a Spanish commission touring the highlands in 1690. The complainants, Alonso Hernández, a former regidor, and Antonio Alvarez, a principal, reported that the recent election of cabildo officers had been disrupted by several other principales, who entered the casa del cabildo threatening to kill the newly elected alcaldes, Domingo Pérez and Jacinto Núñez. The parish priest intervened to end the confrontation and arranged for a second election to be held inside the church, the site of the original vote. In this poll Agustín Pérez was elected alcalde de primer voto. Pérez, it was claimed, then interrupted the balloting and named his own choice to a regidor's seat without a vote. His choice was Francisco Gutiérrez, the *escribano* and assistant to the priest. Once in office, Pérez and Gutiérrez were said to have operated their own repartimiento, stealing pigs and forcing their owners to buy them back. It was this activity in particular that provoked Hernández and Alvarez to bring the case before the visiting commission. Spanish officials ruled against Pérez and turned the cabildo offices over to those who had occupied them the previous year until new elections could be held. They also informed the audiencia that they could not determine the causes of the original quarrel that unseated Domingo Pérez and Jacinto Núñez, though they suspected that much of the blame rested with Francisco Gutiérrez. The escribano, however, was not publicly accused of wrongdoing, because the priest had written a letter praising his fine character. It seems clear that the priest himself was not blameless in the affair, but no accusations were leveled against him.[42]

Cancuc itself was troubled by election disputes in 1665 and 1677. In the first case, a visitador general from the audiencia, Juan de Garate Francia, nullified the election to alcalde offices of Cristóbal Méndez and his son-in-law, Sebastián Velasco. The commissioner found that Méndez had been appointed by the alcalde mayor, Fernando Alvarez de Aguiar, against the will of the rightful electors, the regidores. Moreover, Méndez had been appointed three years in a row, a violation of Crown law. Garate severely reprimanded the alcalde mayor, reminding him that under no pretext was a provincial governor allowed to interfere with the election of village justicias. He also renewed the mandate forbidding native fiscales from holding office on the cabildo, though the relevance of this law to the Méndez case is not clear from the surviving records. The dispute in 1677 involved just such a violation. In this case the incumbent regidores complained that the parish priest had overturned the peaceful and proper election of alcaldes Gerónimo López and Sebastián López. In their place he had appointed Agustín García, his servant, the fiscal and escribano, who, it was said, was a very young man with bad inclinations. A representative of the Crown restored Gerónimo and Sebastián López to their offices, but whether the fiscal or the parish priest suffered any penalty is unknown.[43]

These cases underline the complex dynamics of cabildo officeholding. The system of yearly elections seems to have been a fragile institution, vulnerable to manipulation by colonial authorities or their native allies and easily corrupted by acts of violence among the participants themselves. Yet the audiencia clearly recognized and defended the principle of Indian self-government and was aware that subverting the system could have unsettling consequences for Spanish rule. Though community political life was monopolized by a privileged few, officeholders were expected to conform to certain norms, to meet certain standards, and to respect custom. If they did not, their legitimacy could, and would, be challenged—often by other principales. Finally, cabildo elections offered a mechanism for promoting cooperation among opposing factions within a community. Early in the eighteenth century this mechanism was breaking down as Spanish alcaldes mayores and Dominican parish priests intervened more and more in the political affairs of local communities.

As the system eroded, the potential for violence, among Indians themselves as well as between Indians and Spaniards, increased. A very dramatic example of this dynamic took place in Tuxtla on May 16, 1693. The alcalde mayor, Manuel de Maisterra, his *alguacil mayor*, Nicolás de Trejo, and the Zoque governor, Don Pablo Hernández, were all murdered by an angry crowd, who pummeled them with rocks—an extraordinary event. The confrontation pitted two factions within the town against each other, and though it was the office of *gobernador* that was at stake rather than positions on the cabildo, the episode serves well to expose the kinds of political tensions that could plague native communities.

The violence resulted from bitterness over Maisterra's repartimientos and anger over Hernández's cooperation with the system of forced sales. Because Tuxtla was a center of cacao and cochineal production, the alcaldes mayores had been particularly active there. Hernández was opposed by a faction of four or five leading principales led by Don Julio Velásquez, whose own claim to the governorship intensified their rivalry. Velásquez had complained to Spanish authorities in Ciudad Real about Hernández's conduct, and when those complaints were ignored, he prepared to confront the alcalde mayor on his next visit to the town.

Maisterra arrived in Tuxtla early in the evening of May 16, accompanied by Fray Miguel Presiado, the Dominican curate of the town, and fellow Spaniards Nicolás de Trejo, Joseph de Ochoa, and Juan de Sosoca. A large gathering of townspeople, including women and children, joined Don Julio Velásquez and his son, Don Gabriel, and came out to meet the alcalde mayor's entourage. They demanded that Don Pablo Hernández give up the staff of his office, and when Maisterra tried to put them off, a riot started. Hernández then appeared and helped to defend the Spaniards, but Maisterra, Trejo, and he were all killed. Fray Miguel, Joseph de Ochoa, and Juan de Sosoca fled to the shelter of the church. There the town's fiscales and mayordomos of the cofradías hid them behind the tabernacle near the main altar until they could make their escape. Meanwhile, the rioters converged on the neighborhood (*calpul*) where Don Pablo Hernández and his kinsmen lived. They burned his house to the ground and pillaged the homes of his neighbors. The Spanish later reported that the calpul was nearly destroyed.

News of the violence reached authorities in the capital the next day, and troops under the command of *maestro de campo* Joseph de Cabrera were immediately sent to secure the town. A little more than a week later, on May 27, he reported to the audiencia that the rebels had been captured and the province was again at peace. Some seventy-seven men and women, including Don Julio Velásquez and his son, were held for trial. Eventually, twenty-six of them were executed for their role in the murders, and the others suffered corporal punishment. In a somewhat unexpected twist, after consulting with Bishop Núñez de la Vega, Cabrera attributed the incident to the influence of a sect of *nagualistas* who had been inspired by the Devil. The evidence for such a claim is not known. Over the next decade the Spanish restored and consolidated their control of the town, and in 1712 Tuxtla's governor contributed provisions for the campaign against the rebels.[44]

PARISH OFFICES

From the very beginning of their evangelical mission, the mendicant orders in New Spain had relied on the loyalty and cooperation of native assistants. The figure of an Indian lord moved to accept Christ by the eloquence of a Spanish friar who spoke before a crude wooden cross is a staple element of every chronicle of the Conquest. In a period when European priests had neither mastered indigenous dialects nor won the respect and obedience of native peoples, converted caciques and principales paved the way for the remarkably quick propagation of the faith. Because friars would remain in short supply and because the linguistic skills of later generations did not always match the accomplishments of the first, Indian collaborators continued to be necessary, and their role became institutionalized.

In 1618 the Crown recognized the offices of fiscal, maestro de coro, and sacristán, declaring them free of tribute and personal service obligations.[45] By definition, the fiscal was charged with gathering the congregation for services, the maestro de coro with leading liturgical chants and singing, and the sacristán with serving at the altar during mass, cleaning the church, and caring for church property. Fiscales were to be selected from among men over fifty years old, who were already exempt from tribute because of their age.

There was to be one fiscal for every hundred parishioners, though there were never to be more than two in a parish. Unlike the cabildo posts, parish officers were not elected, nor did they serve fixed terms. Incumbents were appointed by the priest and served at his pleasure, usually for quite long periods. In Yucatán, for example, appointments were for life.[46]

In Chiapas, most pueblos—including both cabeceras and their subordinate towns—had two fiscales, one maestro de coro, and one sacristán.[47] Often the offices of fiscal and maestro de coro were held by the same man, and sometimes, though not always, fiscales also served as escribanos. Records show that parish officers served long terms and that the law requiring them to be past the age of tribute liability was often ignored. It is quite common to find men in their thirties and forties serving as fiscales.

By the seventeenth century the most important elements of Christian observance and ritual had been well integrated into native religious practice. Though the Maya resisted the Dominicans' fees, parish priests sanctified virtually all marriages, baptized all children, and whenever possible gave the dying extreme unction. By law the dead had to be properly buried in sacred ground outside the village church, everyone was required to attend mass, and as a community, Indians enthusiastically celebrated Holy Week and the feast days of numerous saints.

Fiscales and maestros de coro served in some capacity at all these events, guiding the congregation through the ritual, collecting alms, maintaining the parish registries, and overseeing the cofradía account books. A report in 1735, in fact, accused the Dominicans of becoming too dependent on their native assistants and of giving them too much authority.[48] It was said that Maya children learned to recite the catechism not from the parish priests, as was proper, but from the fiscales. Moreover, authorities suspected that some parish assistants actually put on clerical vestments during the priest's absence, said mass, and celebrated the sacraments.[49] During the Tzeltal Revolt, rebel fiscales would do just that.

Who were chosen to be fiscales, maestros de coro, and sacristanes? When first introduced in Chiapas, the offices were filled by principales, as was the common practice among Dominicans and Franciscans in central Mexico, Yucatán, and Guatemala. Like the cabildo system, the parish office structure utilized traditional notions of social hierarchy to establish its legitimacy. Records show that this continued to be the practice well into the eighteenth century. A number of fiscales appear in documents who were kinsmen of alcaldes or regidores, and the cabildo election disputes cited earlier show the close association between civil and parish officeholders. By the mid seventeenth century, however, their legitimacy rested less on the lineage hierarchy than it had earlier. As the institutions of the Church and the authority of the priest became integral to native political culture, parish officials could invoke new sources of legitimacy. In particular, the patronage of the village curate gave them considerable independence and set them apart from those whose status and authority derived from other sources. Many fiscales also had skills no one else in the community could offer: literacy and a knowledge of Spanish. They were free from the controls that yearly elections exerted on cabildo officers, and the length of their tenure gave them more time to consolidate their influence and more time to exercise it.

Because fiscales and maestros de coro wielded substantial power and authority, they were often targets of community dissatisfaction and were often at the center of village controversies, as in Guaguitepeque and Cancuc. Like the cabildo officers, parish officials served several constituencies, including townspeople who sought them out as intermediaries in their relations with the priest, and the priest himself, who depended on them for news and information about events within the parish and expected them to ensure that fees were paid and services rendered. In the new equilibrium that emerged in the seventeenth century, fiscales and maestros de coro contributed much to the balance. When that balance was upset, as it was in 1712, they were at the center of efforts to right it. Some chose to remain staunch allies of their Dominican patrons, but many chose instead to seize the opportunity to construct a new order. These men would be at the forefront of the rebellion.

THE COFRADÍA

In the sixteenth-century world of Mediterranean Catholicism, much of the cost of public worship was shared by cofradías of lay people. They provided the sacramental wine and lamp oil used during church services and paid the priest's fee on Sundays and holy days throughout the year. They also sponsored extravagant street celebrations to honor their patron saint's day or to mark special periods in the religious calendar, like Holy Week. The organizations were as essential to the European Church as the priesthood and were among the earliest ecclesiastical institutions established in New Spain.

Spaniards, of course, formed cofradías, but so too did Indians, under the direction of the friars. Among the first, according to Robert Ricard, was a cofradía founded in San José de los Naturales, in Mexico, less than ten years after the conquest.[50] In Chiapas the earliest cofradías date from the 1560s, but most seem to have been established during the first two decades of the seventeenth century.[51] The population of many communities reached its lowest point in this period, and the Church was looking for new sources of revenue. The cofradías provided parish priests with a means of augmenting the support they received from the caja de comunidad.

Cofradías would become an onerous financial burden, but by all accounts native communities celebrated the rites they sponsored with enthusiasm.[52] The cult of the saints became the focus of Catholic practice in the villages and a means for Indians to hold community celebrations in a traditional style. Public feasts, ritual dancing, and solemn processions incorporated symbols and ceremonial practices that had special meaning for the Maya even though they were carried out under the suspicious eyes of the parish priest. During the campaign to secularize their parishes, the Dominicans would be accused of condoning idolatry, but they defended their support of the cofradías and for the most part seem to have acted with considerable tolerance.[53]

Records suggest that cofradías were poorly supervised for much of the seventeenth century, which eased, for a time, the economic strain they presented.[54] Unfortunately, very little is known about these early years. But in the 1670s, Bishop Bravo de la Serna brought them under stricter control. He dictated a constitution for each organization that carefully outlined their financial obligations, and he insisted that account books be kept up to date. His successors maintained a tight hand, with regular visitas and close supervision of the cofradías' financing. Under the new regime, a heavier burden fell on officeholders in the cofradías, who were pressured to assure the solvency of their organizations. The pressure intensified in the eighteenth century, particularly in the highlands, where the Tzeltal Revolt marked the beginning of an economic crisis in the villages which lasted through the years of famine and epidemics in the 1720s. After the rebellion, mayordomos were expected to recover cofradía funds that had been confiscated by the rebels. They found this impossible to do, and from 1713 until the end of the century, few cofradías accumulated any principal in their treasuries.

Compared to cofradías elsewhere in New Spain, highland cofradías were poor and undercapitalized, and they returned few material benefits to their membership.[55] Within Chiapas, several Zoque cofradías had estancias whose profits supported the local clergy,[56] but in the highlands, only in Ixtapa and Huistán are cofradías known to have owned land or cattle.[57] Nor is there evidence that, prior to the late eighteenth century, highland cofradías loaned money at interest, a common means of fundraising for Guatemalan organizations.[58] In Yucatán, another poor province, cofradías raised crops and livestock on common lands and stockpiled maize and beans to offer as famine relief during periods of crop failure.[59] In highland Chiapas, the only documented benefit to members of cofradías was the sponsoring of yearly requiem masses. Their primary function seems to have been to pay the parish priest for saying the mass on Sundays and holy days, and to provide candles and holy water for the village church.

By 1690 nearly all Maya towns in the highlands had at least four cofradías.[60] The most common dedications were to San Sebastián, el Santísimo Sacramento, la Santa Vera Cruz, and Nuestra Virgen del Rosario. Also represented were cofradías dedicated to Santo Domingo, Santa Ana, Santa Rosa, and las Animas (All Souls). These dedications reflect the evangelical preoccupations of the friars. They were chosen to promote the central elements of the new faith—the miracle of the Holy Eucharist, Christ's sacrifice on the Cross, and the extraordinary virtue of the Blessed Mother. Though the Dominicans, unlike the Franciscans, did not accept the doctrine of the Immaculate Conception, their teaching nonetheless embraced the Marianism of the period. Mary had appeared to St. Dominic to give him the rosary, and this event occupied a special place in Dominican devotions. In Chiapas the popularity of la Virgen del Rosario was enhanced when an image of her, kept in the church at Socoltenango, seemed to have healing powers. In the 1660s the image drew pilgrims, Spaniards, mestizos, mulattos, and Indians alike from throughout the province.[61] In Europe, San Sebastián was the object of special prayers to avert the plague, and so, not surprisingly, was a revered figure in the Americas.

Like Spanish cofradías, Maya cofradías sponsored a mass and other public rituals to commemorate various holy days throughout the year. Some celebrated as many as six fiestas. Others simply paid for a mass one Sunday a month. These fiestas were occasions for elaborate public worship, with processions, bands, dance troupes, and fireworks, much like the festivals that draw anthropologists and tourists to highland towns today.

Not all, or even the most important, fiestas were sponsored by cofradías alone.[62] Towns' patron saint's days, for example, were jointly financed by the cofradías, the cabildo, and contributions from individuals. The costs of Holy Week and All Saints' Day were carried entirely by the justicias and from a collection among the community. Finally, some fiestas were sponsored by individuals, called alferezes, or standard-bearers, rather than by cofradías. Appendix B lists the number of masses and feast days celebrated in each village in the highlands in 1690. The list includes occasions funded by all of the various sponsors.

Each cofradía kept a book to record the names of officers and to account for income and expenditures. Most of these ledgers have been destroyed over the years, some during the Tzeltal Revolt and others during the Cristero Rebellion in the 1920s. Whatever conclusions are possible concerning colonial cofradías in Chiapas are based on the few that have survived.

The book of the Cofradía de San Sebastián, in Chilón, begins with a series of bylaws (*ordenanzas*) written in 1613.[63] They called for the yearly election of two mayordomos, an alcalde and his *diputado*, or deputy, from among "the best Indians in the pueblo, of good life and customs, good Christians." Who the electors were is not indicated. The officials were instructed to purchase a ledger book and a large box with three keys. Two were kept by the mayordomos themselves, and the third by the alcalde del primer voto on the cabildo. Each Sunday the mayordomos were required to solicit alms from the pueblo and to keep careful account of what they received. *Hermanos*, or brothers, of the cofradía were to contribute three reales a year, though how one became a member is unclear. The mayordomos were called upon to make certain that their *hermanos* made confession and took communion. The principal expenditures for the cofradía were the costs of a mass and procession on the saint's day of San Sebastián and a requiem mass for deceased members of the cofradía on the day immediately following. A second requiem mass for past members was to be sponsored on the Day of the Dead.

Following the entry of the ordenanzas, record keeping lapsed until the visita of Bishop Marcos Bravo de la Serna in 1677. He found that the cofradía maintained a principal of 86 tostones and ordered the purchase of a new book. Thereafter, entries were made until 1827. Between 1677 and 1712, the year of the rebellion, annual costs fluctuated between 26 and 28 tostones and were met by alms from the pueblo. After Bravo de la Serna's visit, the principal unaccountably diminished to little more than eleven tostones, but it was gradually augmented over the next thirty-five years, reaching a high of 122 tostones in 1703. The cofradía was still served by only two officers, but many officers served two or more years in succession. After the notorious visit of Bishop Alvarez de Toledo, the cofradía's principal was cut in half, from 90 tostones in 1709 to 42 in 1711. Alvarez de Toledo's visita marked the beginning of a crisis for the cofradía that deepened during the Tzeltal Revolt. The entire principal was lost during the rebellion and was never recovered throughout the whole of the eighteenth century. During an epidemic in the 1720s, the election of mayordomos was suspended for five years when no one would stand for office.

A second book, for the Cofradía de la Parroquia de Santo Domingo, also in Chilón, reveals a similar experience.[64] In 1677, Bishop Bravo de la Serna reorganized the cofradía, ordering the purchase of a new book and outlining a new constitution. Again, two mayordomos were to be elected each year, many of whom would serve two or more consecutive terms. Expenses were to be covered by annual contributions of one *tostón* from members and weekly solicitations from the community. The cofradía celebrated the fiesta of Santo Domingo, sponsored a requiem mass for past members, and contributed to the purchase of holy water and candles. Between 1677 and 1701, the cofradía covered most of its expenses through alms and hardly maintained any principal at all. But in 1701, Bishop Núñez de la Vega established a principal of 10 tostones, probably from contributions from more solvent cofradías in the pueblo, and thereafter the sum grew to a high of 56 tostones in 1707 and 1708. Reduced by half after Alvarez de Toledo's visita, the principal disappeared during the Tzeltal Revolt and was never recovered.

Cofradía books from Yajalón dating from 1713, after the rebellion, reveal some interesting variations in the structure of officeholding.[65] In the Cofradía de Jesús Nazareno, eight women held all the offices. The Cofradía de

Santa María Rosario included both men and women—one prioste, four mayordomos, and eight *madres*. The Cofradía del Nombre de Jesús was run by men—one prioste and four mayordomos. In each case, officers were often reelected. One prioste of the Cofradía del Nombre de Jesús, Juan de la Cruz, served eight consecutive terms.

Far more prosperous than the examples from Chilón, the cofradías in Yajalón rebounded after the rebellion much more quickly. They declared larger sums in principal when reorganized in 1713, and by 1721 all actually had the money in hand. In all three, officers were individually responsible for a share of the principal. For example, mayordomos in the Cofradía de Santa María Rosario handed over 19 tostones and 2 reales annually. This was not a contribution from their own funds, as the language of the document may suggest, but their allotment of principal from the previous year that had been distributed to them for safekeeping. Officers were expected to make up for any shortfall in their share, a considerable burden during bad years. In good years their individual contributions augmented the existing principal.

Yearly expenses, or *gastos*, were balanced by alms from the pueblo, as in Chilón. The Cofradía de Jesús Nazareño sponsored a mass on each of the six Fridays of Lent. The Cofradía de Santa María Rosario celebrated six Marian feast days and paid for a mass each month and on Holy Thursday. The Cofradía del Nombre de Jesús also supported a monthly mass and four other feast days, including the festival of the New Year.

The only expenses listed in all of the surviving cofradía ledgers are payments to the priest. None of them include outlays for food, drink, fireworks, or other costs that may have accrued during the more elaborate fiestas. In contemporary Chiapas these expenses are carried by each year's officers, and their omission from the colonial ledgers is puzzling. The likeliest explanation is that they were paid either out of the caja de comunidad or, as noted above, from alms contributed by the community at large.

Cofradía officeholding has been of enormous interest to anthropologists and historians.[66] In contemporary villages throughout Mexico and Guatemala, a system of parallel "ladders," one composed of offices in municipal government, the other of offices in the cofradías, structures political participation, distributes power, and legitimizes authority. According to the archetype of this civil-religious hierarchy, virtually every young man participates, entering the system at the bottom rung of one of the ladders. The successful completion of his duties, or *cargo*, supports his future rise to higher office. In some communities, he alternates between the two hierarchies as he advances; in others, he does not. Officeholders are expected to fulfill certain ceremonial obligations, which grow more costly at each level, with the achievement of the highest offices demanding extraordinary material sacrifices.

An earlier generation of social scientists viewed the system as a leveling mechanism that dispersed individual accumulations of capital in an activity that promoted social integration and discouraged stratification.[67] They conceived of postconquest Indian villages as communities of equals who depended on communal obligation and reciprocity to survive and who condemned individual enrichment as a violation of that ethos. The civil-religious hierarchy was understood to be a colonial-period adaptation, one that melded distinctly European institutional forms with native American traditions of community service. Indeed, for many scholars, participation in the civil-religious hierarchy came to define "Indian-ness."[68] Where the structure of local government or the pattern of participation in religious ritual deviated from the norm, communities were said to be in the process of losing their ethnic identity and of succumbing to the relentless pressure to acculturate.

More recent scholarship has challenged this idealized version of the civil-religious hierarchy and reexamined its history. In a landmark work, *Economics and Prestige in a Maya Community*, Frank Cancian showed that in Zinacantán the system has not obliterated economic differences among individuals.[69] He emphasizes that the pyramidal structure of the hierarchy reflects sharp distinctions of wealth and status. With many offices at the bottom and very few at the top, the highest positions are within reach of only a small minority whose long-term economic standing has not been affected by the costs of service. Though Cancian disputes the leveling function of the civil-religious hierarchy, he does acknowledge its integrating function. By fulfilling community cargos, prosperous zinacantecos strive to dissipate envy and legitimate their accumulation of wealth.[70]

James Dow has suggested that the cargo system actually contributes to economic stratification among Otomí peoples in the Sierra de Puebla.[71] There the local economy offers few incentives for Otomí peasants to increase production. Markets are controlled by mestizo outsiders, and Indians are denied access to investment capital and new technologies. Under these conditions, Dow argues, the primary motive for individuals to increase surpluses is the opportunity to gain prestige and authority through participation in the civil-religious hierarchy. Taking the argument a step further, he states that the ceremonial exchanges obligated by the cargo system actually redistribute wealth more equitably within the community.[72]

While Cancian and Dow have revised an earlier formulation of the model, like their predecessors they acknowledge the centrality of the civil-religious hierarchy in Indian social and political life. Further, by emphasizing the voluntary nature of participation and the integrating function of community service, they support a positive view of its contribution to Indian cultural survival. Other scholars, though, offer a much more critical interpretation.

Marvin Harris, for example, argues that cofradías were imposed on native communities by a greedy Church anxious to drain away as much wealth as it could.[73] The cofradías simply provided another context for expropriating Indian resources. Moreover, by compelling Indians to purchase goods from outsiders, the system forced native peoples either into wage labor or into producing cash crops and handicrafts for outside markets. Finally, because the system coopted caciques and principales, Harris suggests that the civil-religious hierarchy sharpened class divisions within indigenous communities. His summation is characteristically blunt: "a more inefficient defense against outsiders could scarcely be imagined. . . . Far from protecting the Indian communities against encomienda, repartimiento, debt peonage, excessive taxation and tribute, the fiesta system was an integral and enduring part of the mechanisms by which these noxious influences gained access to the very heart of the village."[74]

Though Harris could not disagree more with scholars who have celebrated the integrating function of the cargo system, he shares their assumptions about its colonial origins. In recent years, however, this too has been disputed, most notably in a detailed and carefully documented essay by John Chance and William Taylor.[75] Chance and Taylor argue that in the colonial period most cofradías were supported either by donations from the entire community or by income from communal property in the form of interest on endowments, rents of house lots, or profits from ranching.[76] Since ceremonial costs were not borne by individuals, cofradía sponsorship had no direct impact on civil officeholding. They suggest that this system was altered as political reforms broke up communal property and as economic changes pushed more Indians into the market economy. Under these conditions, communities lost the resources to support the fiestas collectively. As an alternative, the archetypal modern system emerged, which depends solely on contributions from individual mayordomos, who participate in order to acquire the prestige necessary to hold office in the civil hierarchy.[77] In some regions the transition may have begun as early as the 1770s, but Chance and Taylor argue that more commonly the transformation occurred between 1820 and 1850.

An earlier article on civil-religious hierarchies in Chiapas by Jan Rus and Robert Wasserstrom offers a different chronology but anticipates the basic argument made by Chance and Taylor. Rus and Wasserstrom noted that colonial era cofradías in Zinacantán and Chamula died out after independence as lands were taken from the communities and their populations were forced into labor on lowland plantations. With the 1910 Revolution, however, the seasonal migrations ended, and zinacantecos and chamulas returned to sharecropping closer to home. After 1916, economic and political conditions created new patterns of social stratification within the communities, and new elites emerged who would revitalize the cofradías in order to legitimize their claim on civil officeholding. The "traditional" cargo system, they concluded, is less than a century old.[78]

Rus and Wasserstrom's work focused on the nineteenth and early twentieth centuries, with very little material on colonial cofradías, but research for the present study supports their view of the institution's early history. The evidence available to date also shows that colonial cofradías in highland Chiapas shared many of the characteristics of the cofradías that Chance and Taylor studied. Like the associations in central Jalisco, Oaxaca, and central Mexico, most were founded during the nadir of the Indian population after 1600. Though mayordomos managed their finances, the cofradías did not depend on their individual contributions. Only if the principal of a cofradía was lost, or if donations from the community failed to meet expenses, were mayordomos expected to assume the burden. Moreover, cofradías were not the sole support of community ritual. The entire village bore the cost of public worship through almsgiving and the taxes they paid into the caja de comunidad.

In Chiapas, the cofradías also seem to have been quite separate from the civil hierarchy, and the structure of mayordomo officeholding does not seem to have been designed to accommodate broad participation. Officers frequently served consecutive terms, and some cofradías were administered by only two officials. The records are silent on how mayordomos were selected, but that process must have reflected, as it did elsewhere, the hierarchical structure of society. Considering the hold that principales maintained on civil and parish offices, the assumption here is that they monopolized cofradía offices as well. The supervisory role of fiscales in cofradía affairs, as scribes and caretakers of keys to the treasury box, and the cooperation between mayordomos and civil alcaldes in sponsoring titular saint's day celebrations, suggest that this was likely. The strongest confirmation of the role of the native elite in cofradías is found in the ledger of the Cofradía de Santa Cruz in Sibacá.[79] For one year only, 1728, the gobernador, Don Fabian Alvaro, who had been appointed after the rebellion, served as prioste.

Though questions remain about the politics of cofradía officeholding, there is little disagreement that the fiestas associated with the European cult of the saints contributed significantly to the revitalization of native societies and cultures after the conquest. Today these are occasions not only for the veneration of Christian saints and the observance of Catholic holy days but also for complex ritual performances that evoke historical events, articulate fundamental values, and express a view of the world that is the Indians' very own.[80] They reflect the accumulated experience of native peoples and have been altered in response to social and economic changes that have affected local communities. Colonial fiestas would have reflected the same complex dynamics and served the same functions even though many of the symbols and rituals included in the performances must have been quite different from those found today.

Sponsorship of these celebrations defined the local community, which supported them financially and participated in all the rituals. But the fiesta cycle also had an impact on social relations and cultural processes that extended beyond a single pueblo or even a parish. Today, Indians throughout Mesoamerica often travel to major festivals in other villages, and this also seems to have been common in the colonial period.[81] For Chiapas, Ximénez wrote that the fiesta honoring the Virgen del Rosario in Socoltenango attracted pilgrims from across the province.[82] Early in the eighteenth century, cult activity in Zinacantán and Santa Marta also drew large numbers of participants from outside the pueblos (see chapter 4). The fiestas, then, not only fostered community solidarity but also promoted ethnic consciousness. They provided an opportunity for people who were usually separated by distance or other obstacles to come together, exchange news, trade goods, and share a religious experience that derived from a common cultural tradition.

As noted earlier, cofradía organizations and the festivals they sponsored came under attack at the end of the seventeenth century. The issue was an important one in the debate about the secularization of Dominican parishes, and Joseph de Escals, the Crown visitador, talked openly about abolishing them. Funding for the cofradías was jeopardized as communities strained to meet the demands of provincial bishops and alcaldes mayores. Finally, Dominican reformers began to scrutinize saints' day rituals more vigilantly, looking for evidence of clandestine idolatry. These developments threatened a religious complex that had become essential to the reconstruction of indigenous political culture and to the articulation of local and broader notions of ethnic identity. The birth of the Marian cult that precipitated the Tzeltal Revolt clearly was a reaction to this threat.

THE CONCEPT OF COMMUNITY

For more than three decades, Eric Wolf's paradigm of the "closed corporate peasant community" has served as a model for anthropological and historical studies of Mesoamerican towns and villages. "They are corporate organizations," Wolf wrote, "maintaining a perpetuity of rights and membership; and they are closed corporations, because they limit these privileges to insiders, and discourage close participation of members in the social relations of the larger society."[83] The paradigm was outlined in two essays that Wolf recently described as working papers.[84] In them he offered a brilliant synthesis of contemporary anthropological wisdom about peasants in Mexico and Guatemala, using the work of Sol Tax and the other scholars who had contributed to the Heritage of Conquest project. This aspect of the work reflected the strong functionalist perspective in American anthropology, particularly among ethnographers who were primarily interested in the internal social and cultural dynamics of specific communities. For this reason, anthropologists who have followed in this tradition include Wolf among their conceptual forefathers. But Wolf also attempted to reconstruct the history of modern peasant societies. Like Robert Redfield, he emphasized that peasant communities have never been autonomous but rather have always been part of larger social and economic systems.[85] More specifically, Wolf argued that in Mesoamerica, closed corporate peasant communities grew out of the devastation brought by the Spanish conquest and early colonization. They were the product of the resettlement of native peoples and the imposition of Spanish systems of taxation and local government. This dimension of Wolf's model would influence the new colonial social history that began to emerge in the mid-1960s.

Scholars in this field have shared Wolf's interest in the place of indigenous peasants in larger systems of political and economic exploitation. But with their strong materialist perspective, they have been suspicious of functionalist assumptions that seem to idealize the workings of peasant communities. As a result, in recent years Wolf's model has been reexamined and some of his generalizations challenged. Wolf himself has endorsed much of the critique of the earlier model. He offered his own revision in the essay "The Vicissitudes of the Closed Corporate Peasant Community" and more broadly in *Europe and the People Without History.*

A number of scholars have shown that peasants in Mexico and Guatemala were much more mobile than once was thought and that community social boundaries, regulated by rules of endogamy and other mechanisms, were more open. Nancy Farriss, for example, has distinguished three types of population movements in colonial Yucatán: flight, or escape from pacified areas into unsettled frontier zones; drift, or migration from one pueblo to another well beyond the bounds of a parish; and dispersal, or settlement away from nucleated towns in more isolated *parajes* (hamlets) nearer the milpas.[86] The second type, drift, has been extensively documented for Yucatán by David J. Robinson and Carolyn McGovern,[87] and W. George Lovell has suggested that all three were common in colonial Guatemala.[88]

Historians have long recognized that two of these phenomena, flight and dispersal, also were common in colonial Chiapas. Tabasco and the nearby Petén offered a refuge for tzeltales and choles in the northern and eastern perimeter of the highlands.[89] Despite the threat of attack from unpacified lacandones, Maya from Tila, Tumbalá, and Palenque periodically moved into the rain forest. After the Tzeltal Revolt, other Maya fled to Tabasco to escape Spanish efforts to reorganize their communities.[90]

TABLE 4.2   INDIVIDUALS MARRIED OUTSIDE THEIR COMMUNITY OF
BIRTH AS OF 1715

Pueblo	"Indios" casados"	Indios casados" en otros pueblos"	Indias casadas en otros pueblos"	Others[a]
Cancuc	38%	21%	15%	26%
Guaguitepeque	30	36	25	8
Ocosingo	23	37	30	10
Ocotitán	36	40	15	8
Petalsingo	81	12	3	4
Sitalá	17	20	37	26
Tenango	21	31	28	20
Tenejapa	66	11	9	14
Tumbalá	66	6	5	23
Yajalón	31	11	22	36

SOURCE: AGCA: A3.16 357: Padrones, 1715.
[a]This category includes *reservados* (nontributaries), *viudas* (widows), *viudos* (widowers),
and *casados con ausente* (half tributary; individuals with an absent spouse).

Like their twentieth-century descendants, the colonial Maya preferred to
live in scattered parajes away from the town centers but close to their milpas.
Following the campaigns designed to merge distinct settlements in the late
sixteenth century, numerous reports told of the Maya drifting back to their
original milpa sites,[91] and anecdotal evidence from later periods confirms
that this settlement pattern continued to be preferred.[92]

Evidence also suggests that drift, or the movement from one village to
another, was not uncommon. As shown in Table 4.2, the tribute count for
1715 reveals that many men and women married and presumably lived
outside of the community of their birth.[93] Several pueblos show large propor-
tions of their adult population in two tribute categories: "indios casados en

otros pueblos (Indian men married in other pueblos)" and "indias casadas en otros pueblos (Indian women married other pueblos)." Murdo MacLeod has suggested that these figures are higher than they ordinarily would have been because of population losses and resettlement after the rebellion.[94] However, a more limited count for an earlier period suggests that the 1715 figures may not be unrepresentative.[95]

Whether moves to other pueblos were permanent or temporary, and whether they were confined to parishes or were more widely dispersed, cannot be determined from available records. Nevertheless, the figures show that a surprising number of Maya men and women migrated from one pueblo to another. Since many are known to have traveled widely to attend religious festivals, bring goods to Spanish cities, and work on estates in the Grijalva Valley and near Ocosingo, perhaps this should not be surprising. These visits could easily have provided opportunities to transform ties of friendship into ties of kinship.

But periodic travel is not the same as migration and does not explain why villages were willing to accept outsiders. Other explanations are needed. According to the paradigm, a community's closedness is a response to threats against a scarce resource, usually land. As William Taylor notes, "The essential building block for this kind of village society was landownership."[96] While collective land tenure certainly defined the physical limits of native villages in Chiapas in the seventeenth and early eighteenth centuries, the Maya apparently perceived few threats to their community holdings. Spaniards and mestizos did not settle among them in significant numbers, preferring to settle north among the Zoque or south near Comitán and the commercial artery to Guatemala. Also, while Indian populations were growing, there is no evidence that the pace of growth was causing communities to shelter their territory more aggressively. Even in Oaxaca, central Mexico, Yucatán, and Guatemala, where land litigation between Indian communities was common, most disputes date from the second half of the eighteenth century.

Another feature of land tenure in the highlands would have lessened anxiety about the sharing of land with other Maya. Neither native elites nor cofradías claimed private holdings. Elsewhere in New Spain, litigation was usually initiated by caciques or principales, who represented community interests but who also recognized that inroads onto communal property jeopardized their private estates.

If land pressure did not provide an incentive for strict closure of community social boundaries, there was one very strong incentive for keeping them open. Farriss has suggested that internal migration in Yucatán

> was an attempt to escape, if only temporarily, the burdens of the community which were often intensified by a shortage of people. The burden on the individual Indian of labor drafts, repartimiento goods, and head taxes, both civil and ecclesiastical, could become intolerable when community quotas were arbitrarily raised by greedy officials or not adjusted to a loss of population. . . . [A] common solution was to move to a new town, where old debts were unknown or ignored and where as new contributors to the community's tax rolls and labor force they were asked no questions.[97]

In other words, population drift served the interests of both newcomers, who left old debts behind, and the communities that accepted them, which gained another tribute payer. Of course, the same burdens that prompted the Maya in Yucatán to move were shouldered by the Maya in Chiapas.

Though much remains to be learned about migration, its significance is obvious. The process created a substructure of social relations that reached beyond local communities and added another dimension to the social experience of native peoples that likely promoted a broader sense of ethnic identity. Even if these relations did not include continuing obligations between the parties involved, they imparted a familiarity with conditions in other villages and offered a potential source of aid during hard times. If drift was as common in Chiapas as the figures suggest, one common assumption about the structure of native peasant communities and the potential for collective action among them will have to be reexamined. William Taylor has suggested that regional Indian rebellions were a rarity in colonial Mexico because the strength of "localized village identity" inhibited cooperation among towns and discouraged the development of a broader consciousness of oppression.[98] Brian Hamnett and John Tutino each recently used similar arguments to explain the regional limits of the Hidalgo Revolt in 1810, contrasting the proletarian villages of the rural Bajío, which supported the insurrection, with the peasant communities of central Mexico, which did not.[99]

In contrast, Maya rebels in early-eighteenth-century Chiapas overcame, at least temporarily, whatever constraints the relative closedness of their societies presented. Their success is evaluated later, after the rebellion itself is examined in some detail. But for now, suffice it to say that internal migration seems likely to have been one factor that lowered the barriers to collective action imposed by the corporate character of individual pueblos.

More serious obstacles to effective ethnic solidarity were the continuing factional disputes and internal conflicts within the communities. The election controversies among alcaldes and complaints against Indian fiscales cited earlier offer a picture not of egalitarian peasant democracies but of divided, contentious societies in which contests for political power and economic privilege were sometimes quite violent. The most common cause of conflict was the abuse of power by civil and parish officeholders, whose behavior invited challenges to their authority by other members of the elite. On one level these challenges reflected inevitable power struggles among those entitled to exercise authority. Resources were scarce in these communities, so the right to control them was coveted. On another level, when principales moved to oust one of their peers, sometimes they were acting on behalf of the entire community, upholding norms about custom and the proper use of authority. At other times, they may have been representing narrower constituencies, for within the larger community, individuals identified with a number of smaller social units.

Today the Maya in Chiapas recognize three principles of social organization: kinship, residential proximity, and calpul affiliation.[100] The basic unit of society is the local patrilineal descent group. At marriage, a couple commonly sets up their household near the compound of the groom's father, creating a cluster of families living near one another who are related through the male line. Together these families have claims on land traditionally associated with their patrilineage. Milpa acreage is distributed among nuclear families, with male heads of households doing most of the field labor, though fathers, married sons, and brothers often work together on each others' plots to complete the heavier tasks. Women manage the household, making tortillas, carrying water, cutting firewood, cooking, and caring for the children. They tend sheep, cultivate garden plots, and sometimes help in weeding and harvesting the milpas. As weavers and potters, women also are active in local markets and are important contributors to family income.

Contemporary naming patterns and rules of endogamy and exogamy suggest that in the past these localized descent groups were organized into larger lineages and clans.[101] The Maya typically have three names, a first name followed by two surnames, one Spanish, one Maya. Unlike the Spanish system, which is bilateral, in most Maya communities both surnames pass from father to child. The number of Spanish surnames in each town is quite limited, but each is associated with a larger number of Maya patronymics. Marriage between individuals with either of the surnames the same is forbidden, and these rules of exogamy have led anthropologists to surmise that the Spanish surname once indicated clan affiliation, and the Maya, lineage membership. Today, names simply regulate marriage choices; those who share patronymics do not recognize kinship with one another or assume any mutual obligations.

Residential family clusters are organized into water-hole groups, which in turn form parajes. Modern-day parajes can include more than 1,000 inhabitants, and some maintain their own school and church. The Mexican government recognizes them as official subdivisions of the municipality for census purposes. The Maya almost always choose their marriage partners from within the same paraje.

Parajes, in turn, are affiliated with a calpul or barrio, the largest subdivision within the incorporated town. In highland Chiapas, most towns conform to what Eva Hunt and June Nash have called the dual barrio system, though a few towns recognize three calpules, and one, San Pablo Chalchihuitán, has five.[102] In the ideal type, the municipality is bisected by an imaginary line through the town center. Individuals identify as closely with their calpul as with the town itself. They follow strict rules of endogamy by choosing marriage partners from their own section. Officeholding in the cofradías is limited to calpul members, and some barrios venerate their own patron saint. Offices in municipal government are distributed among representatives of each calpul, with the higher positions commonly rotating between them from one year to the next. In the past, calpules have even recognized their own leaders, to whom town justicias have usually deferred authority to judge minor criminal cases and settle petty squabbles.[103] In some cases, large autonomous calpules have eventually seceded and been recognized as independent towns.[104]

After more than a century and a half of population growth, revolution, and industrial capitalism, contemporary Maya municipalities are, of course, quite different from their colonial antecedents. Nonetheless, most scholars accept that many of the essential principles of modern-day social organization held true for colonial communities as well, and that ethnographic analogy can offer insights into the dynamics of village political conflicts in the seventeenth and eighteenth centuries. Perhaps the important contrasts are those of scale and economic context. With smaller populations, land pressure was much less severe in the colonial period, rural settlements likely were less dispersed, and the tendency for residential subdivisions to push for greater autonomy would have been less pronounced. With fewer opportunities for wage labor, especially in the seventeenth century, economic activity was more concentrated in the village, principally in milpa agriculture and cotton textile production, even after the repartimiento de mercancías intensified. Family life would have been less affected by the long absences of fathers and sons, and newly married couples must have found it easier to find land for nuclear households. In fact, for fear of incest, Spanish civil and religious policy prohibited extended families from living under the same roof. Among their other duties, village alcaldes were to see to it that all married couples lived in separate houses.[105]

Presumably, the basic unit of social organization, then as now, was the localized patrilineal descent group. Historians and anthropologists agree that, among commoners, residential proximity and territoriality were the primary principles of social organization, and had been since long before the conquest.[106] While caciques and principales identified with extended lineages, macehuales apparently did not. Children took their patronymics from their fathers, and the same rules of exogamy that apply today were followed by men and women who shared surnames.[107] But for most Maya, naming patterns simply regulated marriages and did not involve any rights or obligations of kinship. Colonial towns also were divided into two, sometimes three, calpules, which the Spanish termed *parcialidades*.[108] Among the Quiché in Guatemala, these subdivisions were called *chinamital*, and some scholars have recently argued that they exercised considerable autonomy within the larger town. Robert Carmack quotes Fray Francisco Ximénez in arguing that the authority of calpul leaders in Utatlán rivaled that of village alcaldes, "There scarcely was an Indian among them," Ximénez asserts, "who did not obey the head of the calpul in the task given him, and if there were such a case, everyone would turn against him to see that he was punished."[109]

Robert Hill and John Monaghan have shown that the heads of parcialidades in Sacapulas successfully petitioned the Crown for representation on the municipal cabildo in the sixteenth century.[110] Then, in the eighteenth, they went to court to defend territory claimed by their *chinamit*, when pueblo authorities claimed the land as part of the village's communal property.[111] Sandra Orellana has argued that the calpul was the principal social unit among the Tzutujil at Atitlán as well.[112]

Given the comparisons with other highland societies and the strength of the calpul in modern Maya towns in Chiapas, it is tempting to argue that the parcialidad exercised a similar degree of autonomy among the colonial Tzeltal and Tzotzil. Further, one might well assume that disputes among principales reflected rivalries among calpules. The evidence, however, is unclear. Encomiendas were allotted by these subdivisions in the sixteenth and seventeenth centuries, and census counts were often, though not always, recorded by parcialidad.[113] Some documents indicate that village alcaldes and regidores represented individual calpules.[114] However, it is striking how rarely the distinction appears in colonial records on the highlands. For some towns, their existence has not yet been documented,[115] and none of the cofradía ledgers or election disputes cited earlier refer to them. More concretely, the padrones that give counts according to parcialidad show that, in many towns, calpul populations were of markedly different sizes, suggesting that their political and social functions differed as well. In Huistán, a Tzotzil town, the parcialidad of Guaguitepeque had a mere eleven full tributaries (*tributarios enteros*), compared to the parcialidad of Huistán with thirty-eight.[116] The same count in Ocosingo shows the parcialidad of Topiltepeque with four tributarios enteros, the parcialidad of Copanaguastla with forty-four, and the parcialidad of Teultepeque with nineteen.[117] Calpules with counts as low as that of Topiltepeque were not rare, and it is hard to imagine that they were entitled to their own positions on the cabildo, sponsored their own cofradías, or even followed strict rules of endogamy.

The degree of autonomy exercised by individual calpules among the Tzeltal and Tzotzil must have varied considerably. Their claims to certain rights and prerogatives were likely a function of their size and of the process by which individual pueblos were reconstituted after the conquest. Scholars agree that most calpules were created when separate villages were resettled into single towns by the Dominicans during the merging of settlements in the late sixteenth century.[118] In some cases, all of the communities were moved to an entirely new site; in others, smaller settlements and villages were incorporated into preexisting pueblos. In the first case, if communities of comparable size and similar resources were joined, agreements among them may well have given the resulting calpules rights to a share of municipal offices and other entitlements.[119] In the second case, annexed populations may well have found it very difficult to win political concessions from authorities who were well established in the original town, and one would expect the calpul that corresponded to the preexisting settlement to hold the balance of power. Of course, calpul politics would not have been static. Demographic changes, outside interference, and shifts in alliances within the pueblo could all affect relations among competing sections and many political conflicts must not have involved calpul rivalries at all.

Maya rebels in 1712 would face two challenges as they tried to recruit new communities to their cause and hold their movement together. On the one hand, they had to convince the separate towns to cooperate with one another and share their material resources, and local authorities were bound to fear that their own autonomy would suffer in the process. On the other, rebel leaders would also have to overcome the tendency toward fragmentation and division faced by officials in individual communities. Neither task would prove very easy.

CONCLUSION

In his essay on revitalization movements, Anthony Wallace emphasized that chronic stress is common in most societies, but as long as techniques for satisfying basic needs operate reasonably efficiently, stress can be managed and a "steady state" maintained.[120] When those techniques fail, however, levels of stress intensify. Growing numbers of individuals are likely to exhibit various forms of dysfunctional behavior and psychosis, and the social group as a whole may eventually begin to disintegrate. Revitalization movements, like the Tzeltal Revolt, are conscious efforts to reverse this process.

By drawing attention to the techniques for managing stress rather than to the sources of stress, Wallace offers a simple but important insight for students of rebellion. Endemic poverty and new threats to subsistence created the potential for violence in the highlands, but it was threats to the solvency and autonomy of village cajas de comunidad and cofradías that pushed the Tzeltal into open rebellion. The Maya depended on these institutions not only to manage the fiscal burdens imposed by Spaniards but also to support the ritual obligations imposed by their religious beliefs and values. When the costs of the repartimientos and visitas threatened to bankrupt these institutions, an entire moral economy was undermined. Only the intervention of the Virgin herself, it seemed, could resurrect that economy, and only a fundamental reordering of political relations could assure its survival.

5

RELIGION AND THE MORAL ECONOMY
OF MAYA POLITICS

The changing of the flowers is finished,
The changing of the leaves of your tree is done.
Now we have arrived at your great feast day,
Now we have arrived at your great festival. . . .
You will be entertained,
You will be happy,
On your great feast day,
On your great festival.
So receive my candle, my father,
So receive my candle, my lord. . . .
                    —Zinacanteco saint's day prayer, 1969[1]

In September 1584, during an episcopal visita to Chiapa de Indios, a group
of townspeople came to the bishop, Fray Pedro de Feria, to accuse the patri-
arch of one of the principal lineages in the town of leading a clandestine
cult.[2] They said that in nearby Suchiapa a "gran junta" composed of twelve
Indians who called themselves the Twelve Apostles gathered at night to
walk among the hills and caves and to perform "demonic rites against our
Christian religion." With them, Feria was told, went two women, one they
called Santa María, the other Magdalena. Together the cultists carried out
ceremonies in which they were said to transform themselves into gods and
goddesses. In their divine form, the women had the power to conjure storms
and to give riches to whomever they pleased.

The leader of this "gran junta," according to his accusers, was Juan
Atonal, "uno de los más principales indios," an incumbent alcalde and the
father of Pedro Mata, the governor of the town. This news astonished the
bishop, for Atonal was a longtime friend of the Spanish, a model convert,
an "aventajado cristiano" (upstanding Christian) in the eyes of the Domini-

cans. He had been baptized forty years earlier, had made confession for thirty years, and had taken communion once a year ever since.

Feria commissioned the local priest, Fray Manuel Acosta, a Dominican who spoke Chiapaneco, to help him investigate the charges. They visited cave sites and invited other witnesses to come forward. In one underground cavern they discovered an image of a Chiapaneco god and evidence of fresh sacrifices. Several witnesses claimed that Atonal kept another idol in his house and worshipped it "night and day as if he'd never heard the name of Jesus Christ." He was also accused of having publicly repudiated the sacrament of confession and of living openly with a woman who was not his wife.

A number of prominent men from other important Indian towns in the province also were found to have participated in the cult, to have made heretical statements, or to have committed other "errors." Don Juan de la Cruz, from the Tzeltal town of Ocosingo, was charged with having scorned the sacrament of communion and having made claims that simple fornication was no sin. Juan Fernández, a native of the Zoque town of Ocotepeque, was said to have denied the efficacy of confession. Cristóbal Arias, a Tzotzil from Zinacantán, was held because of his special friendship with Juan Atonal and apparent participation in the cult. All of these men were described by Feria as among the most able and acculturated of their respective peoples. They were the very men on whom the Church had come to rely for setting a proper example of Christian virtue. They were also the very men on whom the corregidor had come to rely for sustaining tribute revenues during this time of rapid population decline. For that service they earned the protection of the president of the audiencia, who intervened to see to it that, as new Christians, their lapses in piety were treated with leniency. Atonal was restored to the office of alcalde, and the others apparently also went free. Feria was furious, but there the matter ended.

Like the idolatry trials conducted by Bishop Diego de Landa in 1562 against Maya principales and caciques in Yucatán, the Atonal affair reveals a good deal about the religious origins of political empowerment among native peoples and the ritual imperatives of civil officeholding.[3] For the ancient Maya, the sacred character of profane authority was axiomatic.[4] Kings traced their lineages to mythic ancestors. Rites of royal accession were staged in public spaces carefully configured to symbolize the cosmic order. Kings and priestly elites consumed hallucinogenic plants and committed excruciating acts of self-torture and bloodletting in order to induce the dream states that brought them into direct communication with the supernatural. In addition, they sponsored and supervised the elaborate communal ceremonies of gift giving and sacrifice that mediated the relationship between the people and their gods.

J. Eric S. Thompson described that relationship as a "contract."[5] In exchange for food and other sustenance necessary for their survival, the gods assured that the sun and moon kept to their cycles, brought rain when it was needed, and stilled the earth when it shook or broke apart. They were awesome forces and yet depended on humankind. Without the mundane gifts of corn, beans, and tobacco or the terrible gift of blood, they would go hungry and weaken, upsetting the balance of nature. By carrying the burden of fulfilling this sacred contract, Maya civil authorities assured their legitimacy in the eyes of their constituents, who yielded to their authority and tolerated their privileges.

Times of crisis—military defeat, famine, natural disaster—threatened that legitimacy, not only because such events tested the political competence of leaders but also because they were signs of trouble in the relationship between the community and its divine benefactors. The Spanish conquest, with its catastrophic aftermath of death and disease, was just such a crisis,[6] and the Spaniards' militant evangelism assured that Maya rulers and priests would have to confront its spiritual significance.

As it happened, the Dominicans themselves gave caciques and principales like Juan Atonal and Don Juan de la Cruz an opportunity to restore their place in the moral economy of native politics. Converts among the indigenous nobility were cast as model Christians, and their observance of the sacraments was carefully staged to provide a public example for others to follow. Their selection as fiscales, maestros de choro, and sacristanes reestablished their role as leaders of community public ritual. However, full capitulation required some unwelcome sacrifices. Concubines had to be abandoned, and Spanish rules on incest had to be obeyed. There was also the risk that too close collaboration with the more ruthless of the colonizers would arouse the opposition of their communities or rival members of the elite. Finally and most fundamentally, few individuals could be expected to jettison all of their religious convictions overnight.

As a result, some native rulers, especially among the first generations after the conquest, sought solutions that offered greater independence. For a time, many caciques and principales led double lives. They made their peace with the friars but also moved traditional ceremonies to secret locations outside the towns to carry on older forms of public worship as best they could. In Chiapa de Indios in 1554, for example, Fray Pedro Barrientos discovered that rites to Maviti, said to be the Chiapaneco's principal god, were still being celebrated thirty years after the conquest.[7] He staged a dramatic auto-da-fé in the main plaza and banished the cult's priest to perpetual service in the cathedral at Ciudad Real. Nevertheless, as the Juan Atonal conspiracy shows, local leaders were still reluctant to abandon traditional practices completely. Now, however, as idolatry was driven out of the sphere of public worship altogether, experiments with syncretism began.

In retrospect, the Atonal affair marks a transitional period in the adaptation of Christianity between the last attempts to preserve purer forms of indigenous idolatry and the eventual embrace by native peoples of the European cult of the saints. Feria was horrified by the pagan elements of their activities, but Atonal and his coreligionists did style themselves the Twelve Apostles and were beginning to integrate Christian symbols and images into native practice. Though the friars would not tolerate this kind of creative heterodoxy when it was unsupervised, they were more lenient when it came to saint's day observances, Holy Week, and other Christian celebrations that took place on church grounds under the watchful eyes of the local priest. These festivals offered a workable compromise, one that served both the evangelical goals of the Dominicans and native peoples' deep attachment to community ritual.

For the indigenous elite, the cult of the saints would provide an enduring solution to the spiritual consequences of the conquest.[8] Veneration of the saints meshed well with the Maya view of the reciprocal relationship between human beings and their gods and greatly facilitated a new articulation of the moral economy. As William A. Christian has outlined, in Spain "[v]illage relations with saints . . . were a series of obligations, many of them explicit and contractual, not unlike their obligations to secular lords. They involved the villagers' sacrifice of work time and offerings. They also involved the religious regulation of eating, often a combination of fasting on the saints' vigil and consumption of animal protein in public fiestas, called caridades, on the saints' day or the day the saint helped them."⁹ By assuming sponsorship of the festivals—first as private donors or officeholders on the cabildos, later as priostes and mayordomos on the cofradías, caciques and principales helped to revitalize their community's sacred contract with the supernatural. In the process they also revitalized the religious foundation of their legitimacy.

NAGUALISM

There was more to the Atonal affair than the elites' effort to retain a central role in community ritual. The Twelve Apostles worshipped clandestinely in caves hidden away in the hills and forests outside the towns, and they did not just venerate the saints, they were believed to have actually transformed themselves into gods and goddesses. Today, among the Maya of Chiapas and Guatemala, caves are thought to be openings into the terrestrial homes of the ancestors and of a category of deities known as Mundos by the Quiché.¹⁰ These sites are closely associated with shamanism and with the related concept of nagualism.

Nagualism is an indigenous theory of power found throughout Mesoamerica and is thought to have originated with the Toltecs.¹¹ The term applies to two distinct phenomena. The first is the belief that all individuals are paired at birth with one or more guardian spirits, who usually take the form of animals. In most communities, all such spirits are known as *naguales*, though in some the lesser spirits represented by humble life forms like the rabbit are known as *tonalli*. The most powerful naguales are dangerous predators like the jaguar or awesome natural forces like lightning. According to Núñez de la Vega, in seventeenth-century Chiapas, children were taken to village shamans at the age of seven to have their naguales revealed to them.¹² The shamans consulted almanacs that had been carefully preserved since before the conquest and correlated the child's birthday with the symbols associated with the appropriate day on the 260-day native calendar. It was believed (as it still is) that individuals could actually take on the physical shape of their nagual. In 1713 a woman named Sebastiana González, who was accused of witchcraft during the Tzeltal Revolt, gave this account of a childhood experience: "[she said] that her father and mother, Mateo González and Portensiana de Alvaro had told her she was a raccoon, which is an animal like a cat. They assured her that several times they had seen her transformed into this animal."[13] Today, among the Maya in the highlands, any harm done to an animal thought to be one's spiritual familiar is a bad omen indeed.

The second aspect of nagualism is the actual practice of various forms of shamanism—divination, curing, and witchcraft. The specialists who take up these arts are known as *nagualistas*, and neophytes are taught by elder *maestros*. Núñez de la Vega described a colonial-period initiation rite this way:

> the Master took (the pupil) on different days to some forest, barranca, cave, field, or other secret place. . . . In some provinces it is the custom to place the disciple on some great anthill, and the Master . . . calls upon a large snake which is colored white, black, and red and named mother of the ants. The latter emerges, accompanied by the ants and other small snakes, and they enter the joints of the hands, beginning with the left, emerging at the nostrils, ears, or joints on the right side. . . . After this they go upon the road, where they are met by a ferocious dragon. . . . [O]pening his mouth the dragon swallows the disciple, then ejects him from the rear. Then the Master tells the boy that now he is initiated. These ceremonies continue from time to time through thirteen days.[14]

This may seem like the rawest kind of paganism, but by the seventeenth century, even nagualism had incorporated elements of Christianity. Shamans began their rituals with the Paternoster, Ave Maria, and Credo and ended them by invoking the Holy Trinity.[15]

Ethnographic work among the Maya both in Guatemala and Chiapas suggests that nagualism is an important element in village political culture, sometimes invoked by civil officeholders to legitimate their individual empowerment and sometimes by critics of the political establishment to impose controls on village elites and to legitimate their own moral authority. For example, Maud Oakes reported that in Todos Santos, a Mam village in northwestern Guatemala, several prominent members of the governing civil hierarchy were powerful *chimanes*, or shamans.[16] Similarly, Alfonso Villa Rojas discovered that in Oxchuc, a Tzeltal town, village elders and chiefs were widely assumed to have powerful naguales: "The system finds its justification in its efficiency as a method of social control; it makes possible the continued attachment to traditional custom, and sanctions the moral code of the group. . . . As soon as a man begins to age, rumour spreads that he has a nagual and is able to do harm if his wrath is incurred. People who, in addition to age, are imperious and energetic personalities are most likely to be accused of harboring a nagual."[17] How else would they come by the skill and energy to acquire their rank and status?

On the other hand, June Nash has described a series of quite violent confrontations between civil authorities and the hierarchy of native curers during the 1960s in the Tzeltal town of Amatenango. Over a period of just a few years, nine men were killed in the dispute. She places the conflict in the context of a tripartite system designed to control the abuse of power. In her scheme, incumbent officeholders, recognized nagualistas, and the ancestors were in "structural opposition," their respective powers held in check by those of the others. In comparative terms, then, nagualism is a political "wild card" that can be played both to uphold the legitimacy of an established hierarchy and also to challenge it.

Feria's account of the Atonal conspiracy, though woefully lacking in detail, makes it clear that townspeople in Chiapa de Indios associated the cult with nagualism. For the conspirators, the association offered a second avenue to power and status apart from whatever contributions they may have made to community ritual. It marked them as men and women to be respected and even feared.

Nagualism is part of a broader construction of the supernatural that attaches a sacred dimension to virtually all aspects of the physical world. Ordinary birds, mammals, reptiles, or amphibians can be spirits in disguise and are symbolically linked to deities that influence all the important aspects of human existence. Today in Zinacantán, hummingbirds, hawks, moths, and butterflies are all associated with the ancestral gods.[18] Owls are linked to darkness, death, and the underworld, snakes to male fertility, and rabbits to the moon, mother's milk, and female fecundity. Natural features of the landscape also have cosmological significance.[19] Mountains are the homes of the ancestors, caves the entrance to those homes. Rivers are considered to have female qualities and are associated with certain female deities. The sun, moon, and planets, of course, are deified, and even such intangible forces of nature as earth, wind, and fire are associated with particular gods.

The Maya live in intimate contact with the supernatural, and the possibility of a face-to-face encounter with a member of the spirit world is never remote. Tales Robert M. Laughlin recently collected in Zinacantán are full of stories about chance meetings with spirits, animal naguales, or one of the Christian saints.[20] But it is in the zinacantecos' view of dreams that the immediacy of sacred things is especially evident.[21] Zinacantecos are preoccupied with their dreams. They are careful to remember them in detail and are eager to talk about them with their families. Dreams, they believe, provide a window into the supernatural. They invite contact with dead ancestors, the saints, or simply spooks. They can reveal the identity of a person's nagual or tell of dangers to the individual's soul, and they prophesy the future. Dreams are especially important to shamans. As the following account from Zinacantán by Romin Tanchak explains, they are called to their vocation through dreams, and dreams are an important instrument for curing and divination:

> Whoever sees, dreams well.
> Whoever becomes a shaman is summoned in their dreams to Calvary.
> "We'll give you some work," the elders tell them. "Do you want to accept the responsibility of shamanhood, or don't you want to accept it?"
> If they say, "I'll accept it," then it's fine. If they say, "I don't want to," they'll get a beating. They die.
> If they do what they're told, they are given a little gourd for cooling flower water, the pot for their flowers, and their half gourds for the ritual bath. They are given laurel, wintergreen, peperomia, and savory. They are given whatever medicines are needed to cure sickness. They are given the bamboo staff—the dog frightener.
> After they receive their powers, they are eager to feel the pulse, they are eager to cure. In their dreams they are shown what to give for the illness.
> "Watch over the young and the old," they are told. "Do not rebel! You mustn't refuse the request when the patient's family comes to escort you. If you rebel, you'll be punished for not accepting the command."
> All the shamans are assembled in their dreams at Calvary, the old men and women and the young who have not yet been initiated.
> The ancestral gods are sitting there, the way we see the elders sitting at the Chapel of Esquipulas.[22]

The Dominican friars who worked among the Maya in colonial Chiapas abhorred such beliefs as these, but they brought their own traditions about miraculous visitations and their own convictions about the omnipresence of

God and the readiness of the saints to intervene in the everyday lives of the faithful.

APPARITIONS IN SPANISH TRADITION

In *Apparitions in Late Medieval and Renaissance Spain*, William Christian discusses the place of visions and apparitions in the religious culture of late fifteenth-century Spain. Christian found that the most common by far were visions of the Blessed Mother.[23] Typically, apparitions were seen by shepherds walking alone in the countryside near a location to which rural cultures attached cosmological significance—a cave, a tree, or a spring. Usually the vision led to the discovery of a sacred object, a statue or a painted image. Christian emphasizes that these "are eminently social visions. They attract immediate public attention and call for some sort of verification. If believed, they provoke public devotion, often very emotional. . . . The village (for these are predominately rural events) is the chorus, doubtful of why one of their number should be so chosen, but in the cases we learn about, feeling the pride of a chosen people."[24] Apparitions that captured the public's imagination were celebrated with the construction of chapels or shrines, often in the countryside away from the regular town churches. Shrines based on relics of holy figures were kept inside the churches or monasteries to protect the relics from thieves.

The incidence of apparitions fell off dramatically with the onset of the Protestant Reformation in the sixteenth century as the Holy Office of the Inquisition grew increasingly more suspicious of popular enthusiasm among the laity and intensified its effort to eliminate heterodoxy and standardize Church practices. Whether people actually experienced visions less often is not clear. Nevertheless, the accounts of earlier visitations were preserved in the oral histories of the established shrines and in the libraries of parish priests in the form of books of exempla for sermons. They were standard fare in the sermons of missionary friars throughout Spanish America and were an important vehicle for the spread of what Jacques Lafaye has called American "mariolatry."[25] Among the Dominicans in Chiapas, St. Dominic's own encounters with the Blessed Mother were key elements in his hagiology,[26] and Núñez de la Vega devoted much of his Eighth Pastoral Letter to examples from across the globe of the Virgin's miraculous intercession, each invoked by devoted recitations of the Rosary. Two cases involved Indians, one a woman in Peru and the other a Mexica man in the Valley of Mexico.[27] When joined with indigenous traditions about the immediacy of the supernatural, these stories positively challenged native peoples to experience Marian visions of their own.

VISIONS AND NATIVE RESISTANCE

The most famous vision in the history of colonial Mexico was, of course, the Indian Juan Diego's encounter with the Virgin Mary on the hill of Tepeyac outside Mexico City in 1531.[28] The Blessed Mother was said to have spoken to the man in Nahuatl and to have asked him to tell Archbishop Juan de Zumárraga that she wanted a church built in her name on the hill. The archbishop at first refused to believe Juan Diego's story. However, when Diego brought a cloak to him in which he had gathered roses and unfolded the cloak to reveal an image of the Virgin embossed on the fabric, Zumárraga became convinced. A church was built, and before the end of the century Tepeyac was a busy pilgrimage site for devotees of, as she was now called, the Virgin of Guadalupe.

Scholars once viewed the cult as an archetypal example of religious syncretism because Tepeyac was the site of preconquest devotions to Tonantzin-Cihuacóatl, the principal Nahuat mother-goddess. The fact that the Virgin Mary appeared as a dark-skinned woman standing atop the moon suggested that Juan Diego was simply imposing a new identity on an older icon. In recent years, however, the origins of the celebrated cult have been reexamined.[29] Juan Diego's vision is now widely thought to have been the invention of a seventeenth-century theologian named Miguel Sánchez, who was inspired by the twelfth chapter of the Book of Revelation. The chapter begins, "And there appeared a great wonder in heaven; a woman clothed with the sun, and the moon under her feet, and upon her head a crown of twelve stars." Moreover, research has revealed that, in the early years, the most conspicuous pilgrims to the shrine of the Virgin of Guadalupe were upperclass Spaniards and creoles from Mexico City rather than native peoples from the villages.[30] In fact, the cult seems to have been largely ignored by Indian communities until after 1750, when church authorities began to promote new cofradías in her honor, an expense that many pueblos resisted, at least initially. Its popularity at the end of the colonial period is now understood as more a function of the construction by Mexican creoles of a new national consciousness than the enduring product of an early syncretism.

The Church's endorsement of the myth of Juan Diego's vision stands in stark contrast to its normal response to apparitions of Christian saints among Indians. In parishes throughout Spanish America, while local priests promoted the faith by attributing miraculous powers to religious statuary and holy images, reports of visitations of the Virgin Mary, Jesus, or one of the apostles typically were viewed with skepticism and suspicion. Like the inquisitors in sixteenth-century Castile, clerics in New Spain saw these manifestations of popular piety as potentially dangerous threats to orthodoxy and the authority of church leaders. They understood that apparitions or reports of other kinds of miracles were often a form of cultural resistance and an affirmation of native religious experience. The fact that these incidents occurred more frequently during periods of social crisis made their political significance all the more clear to local Spanish authorities.

The Juan Atonal conspiracy emerged out of the crisis of the late sixteenth century, when native peoples were dying in extraordinary numbers from European diseases and when native elites were confronted with the collapse of the indigenous moral economy. In Chiapas that crisis abated early in the seventeenth century as populations stabilized, economic pressures eased, and principales consolidated their hold on village offices and reconstructed their role in community ritual. But, as outlined in the last chapter, this extended period of relative calm did not last. The surest indicator that tensions were again on the rise was the presence of renewed incidents of violence between Indians and Spaniards, especially the murderous rioting in Tuxtla in 1693, and also the reappearance of popular religious cults that challenged, at least implicitly, the moral authority of the Church. These cults were signs that, from the Mayas' perspective, the balance of sacred forces that sustained their culture and protected their resources had been upset.

In 1708, while accompanying Bishop Alvarez de Toledo on his first pastoral visita, Fray Joseph Monroy, the parish priest of Chamula, received word that a pious man (varón justo), a mestizo from outside the province, was creating an uproar in Zinacantán with his sermons on penitence.[31] The man claimed to have an image of the Blessed Mother that gave off rays of light, which he kept in a hollow tree. Monroy left immediately to investigate, and he later described what he found:

> I came upon a great crowd of Indian men and women from the two pueblos [Zinacantán and Chamula]; I asked them where this man was, and they told me he had now left the tree, moving to another *paraje* nearby. Proceeding a short distance, I discovered a man covered in a blanket, leaning against an oak, his face hidden. I asked him who he was. He did not respond until I asked a third time: I am a poor sinner, who is not allowed to love God. . . . I went to examine the tree, a hollow oak, whose cavity had been covered with a table. On the table I found a *pestanuela* for food received from the hands of the Indians. On this table I found an indentation in which had been placed a wooden image of St. Joseph. Within the tree, I found a small notebook of verses that appeared to be concerned with penitence and love of God. Fixed to the tree was a cross with verses written on paper addressed to the same concerns.[32]

Monroy took the man back to Chamula, where more crowds gathered, and then, after three days, to Ciudad Real, where he was handed over to the Franciscans. The Recollects of the Franciscans, a reform-minded branch of the order, were associated with a popular penitential movement at this time that had been inspiring mass demonstrations of piety throughout the viceroyalty. Monroy decided to make disciplining the hermit the Franciscans' responsibility, though whether or not the man actually had ties to the Recollects is unknown. Monroy apparently decided that they were responsible for the appearance of the hermit.[33]

The man was imprisoned in Ciudad Real for two years. Upon his release he returned to Zinacantán to resume his preaching, and Monroy again went to the pueblo. With the parish priest, Fray Jorge Atondo, he confronted him a second time:

> Knowing that a chapel [*ermita*] had been built in the countryside [*monte*], we went and found it, a *cuadra y media* from the road, in the same paraje as before. The chapel was about eight paces long, divided into a dormitory and an oratorio, with an altar, on which had been placed a small image of the Virgin, with candles, cacao, eggs, tortillas, and other similar things offered by the Indians. With all the conveniences, the ermita was well-adorned, and lined with neatly finished petates. The monte where it was found was

cleared and fenced; the path to it . . . was well beaten due to the continuous arrival of Indians visiting with their candles and liquidambar.[34]

After considerable resistance, the two priests were able to burn the shrine and take the man out of the pueblo. This time he was turned over to the Jesuits, who decided he was being deluded by the Devil and exiled him to Mexico, the province of his birth. He died during the journey out of Chiapas.

News of another cult arrived in March 1712.[35] Fray Bartolomé Ximénez, the parish priest of Totolapa, a Zoque town, became alarmed when attendance at mass became unusually poor. He learned that many in his congregation had gone to Santa Marta, a Tzotzil pueblo, to visit a new shrine. The bishop was informed, and Fray Joseph Monroy was asked to intervene once again.

The Dominicans considered Santa Marta a troublesome parish. Fray Francisco Ximénez remarked that its people were "arrogant and disobedient." At the time that the cult appeared there, their parish priest had left in anger and frustration, and had been in Ciudad Real for several months. Upon his departure he bitterly warned the townspeople that God would punish them for their lack of faith. When the church fell into disrepair and a serious pestilence broke out, that prophecy was fulfilled, or so it seemed to Fray Monroy.

When Monroy entered Santa Marta, he encountered native peoples from virtually every district in Chiapas: tzeltales from los Llanos and the altiplano, tzotziles from la Guardianía, and zoques from the western highlands. He was met by the justicias and principales, who took him to the shrine. There he spoke with Dominica López, a twenty-three-year-old woman, who showed him a small wooden image wrapped in cloth—the work, Monroy believed, of zinacanteco craftsmen. López told the priest that the Virgin Mary had appeared to her one evening as she went to her milpa. "She asked me if I had a mother or father; I responded, 'No.' She told me she was poor, was named María, and had come from the sky to help the Indians. I was to tell the justicias, and they were to build a small shrine at the edge of the town for her to live in."[36] Monroy was asked to celebrate mass at the shrine, but he put them off, saying he first needed permission from the bishop. After four days he left for nearby San Andrés, where he received a dispatch from authorities, ordering him to bring the image, Dominica López, and her husband to the capital. Returning to Santa Marta, he showed the justicias the letter from the alcalde mayor and promised that if they allowed the image to be taken to Ciudad Real, their Virgin would be received with great honor. They agreed, and some two thousand cult followers accompanied Monroy to the capital.

The image was taken to the Dominican convent and respectfully placed in a niche reserved for the Virgen del Rosario. The next day the curious from all classes of the city came to view it, while outside, in the cemetery, the crowd that had come from Santa Marta waited. That night authorities removed the image from the church. When the Indians discovered it missing, they asked for its return. They left the city when their request was turned down, apparently without any threat of violence.

Dominica López and her husband, Juan Gómez, were taken into custody when they came to Ciudad Real and were held for trial by church authorities from the office of the bishop on the charge of promoting a false miracle. Two others were also imprisoned, Gregorio Ximénez, who had briefly served as sacristán at the shrine, and Domingo López, who had been named alférez and put in charge of organizing a fiesta in her honor. Interestingly, none of the alcaldes or regidores who had served in 1711 or who were in office in 1712 were accused of wrongdoing, and none were called individually to testify before the court. The authorities seemed to have decided that they had acted in good faith, and with the situation apparently under control, they also may have feared that arresting the officials might provoke a more dangerous confrontation.

There was little doubt that the Spanish would not condemn them, but duty to their faith and the imperative of maintaining juridical forms compelled the court to hold orderly proceedings and take detailed testimony. Gregorio Ximénez and Domingo López, in fact, were not punished, because the commission decided that they had acted out of sincere belief in the Blessed Mother's intercession. The commissioners' questions focused on the supposed miracle of the Virgin's apparition, a description of the shrine and who organized its construction, and the forms of devotion practiced by the cult. They believed that this was another work of the Devil and suspected Dominica López and her husband of witchcraft, of being nagualistas and curers.

Juan Gómez testified that the Blessed Mother had first appeared to his wife. He did not see the Virgin until four days afterward, when he saw her on a log twenty paces from where his wife had seen her. She was, he said, of "human flesh." The Virgin spoke to Gómez on two occasions. The first time, he asked her why she had come to this place. She replied that for many years God had guarded the town. Now she only wanted the alcaldes, the fiscal, and the maestro de coro to build her a home. Later he asked her why she wanted to be in the pueblo, and she answered, "so as not to die among the sticks and stones" of the forest.[37]

The couple's testimony differs on whether others in the town actually saw the apparition with their own eyes. Both reported that when the justicias and the rest of the town first went to the milpa, the Virgin could not be found. Dominica López testified that when they came a second time, after constructing a shrine, the alcaldes saw the Virgin exactly where she had seen her. Her husband claimed that when they returned, though they "found" the Virgin, no one else actually saw her because he had wrapped her in a manta.

The image was taken to the ermita with great ceremony. Drums, flutes, and horns were played, and the crowd sang as they carried banners, crosses, and lighted candles. A niche was brought from the church, and the Virgin was placed in it as the worshipers recited the rosary and the Credo. Other images were placed beside her, of San Pablo, Santiago, and Santa María Magdalena, the patron saints of neighboring towns. Three days later, Juan Gómez discovered that the figure of the Virgin was now of wood and no longer of flesh. He could not explain the transformation.

All of this had apparently taken place in October of the previous year, 1711, and been overlooked by the Spanish for several months, though there does not seem to have been any deliberate conspiracy to hide the cult from colonial authorities. During the Lenten celebrations in Santa Marta that attracted the attention of Fray Bartolomé Ximénez and Fray Joseph Monroy, a number of Spaniards from Ciudad Real visited the village out of curiosity and were allowed to enter the shrine and talked with Dominica López without incident.[38]

The participants who testified at the trial tried very hard to persuade the court that they were sincere and that they were acting in conformity with accepted Catholic practice. Dominica López, for example, explained in some detail that the fiestas they celebrated were conducted "with the same solemnity that we are accustomed to when we honor our patron, Santa Marta," including recitations of the Credo and the rosary.

She and her husband were appointed caretakers or mayordomos of the shrine by the town alcaldes, and Domingo López was named alférez. Just when Gregorio Ximénez served as sacristán is uncertain. Pilgrims came with offerings of chickens, wax candles, copal incense, flowers, and coins. A few who visited the shrine were sick and came seeking a cure. Gómez admitted that two or three left after several days "clean and healthy." He claimed no role in their cure, saying that he did not know how this had happened, though he seems to have offered this as evidence that the miracle was real.

The court convicted both Dominica López and Juan Gómez and sentenced them to two hundred lashes and ten years' exile outside the province. When the first part of the sentence was carried out, they were carted through the streets of Ciudad Real and beaten until finally the bishop intervened for fear they would be killed. They were then taken to Guatemala and on to the Golfo Dulce on the Caribbean coast of Honduras to serve their exile. Deprived of its sacred image and its mayordomos, and having failed to win the approval of the bishop, the cult ended with little fanfare. There was no talk of rebellion.

While these events were being played out, two other miracles were said to have taken place in San Pedro Chenaló, another Tzotzil town.[39] On the eve of the feast day of San Sebastián, an image of the saint kept in the town church was seen to sweat on two occasions, and townspeople built a new chapel to honor the miracle. Then, on two Sundays in a row, an image of San Pedro, the town's patron saint, was seen to throw off rays of light.

These events were met with a somewhat different response than had the appearance of the Virgin in Santa Marta. According to Fray Francisco Ximénez, the people of San Pedro Chenaló became fearful, thinking these were signs of God's anger, portents of disaster. They responded not with joyful processions and celebrations but with prayers and solemn acts of penitence. When Fray Joseph Monroy came to investigate, he calmed the town. After a few days he had persuaded them that no miracles had taken place and was allowed to burn the shrine without incident.

When the Virgin appeared in the Tzeltal town of Cancuc twelve months later, officials in the provincial capital hoped to put down the new cult with the same success they had had in Zinacantán, Santa Marta, and San Pedro Chenaló. They were ill prepared for their failure.

THE HIGHLANDS IN REVOLT

"This was the beginning of a new world."

—Francisco de Torre y Tobilla
rebel priest[1]

The Virgin spoke to her with these words, "María,
you are my daughter."
She responded, "Yes, Señora, you are my mother."
The Virgin continued, saying, "Daughter, make a
cross on this place and mark the earth. It is my will
that a shrine be made here for me to live in with you."
She appeared as a woman, very pretty and white.

—Agustín López
the father of María de la Candelaria[2]

The first to warn of trouble afoot in Cancuc was the parish priest, Fray Simón de Lara. On June 15, 1712, he informed his counterpart in Tila, Joseph Francisco Moreno, a secular curate, that a new miracle had been "invented" and that, without his consent, his townspeople had built a shrine.[3] The two considered tearing down the structure at once but decided to call the entire pueblo to the church to learn what had happened before taking any action. There, María López, the thirteen-year-old daughter of Agustín López, Cancuc's sacristán, willingly confessed that while she was walking on the outskirts of town, the Virgin Mary appeared and spoke to her. The Blessed Mother told María that she had come to offer the Indians her help and that they were to construct a shrine for her. The young woman reported that she went home to tell her parents of the visitation and that her mother urged her to proclaim the miracle to the pueblo. Her father went with her to the site of the encounter, a place near their house and near the *monte serrado*, the rough terrain that led higher into the mountains. He placed a wooden cross there as the Blessed Mother had asked. Soon afterward, with the support of

Cancuc's justicias, especially that of the first alcalde, Domingo Pérez, everyone in the village came out to help build a small chapel. Apparently María, the *indizuela* (little Indian girl), as the Spanish often referred to her, did not tell the two priests that the Virgin continued to visit and to speak with her in a hidden room within the ermita.

Fray Simón did not hesitate to denounce the miracle as a fraud, the work of the Devil. He chastised María and her father and gave each a severe lashing of forty *azotes*. But the girl, in tears, held to her story, and townspeople defied their priest by continuing to pay their respects at the shrine. The two clerics apparently did not feel confident enough of their safety to attempt to dismantle the chapel on their own. Fray Simón left Cancuc for Tenango, his other parish, where he was more welcome, at least for the moment.

A week later, sixteen cancuqueros arrived in Chamula on the evening before the great festival of el Día de San Juan. The bishop, Fray Bauptista Alvarez de Toledo was there, along with the justicia mayor of the province, Juan Francisco de Astudillo, and Chamula's curate, Fray Joseph Monroy. The three Spaniards heard an account of events in Cancuc that recalled the Gospel stories of Christ's birth. "In our pueblo, at midnight, we saw beneath the heavens many brilliant lights [*resplandores*] over a certain place on the edge of town. And going there to look, we found a shrine [*ermita*]. Of this we have come to tell you."[4] As with María and her father in their exchange with Fray Simón de Lara, these tzeltales made no attempt to keep secret the miracle of the visitation. Quite the contrary. Flushed with the excitement of so extraordinary an event, they hoped to convince the bishop of the authenticity of the apparition and win his approval to carry on the new cult. Instead, he locked them up and threatened to send troops to burn the shrine if the cancuqueros did not dismantle it themselves.

Soon afterward, Fray Simón de Lara returned to Cancuc and found the cult flourishing. He informed the authorities in Ciudad Real, who instructed Cancuc's justicias to come to the capital. They were imprisoned there (presumably to their surprise), and new, more compliant officials were named by Francisco de Astudillo and Fray Simón to replace them.

Despite these efforts, pilgrims from nearby towns—first from Bachajón and Oxchuc, and then from others—came to Cancuc in ever greater numbers to offer alms and gifts to María López, and to hear the Virgin's message.[5] Beyond this, and unbeknownst to the Spanish, Agustín López began to attract more active support from village leaders in nearby communities and to put together a more formal political apparatus to administer the cult. As the bishop and justicia mayor took more aggressive steps to suppress the movement, these conspirators moved closer to open rebellion.

Four years later, when he was finally captured, Agustín López testified that the original conspiracy was made up of his daughter and him, together with four others with whom he consulted before revealing the miracle to the town as a whole.[6] He described the four men—Gerónimo Saroes, Sebastián García, Gabriel Sánchez, and Miguel Gómez—simply as "amigos." All but Gabriel Sánchez had been civil or parish officeholders. Saroes had served for many years as fiscal and escribano in Bachajón. But in March 1712 he had quarreled with the local priest and had been outlawed by the town's justicias. He left Bachajón and came to live in Agustín López's house. Sebastián García and Miguel Gómez were former regidores in Cancuc. López himself had been sacristán in Cancuc for forty years. Of this group he said: "all four were men of authority in [Cancuc] and all the Indians had much respect for them. In this time and occasion they were poor; myself and the others could scarcely put our hands on a single manta."[7] They were obviously bitter men for whom cooperating with Spanish governors and priests and participating in local officeholding had brought only poverty. Agustín López was the only one among them who still held office at the time of the miracle.

According to several accounts, their claim that María López had spoken with the Blessed Mother was not immediately accepted by all who heard the story. As one young woman testified, "[T]hey were afraid of what she told them, even though they knew she was an Indian woman just like others."[8] But when the incumbent officeholders in Cancuc threw their support behind the cult, their claims gained wider acceptance. Agustín López recalled that "although at the beginning some Indians doubted, seeing that others believed, who were capable and of authority because of the offices they had occupied and still occupied, they were convinced, and all believed alike."[9] All the people of Cancuc, he said, helped erect the shrine. Then, when the justicias were imprisoned and people lost hope that the miracle would be recognized as legitimate by the Church, public sentiment for the cult solidified. Sometime in late June or July, both of Cancuc's fiscales, Domingo Méndez and Nicolás López, began to cooperate with the conspiracy. With their recruitment, all the standing members of Cancuc's political hierarchy now backed the cult.

They were joined by Lucas Pérez, fiscal in Chilón, and Antonio López, fiscal in Tenango, who also were invited into the shrine's inner circle.[10] Lucas Pérez, like Gerónimo Saroes, had had a recent falling out with his priest. During Bishop Alvarez de Toledo's visita in 1709, he had refused to pay a fee for having his child confirmed and was turned out of office. For the moment, however, no other officeholders from towns in the highlands participated in the plotting.

One other significant recruit arrived in Cancuc sometime in July before the rebellion ignited. His name was Sebastián Gómez, a Tzotzil from San Pedro Chenaló, and he told an extraordinary story.[11] He brought with him a small statue of San Pedro and claimed he had risen to heaven and had spoken with the saint himself. He said that San Pedro had invested him with the authority to ordain priests and bishops, and that he was to be known thereafter as Sebastián de la Gloria. Fray Francisco Ximénez, the chronicler, believed that Sebastián Gómez had been the "inventor" of the miracles in San Pedro Chenaló that were reported in 1711, but no other evidence supports this supposition. Gómez himself was never captured and thus never told his side of the tale.

At about this time, late July 1712, the newly appointed alcaldes in Cancuc warned Fray Simón de Lara that his life was in jeopardy.[12] The conspirators, anticipating his flight, blocked the roads to prevent his escape, but the priest somehow found his way to Tenango. There, the loyalist fiscal, Nicolás Pérez, persuaded him to return to the safety of the provincial capital. Cancuc was on the brink of rebellion.

Two events followed close on the heels of Fray Simón's retreat. From the perspective of the Spaniards in Ciudad Real, they could not have come at a worse time. First, despite Fray Joseph Monroy's efforts to dissuade him, Bishop Alvarez de Toledo announced that his second pastoral visita of the highlands would begin on August 5. Second, the former alcaldes from Cancuc who had been imprisoned in Ciudad Real escaped. They returned to their town to reclaim their offices and to roust their Spanish-appointed successors, who fled to the capital.

Cancuc moved quickly toward a complete break with Spanish rule. Townspeople took statues of the Virgin, San Antonio, and San Pedro from the town church to decorate the altar inside the shrine, where María (now known as María de la Candelaria after the Virgen de la Candelaria) and her family had already taken up residence. Next, Sebastián Gómez de la Gloria ordained the first rebel priests, or *vicarios generales*.[13] Among them were the fiscales who had joined the conspiracy earlier—Gerónimo Saroes of Bachajón, Antonio López of Tenango, Lucas Pérez of Chilón, and Domingo Méndez and Nicolás López of Cancuc—and three newcomers: Sebastián Gonzales of Guaguitepeque, Francisco Pérez of Petalsingo, and Francisco de Torre y Tobilla of Ocosingo. According to Torre y Tobilla:

> they placed the witness on his knees about three feet in front of the altar and to one side of three lighted candles. Before him was Sebastián Gómez de la Gloria, who at the time of the consecration ceremony in the Mass seized a candle from the altar and put it on his head and lifted it three times and rested it [on his head] three times and then returned it to the altar. And when the Mass was finished Sebastián Gómez went out leaving the witness kneeling with three candles until midnight.[14]

Torre y Tobilla was apparently the last of the eight to be made a priest and was ordained separately. Before the priests began their duties, they also received a formal baptism: "[A]t midnight Sebastián García summoned him and brought him to the chapel, where Sebastián Gómez baptized him, pouring water on his head and placing his hand on it and lowering it onto his forehead and from there to his nose, saying, 'in the name of the Father, the Son, and the Holy Spirit' in his mother tongue; and afterward he went out in the procession with the Holy Sepulchre singing the misericordia." Priestly vestments, chalices, patents, and other ceremonial paraphernalia were brought from the church, and the first rebel masses were said. According to Domingo Méndez, María de la Candelaria herself also wore an alb during these ceremonies.[15]

REGIONAL MOBILIZATION

In the first week of August, cult leaders in Cancuc issued a call to war, formally renouncing their obedience to God and king in a letter written in Tzeltal and carried to the alcaldes in each of the pueblos in the province of the tzeltales, the Guardianía de Hueytiupán, and several towns in the provinces of Los Llanos and the Zoque. It read, "Jesús, María, and Joseph. *Señores alcaldes*: I, the Virgin of Our Lady of the Rosary, command you to come to the pueblo of Cancuc. Bring all the silver from your church, and the ornaments and bells, with all the *cajas* and drums, and all the books and money of the cofradías, because now there is neither God nor King. Come at once, because those who do not come will be punished. Y a Dios. Ciudad Real de Cancuc. La Virgen Santissima María de la Cruz."[16]

On August 10, five days of public processions began. They were in the style of community fiestas, with fireworks and ritual dancing. María de la Candelaria held court at the shrine, constantly preaching the truth of the Virgin's intervention. The rebel priests said mass, both inside the village church and at the ermita, and gave their own sermons exhorting the assembled crowds to show their loyalty and obey the commands of the rebel leaders.

It is impossible to offer an exact count of just how many pueblos were represented at the convocation. Ximénez simply wrote that "many pueblos or most of the tzeltales" responded to the summons.[17] Neither Gerónimo Saroes, Agustín López, nor other eyewitnesses gave precise accounts, and the estimates of recent scholars have varied. Herbert Klein reported that "some twenty-eight" towns attended, while Robert Wasserstrom indicated "nearly twenty-five."[18]

The trial testimonies collected after the revolt help clarify the extent of regional participation, and provide the names of the native towns of rebel captains, cult priests, and others accused of more specific crimes. Witnesses also named the towns that contributed Indian soldiers during engagements with Spanish troops or forays against pueblos disloyal to Cancuc. This record shows that the twenty-one communities listed in Table 6.1 provided captains, supported a rebel clergy, or took part in the fighting. This tally corresponds to a reckoning offered by Fray Gabriel de Artiaga, a contemporary observer who reported that twenty-one pueblos had been active, "twelve from the region east of Ciudad Real, nine from the north."[19] Individuals from other pueblos are known to have participated—a Domingo García of Comitán was captured at Cancuc, for example—but in these cases there is no evidence that their towns contributed as a whole community. After the fall of Cancuc, audiencia troops would visit several towns not on the list—

TABLE 6.1   THE REBEL PUEBLOS

TZELTAL	TZOTZIL
Bachajón	Hueytiupán
Cancuc	Huistán
Chilón	Mitontic
Guaguitepeque	San Pedro Chenaló
Moyos	Santa Marta
Ocosingo	
Petalsingo	CHOL
San Martín Teultepeque	Tila
Oxchuc	Tumbalá
Sibacá	
Sitalá	
Tenango	
Tenejapa	
Yajalón	

San Andrés, Santa María Magdalena, and San Pablo—but no active participants are known to have come from these pueblos.

The revolt was confined to the eastern half of the central plateau. None of the Tzeltal towns in valleys south of Ciudad Real participated. These included Amatenango, Aquacatenango, Pinola, Soyatitán, Socoltenango, Chalchitán, Istapilla, Tecoluta, and Zapaluta. Nor did the revolt gain the support of the majority of Tzotzil towns north and west of the capital, notably Zinacantán and Chamula.

With the great celebrations in Cancuc, cult leaders mobilized a large regional constituency. To coordinate their efforts, the original group of conspirators, led by Agustín López, imposed a more formal political apparatus on the cult, transforming their small circle into a more linear and symmetrical hierarchy. Gerónimo Saroes and Lucas Pérez were appointed as secretaries

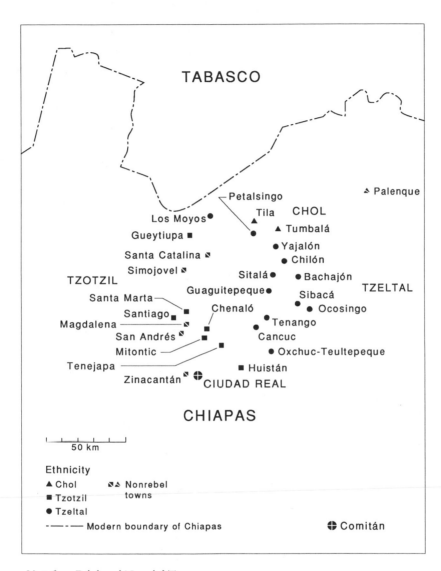

Map 6.1. Rebel and Nonrebel Towns

and charged with serving María de la Candelaria at the shrine. It was Saroes, one of the very first conspirators, who wrote the proclamation summoning the pueblos to Cancuc.[20] Domingo Pérez (the first alcalde of Cancuc) and Sebastián García were appointed as mayordomos, a level of the shrine hierarchy that eventually numbered twelve. The mayordomos were ranked and were given seats before the shrine's altar, with the senior officials occupying the forward rows.

The first rebel captains general were also named during the August 10 convocation: Nicolás Vásquez of Tenango, Jacinto Domínguez of Sibacá, Juan García of Cancuc, and Lázaro Ximénez of Hueytiupán.[21] Vásquez became the senior capitán general, a mayordomo at the shrine, and a new member of the leadership. They were installed with great ceremony by Sebastián Gómez de la Gloria.

The social and political origins of these men remain uncertain. All were chosen before any actual fighting took place. Only one of them, Jacinto Domínguez, a former regidor, had held civil or parish office. All were adults in their thirties and forties, apparently physically vigorous and well respected in their communities. They must have been known to Agustín López, Gerónimo Saroes, Domingo Pérez or others among the inner circle, who must have been confident that their loyalty could be relied on, and they did in fact acquit themselves well once the insurrection was underway.

More captains were recruited when the rebel armies were mobilized, though these men were apparently chosen by the captains general in charge of each band rather than by the central leadership. It is striking how few were current or former village officeholders. Of more than fifty captains identified in the records, only three—an alcalde and a regidor from Yajalón and Jacinto Domínguez, the former regidor from Sibacá—are known to have served as justicias. The cult's leaders seem to have deliberately turned to men outside the established elite to lead their army.

Once the fighting began, certain men probably were singled out for their bravery, skill, and good battle sense, or for their fervent loyalty to Cancuc. But the president of the audiencia, Toribio de Cosío, who led the campaign against the rebels, suggested that there were other criteria as well: "I must observe that the process of selecting young captains is governed according to the nagual each one has; they are taught to think by witches [brujos]."[22]

Except for Edward Calnek, modern observers have dismissed Cosío's theory as simply another attempt to discredit the rebels and attribute the uprising to the work of the Devil.[23] Indeed, very little in the record sheds light on Cosío's claim. Maya witnesses were remarkably close-mouthed when questioned about witchcraft, and, surprisingly, Spanish interrogators displayed no great zeal when probing the issue. The one exception—and an important one—is in the testimony of Jacinto Domínguez. Domínguez claimed that two local captains, Miguel Martínez and Andrés Sánchez, both of Sibacá, had powers that exceeded his, despite their lower rank, because they were nagualistas. "Miguel Martín[ez] was his nagual rayo," he said, "and Andrés Sánchez had fifteen naguales."[24] He testified that they used their power to start an earthquake at Ocosingo that created a landslide to block the advance of Spanish troops. Both survived the revolt to stand before the court, and both (not surprisingly) denied Domínguez's testimony.[25]

Despite the lack of solid evidence, if (as discussed in chapter 5) nagualismo is understood as an indigenous theory of power and if the distinction between the attribution of power and the actual practice of shamanism is recognized, a link between nagualismo and the choosing of captains is certainly plausible. Such a link would explain, for example, how men without battle experience could be chosen for the rank and why such men were obeyed even by cabildo and parish officeholders and even though nearly all of them apparently lacked the status of *principal*. Finally, of course, the extra protection a nagualista's spirit guardians offered and their power to mobilize natural forces like wind, rain, and lightning, were likely to be especially valued in time of war. Indeed, María de la Candelaria would call upon acknowledged witches at crucial times during the rebellion even though she had not, as a rule, appointed them captain.

When the alcaldes from other towns led their people to Cancuc in the second week of August, they declared their commitment to the cult and to the revolutionary stand taken by the alcaldes of Cancuc. Yet they remained apart from the central leadership, and, as just noted, very few of them were appointed captain when the fighting began. Although twenty-three justicias were later convicted of participating in the uprising and eight of them were executed, their primary role, as before, was to serve as mediators between their local communities and the regional government now located in Cancuc.[26]

THE REBEL OFFENSIVE

The Tzeltal towns of Bachajón, Sibacá, and Ocosingo were the first to respond to the summons to Cancuc, and while nearly all the other pueblos in the province followed, some held back.[27] Chilón, Tenango, Guaguitepeque, and Oxchuc were among the latter, and the rebels moved first against them. In Tenango, Nicolás Pérez, the fiscal who earlier had helped Fray Simón de Lara escape, rallied at least some portion of the town to help defend the church and to resist villagers who were eager to take ornaments and other objects to the convocation in Cancuc. When the rebels arrived, he stood, machete in hand, on the steps, exhorting them not to obey the Devil. He and others from the four towns were captured and taken to Cancuc. There they were paraded before the shrine and put to death. A description of their executions by Fray Francisco Ximénez evokes the passions of the traditional Christian martyrs.[28] Some were given fifty lashes at thirty-four stations proceeding toward the rebel chapel, where a final whipping finished them. Others were suspended by their wrists and flogged to death. Some were simply hanged by their necks. Nicolás Pérez was beaten and then burned to death. Among the dead—the number is uncertain—was another fiscal, Fabián Ximénez, from the Tzeltal town of Oxchuc.

As the violence escalated, provincial authorities in Ciudad Real took the first steps to mobilize their own forces. Their efforts were hampered by an administrative vacuum left by the death at the end of May of Martín González de Vergara, the alcalde mayor, whose office remained unfilled. The task of raising a military force to confront the rebels fell to Juan Francisco de Astudillo and Fernando de Monge, who were alcaldes in Ciudad Real and officers in the local militia.[29] At the start, militia forces in the province numbered little more than two hundred men, mostly mestizos from the capital and outlying settlements near Comitán and Ocosingo who were led by a handful of local Spaniards. These troops proved unable to end the rebellion by themselves.

Soon after news of the convocation in Cancuc reached Ciudad Real, a small militia force of some thirty men, led by Pedro Ordóñez, a Spaniard who owned land near Chilón, was called up and ordered to the capital.[30] Chilón, however, had not yet joined the rebellion, and Ordóñez lingered there to support the loyalist alcaldes and protect the Spanish and mestizo families living nearby. Meanwhile, Nicolás Vásquez, the rebel captain general, left Cancuc with twenty Indian soldiers from Bachajón and more from Tila, Petalsingo, and Yajalón to bring Chilón into the fold.[31] The parish priest, Fray Nicolás de Colindres, bravely went out to confront the rebels as they approached, while Ordóñez's militia and their families retreated to the church. Vásquez offered to let the Spaniards go free if they turned over their weapons. Colindres persuaded Ordóñez to accept the proposal, arguing that he had little choice but to accept. However, despite Vásquez's assurances, when the rebels came to the church they attacked the militiamen with machetes and sticks. Twenty-six of the militiamen, including Ordóñez, were cut down, though all of the women and children, along with Colindres, were spared.

Another rebel band, two hundred men from Yajalón and Tila, led by Jacinto Domínguez and Sebastián Gómez (not the cult's bishop but a captain general of the same name from Tumbalá) set out for Ocosingo.[32] Located in a valley with several Dominican-owned estancias and a sugar mill, Ocosingo had the largest number of Spanish and mestizo settlements within the territory of the highland Tzeltal. The rebels arrived on August 14 to find only women and children under the care of their priest, Fray Marcos Lambur. Their menfolk apparently had heard of events in Chilón and expected that their families would be safe while they fled south to join militia forces at Comitán. The rebels were enraged to find them gone, and after a fruitless search of the estancias, Domínguez's band returned to Ocosingo and massacred all the children. They took twenty-six women and Fray Marcos Lambur back to Cancuc. Two former alcaldes from Ocosingo, Jacinto Vásquez and Sebastián de la Cruz, saw to it that the Dominican convent was ransacked and their *trapiche*, or sugar mill, burned. The Spanish viewed the murder of the children at Ocosingo as one of the worst atrocities committed during the entire rebellion.

In Cancuc the ladino women taken at Ocosingo were told that the Virgin ordered that they take Maya husbands, "for in the future, there would be no difference among them."[33] Juana Bárbara Gutiérrez, a thirty-year-old mestiza from Ocosingo, later testified about the experience:

[O]n the fourteenth of August, when Indians from different pueblos entered
[Ocosingo], they beat her and, tying her up, imprisoned her in the town
jail with the other women. They took her to Cancuc and then entered the
new shrine. They made her pray before images of Nuestra Señora del Rosario,

San Juan Evangelista, and San Antonio that were on the altar. They asked for the rosary around her neck and placed it on a silver cross that was on the altar, and when they returned it, it was with a flower taken from a pile at the foot of the cross. Threatening to beat her, they made her listen to masses that the Indians said, sermons that they preached, and processions that they made. One night, at two or three o'clock, the Indian who was called the vicario de San Pedro entered her lodging and told her that that day she would have to marry an Indian from Yajalón. She resisted, because of the reverence she had for the Blessed Sacrament and to spare her husband the hurt. Then they commanded her to undress and tied her to a chair and gave her many lashes. Finding that she lacked the strength to endure the beating and afraid of being killed, she gave her word to marry.[34]

They carried her to the house of another Tzeltal priest, who exchanged her rosary for that of her intended husband, Jacinto de la Cruz of Yajalón. On the following day, in Cancuc's parish church, Juana Bárbara Gutiérrez and fifteen to twenty other Spanish and mestizo women were married in a nuptial mass said by a rebel priest. Most of the grooms were prominent rebels or their sons, including two sons of Antonio López, the fiscal from Tenango who served as a mayordomo, and a captain, Juan Hernández of Yajalón.

Apparently Fray Marcos Lambur was well treated when he was first brought to Cancuc, but after he insisted that he be allowed to say mass, he was shot while standing in the doorway of the church by Nicolás Vásquez and Joseph Díaz of Yajalón with rifles they had pillaged in Chilón.[35] His body was dragged by a rope tied around his neck to a cave outside the town and left to decay, depriving the priest of a proper burial. Vásquez claimed the murder was ordered by Sebastián García, a member of the original inner circle who was told to do so by María de la Candelaria. Agustín López later denied his daughter had been involved.

Around the same time, three more Spanish priests were added to the list of casualties.[36] Fray Manuel de Mariscal, the curate of Yajalón, and Fray Nicolás Colindres, who served Bachajón and Chilón, were ambushed along the road between Sibacá and Guaguitepeque by a band led by Nicolás Vásquez. According to Fray Francisco Ximénez, who was always eager to report the heroic deeds of the Dominican clergy, they had decided to go to Cancuc to minister to the ladinas taken hostage in Ocosingo. The third, Fray Juan Gómez of Guaguitepeque, was killed near Oxchuc. Like the others, he had chosen not to abandon his parish but to stay among the Tzeltal no matter what the risks.

Despite the success of these early raids on ladino settlements, the cancu-queros faced a serious challenge from within their own ranks before the insurrection was a month old. In Yajalón, a rival cult formed when a woman named Magdalena Díaz announced that the true Virgin had appeared to her.[37] The Cancuc visitation, she said, was a fraud. Just what Díaz's inten-tions were is unknown. Perhaps she hoped to wrest control of the rebellion away from the leaders in Cancuc, or perhaps she intended to offer an alterna-tive to war with the Spanish. Francisco Ximénez wrote that she was María de la Candelaria's *tía*, or aunt, and after the rebellion one informant said that she had been the first person that María had consulted after the visita-tion, but nothing is certain.

According to Ximénez, many in Yajalón, Petalsingo, Tila, and Tumbalá accepted Díaz's claim. The defection of these towns would have dealt the cancuqueros a serious blow, for they were among Cancuc's earliest and most militant supporters. Cancuc loyalists moved swiftly to put down their rival. They swept into town at dawn one morning, captured Magdalena Díaz, and took her to Cancuc, where she was promptly hanged. Ximénez reported that a young man from Tila who claimed to be Jesus Christ was also executed in Cancuc around this time, but even less is known about his case.

Throughout the Tzeltal Revolt, leaders in Cancuc demanded absolute loyalty, and they treated fellow Mayas who were reluctant to obey with the same ruthlessness they applied to the Spanish. Some weeks after the incident in Yajalón, rebels led by Nicolás Vásquez descended on the Tzotzil town of Hueytiupán to assure their support and then moved on to Simojovel, another Tzotzil town that had refused to join them.[38] There, they killed still another Spanish priest, Fray Juan Campero. He was shot inside the church and then hacked to death. His body was left at the foot of an orange tree in the plaza. An Indian servant, Bartolomé Sánchez, died defending him. When towns-people continued to resist, several hundred were massacred. The people of Palenque, a small Chol pueblo near Tila, one of the more active rebel towns, feared similar treatment.[39] They evacuated the entire village and took refuge in the Petén.

In the last week of August the first Spanish counteroffensive began. A new alcalde mayor, Pedro Gutiérrez de Mier y Theran, had been appointed by the audiencia and was on his way to the highlands from Tabasco. In the meantime, Fernando de Monge marched toward Huistán with 140 militiamen, hoping to keep a gathering rebel army at bay until reinforcements arrived with the new alcalde mayor.[40] This was to be the first great battle of the war. Huistán was just east of Ciudad Real, the rebel town closest to the capital. The tzeltales had begun to marshal their forces there as early as August 20. They dug a trench across the main approach to the town from Ciudad Real. Its walls were reinforced with wooden poles and woven fiber, and its floor was lined with stones. Later the Spanish estimated that by August 25 Nicolás Vásquez was in command of 4,000 "soldiers of the Virgin"—for the first time, Mayas from all the rebel towns had massed as one army.[41] María de la Candelaria herself was there, preaching, rallying the forces, and promising greater glory for those who fell in battle.

As the siege in Huistán got underway, Gutiérrez arrived in Ciudad Real and soon marched with a second force of 150 Indians from Chiapa de Indios led by their governor, Don Agustín Ximénez, and 200 "caballeros, mulatos, negros, y mestizos" from the capital.[42] They split into two groups. One joined Monge's men to face the main rebel force in the trench. The second moved to intercept rebel reinforcements making their way toward Huistán.

Accounts of the battle are reminiscent of descriptions of the wars of the conquest. A few captains had rifles taken at Chilón, but most of the rebel army was armed simply with wooden pikes and slingshots. They also carried drums, horns, and banners. While they must have presented a noisy, colorful, and intimidating sight, they withstood the Spanish assault for less than a day. Horses, muskets, and crossbows gave Gutiérrez's army a decisive advantage. Only nine of them were killed and nine wounded.[43]

On August 27, Gutiérrez saw that the rebel army was in disarray. He burned all the houses in Huistán and, hoping to pursue his offensive deeper into the highlands, sent to the capital for more ammunition and provisions. However, Ciudad Real had received news of trouble elsewhere. In nearby Zinacantán, three ladinos had been imprisoned by angry townspeople, and rumors were flooding the capital that the zinacantecos planned to enter the city to set fires and kill all the Spaniards.[44] With nearly all able-bodied militiamen and city officials in the field at Huistán, Fray Jorge de Atondo and Fray Joseph Monroy organized those families who remained behind, preparing horses to evacuate the city. Then Monroy went alone to Zinacantán to try to calm the town. He found the townspeople milling around in the plaza, disorganized and without leaders. He preached to them and persuaded them to disperse to their homes and milpas. Spanish fears of a serious uprising in Zinacantán, heightened by their anxiety over events in Cancuc, turned out to be greatly exaggerated. Those tzotziles believed responsible for the unrest were taken without resistance to Ciudad Real. Four were hanged, the only zinacantecos to be punished. The incident, however, stalled the alcalde mayor's offensive against Cancuc. Gutiérrez had quickly withdrawn from Huistán to defend the capital, and rather than march right out again, he stayed in Ciudad Real to regroup.

During the next three weeks, Gutiérrez gathered resources for a more ambitious campaign into the highlands.[45] Sizable contributions arrived from the Dominicans and from several Indian pueblos. The convent in Comitán sent fifty-four African slaves and a hundred of its best horses. From the convent in Ciudad Real came a thousand pesos. The chiapanecos remained with the provincial army, and Tuxtla and San Bartolomé de los Llanos sent horses, corn, and other provisions.

In Guatemala the president of the audiencia, Toribio de Cosío, prepared to lead a force to Chiapas himself and to take over the pacification effort. Nicolás de Segovia was named *gobernador de las armas*. They left Santiago early in September, passing through several Cakchiquel and Quiché towns in the western highlands to gather supplies. Concerned that the rebellion might spill over into the southern province, Cosío also wanted to make a dramatic show of force to discourage any feeling of solidarity with the rebels in Chiapas.

Segovia marched from Ciudad Real around September 19 with 400 Spanish and mestizo soldiers, 54 slaves, 150 chiapanecos, and 3 priests, Fray Juan Arias, Fray Joseph de Parga, and Padre Agustín Rodríguez.[46] Half his forces went directly to Huistán, apparently to assure that it remained pacified. The other half headed for Tenango, the closest Tzeltal pueblo to the city. They found the town abandoned, its people hiding in the hills.

On September 28, Gutiérrez marched toward San Pedro Chenaló with 400 soldiers armed principally with pikes and broadswords, 150 *arcabuceros*, and an indeterminate number of Indian lancers from Chiapa de Indios and from among the mexicanos in Ciudad Real.[47] Two Dominicans, Fray Pedro Marcelino, and Fray Joseph Monroy, joined him. In San Pedro Chenaló, they engaged a rebel army of a thousand whose members were carrying colored banners, drums, and trumpets and who were entrenched some distance from the road at the bottom of a small hill. This time the rebels prevailed, though just why is unclear. They pelted the Spanish with such a steady barrage of stones that the provincial forces were unable to advance. The next day, Gutiérrez decided to go back to the capital.

Segovia departed Huistán, which he found as the alcalde mayor had left it weeks earlier—burned to the ground.[48] On September 22 the troops who had gone to Tenango rejoined him, and together they converged on Oxchuc, where a rebel army they estimated at six thousand was entrenched nearby. On the morning of the twenty-third the battle began. The fighting raged for hours until Segovia ordered a cavalry charge that forced the rebels to retreat into the mountain forest. Several tzeltales were captured, and like Huistán, Oxchuc was set aflame. The next day Juan de Losada, maestro de campo, came from Ciudad Real with three hundred reinforcements to call Segovia back to the capital. President Cosío had arrived and was prepared to make plans for the next stage of the pacification. It would begin in November.

REBEL POLITICS

During the hiatus in the fighting, the rebels confronted a number of political problems created by both the successes and the failures of the several weeks just passed. The cult treasury in Cancuc was now overflowing with wealth, perhaps 4,000 pesos, most of it taken at the expense of the other rebel towns: every celebrant at the August convocation had been told to offer one real in alms to the shrine, and the mayordomos of many (though not all) local cofradías had deposited their cajas with cult leaders.[49] The churches in the rebel towns and the convent in Ocosingo had been sacked, and a rich trove of silver crosses, candlesticks, wooden statuary, musical instruments, and decorated banners were stored in Cancuc at the shrine and in the church.[50]

Many officeholders in other communities were not happy with Cancuc's newfound riches. Led by Juan López, a *principal* in Bachajón, they confronted María de la Candelaria with demands for a more equitable distribution of the loot.[51] On the advice of the captains general and her father, she agreed to allot a share of the booty according to the number of people in each town. In addition, each captain would receive two *platillos* for his services, and henceforth Cancuc would retain only the alms and gifts received at the shrine or the town church.

The compromise was made grudgingly and did not signal any willingness among the cancuqueros to yield a portion of their authority. During the disturbance, the leadership threatened to go to the Ciudad Real to make a separate peace, leaving the others to defend themselves without the aid of the Virgin. For the dissidents, the cost of winning a settlement was the loss of their leader. Juan López was hanged as a traitor.

Another development also served to bolster regional ties while reaffirming the authority of the central hierarchy over local affairs. As noted above, in early August some eight fiscales had been ordained as native priests and had begun to say the Mass in Cancuc. Now, more than six weeks after the pueblos had declared their independence from God and king, the fiscales, maestros de coro, and escribanos from other rebel towns were summoned to the cult center. In an elaborate ceremony on September 23, Sebastián Gómez de la Gloria ordained at least thirteen more of these officials and instructed them to return to their communities, say the Mass, and offer the sacraments. Nicolás Vásquez also preached to them at the close of the ordination ritual.[52] The new native priests should not be considered as new members of the leadership, however. Latecomers to active cooperation with the cult, none were later convicted of participating in or encouraging violent acts against the Spanish. Most claimed they feared that the cancuqueros would kill them if they did not obey the summons.[53] This was a credible enough anxiety in view of the earlier fate of their counterparts from Oxchuc and Tenango, and the Spanish court that later tried them believed their statements. The thirteen did, however, carry out their responsibilities as priests, even dutifully recording baptisms and marriages in the parish registers.

By October the chain of command within the central hierarchy had become more clearly defined. Recent students of the Tzeltal Revolt have followed the lead of Fray Francisco Ximénez and named Sebastián Gómez de la Gloria as the most powerful figure in the hierarchy.[54] But testimony from the rebels themselves presents a different picture, for Gómez does not figure prominently in their accounts. He was not among the original conspiracy identified by Agustín López, and the cult was well established before he even arrived in Cancuc. The only major act promulgated by Gómez himself was the decision to create an indigenous priesthood. Most of the other critical steps taken by the leadership were attributed to others. Gerónimo Saroes wrote the August 10 summons. According to Nicolás Vásquez, the orders to attack Chilón and Ocosingo and to murder Fray Marcos Lambur were given by Sebastián García. The compromise over loot was negotiated by the leading captains and Agustín López. Finally, an episode during the early weeks of the rebellion revealed the limits of his power. Gómez had been joined in Cancuc by his brother, Domingo Gómez. According to Gerónimo Saroes, Domingo "carried himself with much arrogance, wanting all to kiss his feet; he mistreated the Indians."[55] The entire pueblo rose against him, and he was put to death.

If Sebastián Gómez de la Gloria was not the paramount leader, who was? According to Jacinto Domínguez, it was Nicolás Vásquez. Domínguez described him as "el principal" of those in Cancuc.[56] Vásquez himself testified that "I was superior and had command over all the other captains, vicarios, and curas."[57] Still, the evidence shows that Vásquez shared power with others. In matters concerning the cult, Vásquez acted in consultation with Agustín López and the senior mayordomos, particularly the members of the sacristán's original circle of friends. Such was the case in both the execution of Fray Marcos Lambur and the decision to redistribute the plunder. As another sign of the collective nature of decision making, Agustín López and Jacinto Domínguez, like Nicolás Vásquez, were also to be named "king" after all the Spaniards had been killed.[58]

Even if Vásquez did not have sole authority, his rise to power reflects a growth in the political influence of the captains.[59] By creating the captaincy structure, the cancuqueros tied the regional chain of command more closely to the central leadership. By filling the posts with men who held no traditional offices, they gave authority to those whose loyalty they could count on. This arrangement necessarily undermined the authority of incumbent officeholders and other principales in the rebel towns. For example, Francisco Sánchez, a rebel captain and mayordomo at the shrine, was described by a principal from Yajalón as "el principal cabeza" (principal leader) of Yajalón,[60] and an alcalde from Yajalón was reported to have been appointed by local captains to a seat vacated during the revolt. Shrine leaders apparently believed that, except in the most militant towns, local justicias could not be trusted.

Robert Wasserstrom and Victoria Bricker have insisted that the political organization of the revolt was carefully and systematically modeled on Spanish institutions.[61] Wasserstrom writes of "empire-building" on the part of the leadership and interprets the rebels' recasting of Cancuc as "la Ciudad Real Cancuc de Nueva España" and of Hueytiupán as "Guatemala," to be literal attempts to establish a native audiencia. Bricker describes a tidy, functioning confederacy of four levels (town, province, audiencia, empire) that was structured around the equivalent of the colonial offices of the cabildo, captain general, alcalde mayor, audiencia president, and king.

The rebels did borrow the nomenclature of the colonial political and military bureaucracy, but their intentions should not be taken so literally. Adding "Ciudad Real" and "Guatemala" to the place names of the two towns was a rhetorical gambit. In the context of cultural revitalization and rebellion, this rhetorical inversion was a powerful symbolic assertion of the legitimacy of the rebel cult and of Cancuc's political supremacy. But given the relatively small scale of highland Maya societies, the four-month lifespan of the rebellion, and the rebels' preoccupation with the military effort, the Cancuc leadership had neither the time nor the resources to put in place so formal and tightly organized a political apparatus.

In fact, rebel politics remained volatile, and resistance to the Cancuc regime continued right through the later stages of the revolt. In September a new political problem arose when the newly ordained native priests returned to their villages and began to demand the same fees for their services as the Dominicans had received. The townspeople balked at the charges and withheld recognition of their authority, actions that implicitly threatened the legitimacy of the cult and its leaders. Cancuc took the challenge very seriously. Nicolás Vásquez sent an angry message to the pueblos reminding them how important it was to obey their new clerics. "[I]n all the pueblos," he said, "there must be a priest who has power before God by means of the mass, because if there were not, and since it is necessary that there be sinners in the world, the world would end. Because of the masses that these fathers celebrate, God's anger is calmed."[62]

The problem of arrogance and avariciousness among the rebel clergy may also have been behind a purge within the inner circle. Though the exact nature of their transgressions remains uncertain, Gerónimo Saroes and Lucas

Pérez were dismissed from their offices as secretaries to the Virgin in early November.[63] Pérez was ceremonially disgraced with a public whipping, though Saroes apparently remained close to Agustín López and his daughter. The fiscales Mateo Méndez of Sibacá and Nicolás López of Cancuc were chosen to replace them.

These controversies suggest the limits of Cancuc's political success. Other evidence suggests that the scale of the rebellion, measured in terms of the commitment of other Tzeltal and Tzotzil pueblos, also should be reevaluated. Some of the twenty-one towns directly implicated in actions taken by the rebels were much less involved than others. For example, Tenango, Guaguitepeque, and Oxchuc were not well represented at the August convocation and were among the first to reaffirm their obedience to the Crown once Cancuc had fallen.[64] The only individuals held for trial from Tenejapa, San Pedro Chenaló, Mitontic, and Santa Marta were the fiscales, maestros de coro, and escribanos accused of saying the mass, none of whom were charged with actually fighting. Further, none of these four towns was mentioned when witnesses accounted for participants in the major military engagements. In contrast, records show that rebels from Cancuc, Bachajón, Yajalón, Hueytiupán, Tila, Petalsingo, and Tumbalá fought in all the major battles, and all of the retaliatory raids against other pueblos were undertaken by one or more of these seven towns. Ocosingo and Sibacá also are known to have contributed soldiers to the Virgin's defense. Finally, nearly all of those held for trial were natives of one of these nine towns.

This evidence suggests that Spanish estimates of the size of rebel armies are likely to have been exaggerated. An army of 6,000 Mayas was said to have confronted Segovia's force at Huistán. If this figure is accurate, virtually the entire adult male population of the twenty-one rebel towns had been mobilized, which seems very unlikely in light of the reluctance of many Maya to commit themselves fully to the rebellion.

THE CULT

When the Tzeltal first took up arms against the Spanish, they did so to defend the cult of the Virgin, and they would hold the support of their neighbors only as long as the cult could sustain itself. As a cofradía of mayordomos who sponsored masses and public fiestas honoring a saint, the sect's political organization derived from that of local cults of the saints. The cult functioned as a cofradía writ large, a cofradía that gave new meaning to the concept of community. Like local sodalities, its most important public ceremonies—the mass, ritual dancing, music making, fireworks displays—served to reinforce a sense of common identity among its celebrants, heighten their emotional affiliation with Cancuc, and intensify their commitment to shared ideals of the rebellion.

Still, this was not like any other cofradía; the political context in which it operated made for some important differences. Cofradías were normally sanctioned by the local curate, who allowed images of the saints to be housed within town churches and who participated in the observances sponsored by the mayordomos. The Spanish had an opportunity to incorporate the Cancuc cult into this system when the small group of cancuqueros went to Chamula on the eve of el Día de San Juan to seek the bishop's approval. When the bishop denounced the miracle, he promoted the cult's transformation into something fundamentally new.

The cancuqueros recast their sect as the one true church and, turning the tables, rejected the legitimacy of the Church itself. They called the Spaniards Jews, demons, and devils, and mocked Ciudad Real as Jerusalem, but they did not reject Christianity. They held strictly to the ceremonial forms of European Catholicism and replicated the institutional structure of the Church, a deliberate and self-conscious assertion of their own version of orthodoxy. Even in private and secret correspondence, rebels invoked the formulaic blessings and formal salutations of the Church. A letter to Nicolás Vásquez from Antonio de la Cruz, maestro de coro in Ocosingo, begins: "To our vicar general, Don Nicolás Vásquez, a thousand times I prostrate myself at your feet, saluting you in the grace of God the Father, God the Son, and God the Holy Spirit, forever by my Jesus. I, your son, Antonio de la Cruz, remain well, thanks to God, in order to serve you."[65] Native priests wore the vestments left behind by Spanish curates; used all the customary ritual paraphernalia, including chalices, patents, and ciboriums; led their congregations through the recitation of the Rosary, the Paternoster and the Ave María; and even in Cancuc celebrated the Mass inside the town churches, the most visible of all symbols representing the Holy Mother Church.

The rebels' careful conformity to Catholic ritual was fundamentally an act of defiance, a deliberate usurpation of Spanish symbols of authority and

cultural superiority that aggressively declared the legitimacy of their movement. Ultimately, of course, their claim rested on the Virgin's intervention
and miraculous visitation. In making this claim, the cancuqueros invoked a
long tradition in European Catholicism. Other elements of the cult also
reveal its leaders' preoccupation with asserting their legitimacy. The myth
told to Bishop Alvarez de Toledo in Chamula—of having been drawn to the
site of the shrine by bright lights in the sky—is one example of this.
Sebastián Gómez de la Gloria's claim to having had an audience with San
Pedro, which empowered him with the authority to ordain a clergy, is
another, and the ritual ordeal that rebel priests were subjected to during
their ordination is a third.

While the Cancuc cult was an emphatic defense of Catholic practice and
belief as exercised by the Maya themselves, their militant Catholicism by no
means implied a rejection of native custom. The myths, symbols, and rituals
of the cult also drew on older Maya traditions about the supernatural and
spiritual empowerment that added another dimension to their meaning and
social significance.

The Virgin appeared in Cancuc on a hill near the outskirts of town and,
according to Agustín López, near the monte serrado. As discussed in the
previous chapter, Maya everywhere have associated places like hills, caves,
water holes, and trees with the spirit world. When María López walked
away from town that day in early May, she would have been conscious of her
proximity to the supernatural. The Virgin's appearance, however startling
and miraculous, was consistent with a broad set of Maya beliefs about the
omnipresence of spiritual beings in nature. This is not to argue, as Edward
Calnek has, that the Virgin of Cancuc was identified with an indigenous
deity.[66] Today, in Chamula and elsewhere, the Tzotzil associate the Blessed
Mother with the moon. It is entirely conceivable that María, perhaps having
gone to draw water, confronted the Virgin in a place traditionally associated
with the Tzeltal moon goddess. But by the early eighteenth century, though
the Blessed Mother may have had additional associations for the Maya, she
had become a compelling symbol in her own right. Agustín López, María's
father, was very definite: the Virgin appeared as a beautiful *white* woman.

María's experience also was similar to the process that empowered shamans and nagualistas, and was consistent with the Mesoamerican model of
the man-god articulated by Alfredo López-Austin and Serge Gruzinski.[67]

She had a vision: the appearance of the Virgin. She formed a pact: the Virgin promised to live at the shrine with her. And she continued her visions while claiming exceptional powers. During the siege of Cancuc, for example, she promised to bring back to life any of the soldiers who died defending her. One witness, María Hernández, a kinswoman of María López, reported that López actually claimed to be the Virgen de la Candelaria and to believe that she would live forever.[68]

The syncretic character of María's experience is also reflected in the mechanism she used to continue her conversations with the Virgin. The use of an inner sanctum behind the altar inside the shrine, where the Virgin was said actually to speak to her, brings to mind the artifice of "talking saints" in contemporary Zinacantán.[69] These saints are used by shamans to confirm the divinations of illness or the identification of witches. Though unseen, they "speak" through the medium of a box kept in the home of the curer. Talking icons are also well known to students of the Yucatec Maya. At the time of the conquest, on Cozumel, a pottery idol inside a shrine was said to be the conduit through which Ix Chel, the Yucatec moon goddess, replied to her celebrants' prayers.[70] The idol was mounted on a wall that enclosed a hidden room where the priest sat, an oracle for the goddess. The famous "talking cross" used by the rebels at Chan Santa Cruz during the Caste War (1847–1901) offers another example.[71]

Some readers may find the idiom of the cult surprising. Why, as an act of rebellion, would the Maya embrace Christianity and preserve the institutional forms of the Church? These were, after all, elements of a cultural system that constantly espoused its own superiority, and they were part of a colonial administrative apparatus that took an enormous toll on community resources. Why not revive ancient gods and revitalize pagan ceremonies that celebrated the Maya's own ethnic identity and recalled a time before colonial domination? These questions reflect lingering doubts about the authenticity of native conversion, doubts a European cleric of the period, like Núñez de la Vega, may well have shared. However, they make a conceptual distinction between pagan and Christian that the Maya would not have acknowledged. The archaeologist may legitimately explore ethnographic survivals in pursuit of clues about preconquest culture, and the historian may legitimately seek to distinguish religious idioms in an effort to understand the processes of cultural change. But the choice of symbols, myths, and rituals in the Cancuc cult shows the syncretic practices of highland Maya religion to have been an integrated system in which Christian and Maya elements merged so completely that their derivation was of little consequence to the believer. J. Eric S. Thompson called this "unconscious eclecticism."[72] In November 1712 the Maya rebels at Cancuc prepared to defend this eclecticism to the death.

THE REVOLT FAILS

During the October hiatus, most of the rebels returned to their own communities to work their milpas. María López de la Candelaria and the more prominent cult leaders visited other pueblos in the Virgin's dominion to conduct fiestalike celebrations. The new local native priests celebrated occasional masses and even performed baptisms and marriages, dutifully recording the names of the principals in the regular parish ledgers.[73] Meanwhile, the rebel captains general prepared for the next round of fighting by directing the construction of heavily fortified trenches along the main roads leading toward Cancuc.

The hiatus was short-lived. Hostilities resumed in the second week of November, when some four hundred Spanish troops led by President Toribio de Cosío, Nicolás Segovia, and Pedro Gutiérrez marched out of Ciudad Real toward Cancuc.[74] The friars Juan Arias and Joseph de Parga accompanied them as guides and as consultants knowledgeable in the ways of the Maya. At the same time, a second entrada was being prepared in Tabasco by the alcalde mayor there, Juan Francisco Medina Cachón.[75] News of the Tzeltal rebellion had reached the north as early as August 19, and a militia force had been sent at that time to guard the frontier and prohibit trading with the rebel towns. Care had also been taken to prevent any contact between the rebels and British privateers active in the Laguna de Términos. In November, Segovia had written to Cachón requesting military support, but the Tabascans, preoccupied with the British, had not gathered sufficient troops by the time the Guatemalan junta began its entrada.

Cosío's army spent its first night encamped outside Oxchuc, planning to move on to San Martín Teultepeque the next morning.[76] Scouts had spotted a deep trench across the road to San Martín, marked by two rebel banners. The next day the Spaniards met only token resistance there, killing nine Tzeltal soldiers, including one captain, before reaching San Martín. They stayed the night, and in the morning they set fire to the small village before setting out for Cancuc. A quarter league from the town, scouts encountered another fortified trench, and Cosío made camp. Some of the troops were already showing signs of faintheartedness. The day had been unseasonably hot, many were complaining of thirst, and their campsite was without fresh water.[77] Moreover, some three thousand rebels were sighted moving into positions along their left flank. Scattered exchanges occurred that evening, but a violent thunderstorm put an end to all fighting until the next day.

In the morning, Segovia sent Francisco Xavier, a veteran of campaigns in Portugal and North Africa, with a hundred men to try to break through the trench and cut the timbers that supported its walls.[78] They made three attempts, each repelled by rebels who pelted them with stones and rolled dislodged boulders down at them. Xavier's soldiers were finally reinforced by a hundred men led by Miguel Ramírez and two hundred others under Juan de Quintanilla. A mortar round was fired and one of the rebel banners was shredded, but still the tzeltales held back the advance. Segovia himself led an attack on the trench, but when he was wounded in the head, his army became confused and disheartened and withdrew to regroup. They decided to try a different approach along the road from Ocosingo to Cancuc the following day.

Despite having held the trench and forced a Spanish retreat, a segment of the rebel leadership argued for abandoning Cancuc and carrying on the war guerrilla-style from hideouts in the monte serrado.[79] María López de la Candelaria rejected this strategy and promised that the Virgin would restore to life anyone killed defending the town and her shrine. That evening, processions and prayer vigils were held and Maya shamans were enlisted to work their magic. Sometime in the night, however, María and her father, Agustín López, along with Sebastián Gómez de la Gloria, Gerónimo Saroes, and other members of the shrine's inner circle, slipped out of Cancuc and escaped to the hills. They eventually made their way to San Pedro Chenaló. The captains general Nicolás Vásquez, Juan García, and Lázaro Ximénez remained behind to lead the rebel defense.

For the Spanish and their army of *casta* militiamen, the next day's fighting proved to be no easier.[80] They confronted another well-fortified trench, and because the road toward it sloped uphill, they found themselves even more vulnerable to the stones and arrows of its defenders. There was talk of abandoning the effort altogether, but the commanders managed to rally their men. They fought for more than five hours until they finally opened a breach in the trench. With that, the rebels began to scatter in confusion, and the principal captains made their escape into the forest. The Spaniards' siege turned into a rout, and as a portion of their army pursued the Maya fugitives, the main body marched on the town center with Cosío in the lead. They encountered little resistance except for a handful of rebels who tried to keep the soldiers away from the shrine and were killed. Inside the chapel, the Spaniards found some old men, one holding a missal, the other a small statue of Christ. Two others were hiding under the altar. They also found a group of women who had taken refuge inside the town church. That afternoon, on November 21 (el Día de la Presentación en el Templo de María Santísima Señora Nuestra, as Fray Francisco Ximénez reminded his readers), Cancuc was secured. Only one member of the Spanish forces had died in the siege, the *ayudante general*, Juan de Corona, who had taken a pike in the eye during the assault on the trench the previous day.

After giving thanks at the altar in the town church, Cosío inspected the shrine and ordered the arrest of any captains found among the wounded or those who had surrendered. One captain was found, and he was immediately hanged. Others were captured over the course of the next several days and held for trial. The town was filled with rebels hurt in the fighting and many others who were suffering from sickness. Fray Parga heard the confessions of at least seven who were near death. At one point, when two Mayas called to him under cover of the forest, he also went out onto the hillside accompanied by a soldier. The first turned two of his young sons over to Parga for safekeeping. The second gave him his daughter, who had a bullet wound in her hand. They then fled into the monte serrado. Cosío's troops searched the town, hoping to find the indizuela, but they found no sign of her.

On November 22, Cosío offered a pardon to the members of the towns that had participated in the rebellion who would voluntarily come to Cancuc and reaffirm their obedience to the king. "I command you in the King's name," he declared, "that as soon as you see this, come to this pueblo of Cancuc in order to talk and to arrange the matters of your pueblo in such a way that you are treated with kindness and forgiveness for the crimes that were committed following the deceit of those who gathered in this pueblo."[81] Copies of the proclamation were distributed by the friars Arias and Parga, and sent with individual tzeltales and tzotziles to all the pueblos that the Spanish believed had been involved in the rebellion. Three days later, twenty-five families from Tenango arrived. Their fiscal, Antonio López, spoke for his townspeople.[82] People from Guaguitepeque, Tenejapa, Oxchuc, and Huistán followed soon after.

As these towns surrendered, Cosío learned that a pact to continue the rebellion had been concluded among seven of the hardcore rebel communities.[83] He was told that the Virgin had promised to protect the insurgents for at least three more years and that she had assured the rebels that in five years all the Spaniards would be conquered. Thus, while Cancuc had fallen, the rebellion was not yet played out. Nicolás Vásquez, Lázaro Ximénez, Jacinto Domínguez, and other prominent captains were still at large, as, of course, were María López de la Candelaria, Agustín López, and Sebastián Gómez de la Gloria. Rebel scouts roamed the countryside monitoring Spanish troop movements, and hundreds more were hiding in the forested hillsides, prepared to continue the rebellion and waiting for orders from their captains.

On December 4, Nicolás Vásquez brought insurgents from Yajalón, Sibacá, Bachajón, Ocosingo, Tila, Tumbalá, and Petalsingo together in Guaguitepeque to consider an attack on Cancuc.[84] He also enlisted five nagualistas to use their powers against Cosío's troops: Sebastiana González and Dominica Aguilar of Yajalón, two women from Tila, and an old blind man, also from Tila.[85] The women were carried on litters to a nearby riverbank to conduct their ceremonies, but when they had worked for five days with no result, the gathering lost heart, and the rebels returned to refuges near their pueblos. The Guaguitepeque incident proved to be the last time so large an aggregation acted in concert. Thereafter, action was undertaken by much smaller bands of rebel fugitives.

On December 18 a group of insurgents from Yajalón, led by the captains Francisco Sánchez and Juan Hernández, swept into Chilón to retaliate against the townspeople there who had accepted the surrender.[86] An alcalde, Diego Pérez, and the regidor Agustín Ximénez had gone to Cancuc to declare their loyalty to the Crown personally. The yajaloneros killed Dominica López (Ximénez's wife), who had delivered Cosío's offer of amnesty. Then they set out to terrorize the onlookers, killing two, Miguel Solvano and Diego de Avedaño, stabbing another, Juan Méndez, in the shoulder with a lance, and threatening others with torches and machetes. The foray ended when the men from Yajalón were joined by chiloneros from the calpul of Santo Domingo, who remained loyal to the Virgin, and together they sacked the calpul of San Juan, the home of Diego Pérez, burning all the houses. Similar reprisals were made in Tila and Tumbalá against fellow Mayas who carried Cosío's proclamation. In Tila, several of the ladinas who had been forcibly married to Maya men also were killed.[87]

President Cosío spent several weeks in Cancuc, interrogating prisoners and making an inventory of property found inside the shrine and the church. Much of that time was also given over to religious devotion. Each day the mass was celebrated, and Arias and Parga gave sermons and lessons admonishing the tzeltales to denounce the Devil and to obey the Gospel as preached by the Dominicans. On December 24, Cosío left with four hundred men for Chilón, and on Christmas Day he moved into Yajalón. Spanish practice during these reducciones was to occupy the pueblo center, appoint new alcaldes and regidores, inspect the church, and bury the dead. New justicias were appointed from among those who had voluntarily surrendered, and it was not uncommon for an official who had held office during the rebellion to continue to serve if he had initiated his pueblo's capitulation.[88] Along with soldiers from the occupying force and the priests who accompanied each entrada, these alcaldes helped round up fugitives hiding in the monte. Any Mayas who did not surrender voluntarily was held for questioning when they were captured. Those implicated in specific acts of violence were imprisoned to await trial.

Cosío established a field camp in Yajalón and remained there through January. During this time, as president of the audiencia and the senior judicial officer for the province, he held the first of a series of trials. Thirty-two rebels were brought before the court at this time. Seven were accused of crimes committed since the fall of Cancuc: five for participating in the foray into Chilón when Dominica Gómez and the two others were killed, and two for killing two ladinas and their four children in a milpa near Tila. Of the twenty-five others, ten were accused of serving as captains, thirteen of accompanying the captains, one of being a witch, and one of carrying a firearm.[89]

The trials themselves were formal, deliberate proceedings. Each case opened with a statement of the charges. This was followed by a declaration taken from the accused at the time of their capture and then by additional testimony from witnesses called to provide accounts of what had taken place. This testimony came in response to specific questions asked by the court. Though not recorded verbatim, the witnesses' responses were summarized by the court secretary with care and attention to detail. While designed primarily to determine the culpability of each individual, Cosío's inquiry was also aimed at obtaining a complete account of the key events of the rebellion and some explanation of the rebels' motives.

In each case, just before a verdict was determined and the sentence announced there was a formal "confession" by the defendant. Like all of the testimony, these confessions were elicited in response to a series of questions asked by the court. They gave defendants an opportunity to deny their guilt one last time or to revise their earlier declaration in light of evidence introduced during the trial and to show some remorse. Before sentencing, a court-appointed "defender" spoke in behalf of the defendant. In Yajalón, the *defensor* was a Spanish lawyer named Tomás de Mora. Typically his statements were pro forma requests for leniency, not systematic refutations of the charges and the evidence.

The sentences of the thirty-two rebels were carried out in Yajalón on January 26, 1713. Nine who were condemned to death were decapitated, drawn, and quartered. Of these, five had served as captains, one had carried a firearm, two had murdered the ladina women, and one, Sebastiana González, was condemned as a witch. Eight others were given two hundred lashes and were exiled in perpetuity to Jiquipilas, a town in western Chiapas. Of these, three were captains who had surrendered voluntarily and five were simple soldiers who had marched with them. The five accused of going to Chilón on December 7 also were given two hundred lashes and were prohibited from serving as justicias for five years. Four more were given a hundred lashes and forbidden to hold office for ten years. Two received fifty lashes. The three caught hiding in the monte serrado were found innocent of any crimes. They were released without any corporal punishment. Two of them were prohibited from serving as officeholders for four years, and the other was told to go to Esquintenango because the town needed labor. The sentence of one of the accused, Sebastián Martín, is inexplicably missing from the record.

While Cosío remained in Yajalón, he sent part of his army toward Tila and Petalsingo and a second detachment to Tumbalá to consolidate the Spanish victory. Meanwhile, the alcalde mayor of Tabasco, with 370 men, including a hundred Indians from that province, had begun his own entrada soon after the siege of Cancuc.[90] On November 25 he occupied Moyos and from there completed the pacification of the Tzotzil towns of Hueytiupán, Santa Catarina, San Pedro Chenaló, and San Andrés. He also saw to it that tzotziles from Simojovel, who had steadfastly refused to join the rebellion and who had spent the last several months hiding from the cancuqueros, were peacefully resettled in their village. Rebel resistance was strongest near Hueytiupán, where Cachón encountered a band led by Lázaro Ximénez, one of the highest-ranking captains. Ximénez escaped, but Cachón imprisoned forty-eight insurgents and shipped them to Tabasco. After passing through Petalsingo on January 7 and meeting with some of Cosío's men, the Tabascans went on to Yajalón to confer with Cosío himself. For reasons that are unclear, Cachón had disobeyed orders when he took his army into the Tzotzil towns. His instructions had been to occupy Tila, Tumbalá, and Petalsingo. Now, though Cachón hoped to command the pacification of Bachajón, Ocosingo, and Sibacá, Cosío sent him back to the three northern towns. Audiencia troops under the command of the maestro de campo, Pedro de Zabeleta, entered Bachajón, Ocosingo, and Sibacá during the last weeks of January.[91]

In the first week of February, Fray Joseph Monroy, with a hundred militiamen under the command of sargento mayor Juan Martínez de la Vega, moved out into the districts known as las Coronas and las Chinampas, pursuing rumors that both María López de la Candelaria and Sebastián Gómez de la Gloria were hiding somewhere near San Pedro Chenaló.[92] He received a peaceful reception in San Miguel Mitontic, Santa María Magdalena, Santiago Huistán, and Santa Marta, and made plans to go on to San Andrés in the first week of February to celebrate the feast day of the town's patron saint. He was warned, however, that Nicolás Vásquez had been agitating in the village and intended to set a trap and kill the friar while he was saying mass inside the town church. This news gave him pause, and troops were sent to survey the road to San Andrés. They discovered a trench outside the village but no rebels, and Monroy decided it was safe to go in. San Andrés was secured and the trench dismantled, and Monroy celebrated the fiesta as planned.

From San Andrés, Monroy returned to his parish seat at Chamula. Some days later he walked alone to Santa Catalina and San Pablo, where he persuaded the local justicias that they should go to Ciudad Real to make a formal acceptance of Cosío's peace. In San Pablo he came upon one of the ladinas from Ocosingo, who warned him that Nicolás Vásquez also had been there, denouncing the Spaniards as Jews and dismissing the offer of amnesty as trickery. She also told him that a woman rebel captain, who had served as a mayordoma at the shrine, was active near San Pedro Chenaló, leading a militant band from Hueytiupá. Soon afterward, Monroy led a force of ninety-six chamulas and a sizable number of Spanish militiamen toward San Pedro Chenaló, which had already been reduced to ashes earlier in the war. There they easily subdued a small rebel force and captured the notorious capitana, along with some others, who were taken to the jail in Ciudad Real. Unfortunately, this is the last record of a female captain; her name does not appear among those tried in Ciudad Real by Toribio Cosío. Monroy and his Chamulan allies stayed in San Pedro Chenaló for twelve days to make a thorough search of the countryside for the elusive indizuela and her bishop, but with no luck.

During the pacification, the Spanish had anticipated more fighting, and each entrada included 100 to 300 lancers, arcabuceros, and lightly armed foot soldiers, but the Cancuc loyalists proved unwilling to engage them. Yajalón, Petalsingo, Bachajón, and Ocosingo were all empty when the Spanish arrived, save for a few tzeltales who were too ill or too old to flee.[93] In Tila, a large rebel force was sighted by scouts, but they had deserted the pueblo as the Spanish approached. Once a town was occupied, the local inhabitants usually began to filter back to accept the amnesty within a few days. Rebels taken in the monte serrado rarely resisted. Thus, by the second week of February the pacification was complete. Among the last rebels taken were Nicolás Vásquez, Jacinto Domínguez, and Marcos Méndez, one of the Virgin's secretaries.[94] Sometime around February 17 they were brought to Pedro de Zabeleta in Sibacá by alcaldes from the town who were cooperating with the pacification. They apparently surrendered without a fight, the last of their ragged forces having abandoned the cause and dispersed to isolated milpas near their home villages.

During February, March, and April, more trials were held. In Ciudad Real, Cosío carried out hearings against 122 rebels. Most had been captured at Cancuc, but others had been rounded up near Yajalón, Bachajón, Tila, and other towns during the entradas led by Cachón and Zabeleta. Of these, fifty-five were condemned to death, nearly all of them captains (including

Nicolás Vásquez and Jacinto Domínguez), fiscales close to the inner circle (Gerónimo Saroes, Lucas Pérez, and Agustín García), or rebels directly implicated in the deaths of the priests Colindres, Mariscal, and Gómez, or the murders of ladina women or loyal Indians. Some nineteen others were given two hundred strokes and exiled in perpetuity to Jiquipilas, or Aquespala. Fifteen received a hundred lashes and exile for five to ten years. Ten got a hundred lashes and were assigned to work on the Dominican estancias near Ocosingo or in the nunnery in Ciudad Real. One man's only penalty was to be denied office for four years. The other twenty-two accused were either judged innocent and freed without penalty or, though held for trial, released without their cases coming before the court. Among the latter were three men from towns outside the province, petty traders who had been en route to the capital and who had been unwillingly pressed into service by the rebels at Cancuc. They were sent back to their homes.[95]

Under ecclesiastical law, Bishop Alvarez de Toledo prosecuted eighteen fiscales who were accused only of having served as priests and who were not liable for secular crimes in Cosío's jurisdiction.[96] Upon conviction they received no corporal punishment but were exiled for ten, eight, six, or four years, according to the number of times they admitted to celebrating the Mass.

A third series of trials was held in Sibacá, Ocosingo, and Bachajón by Pedro de Zabeleta, to whom Cosío delegated judicial authority. He conducted hearings against fifty rebels from the three towns. In contrast to the pattern found in other towns, a significant number of incumbent and former justicias were among the accused, a reflection of the militancy of these particular villages. Zabeleta condemned twenty-one to be hanged for participating in the massacre in Ocosingo, most of whom were either captains or incumbent officeholders. Twenty-nine others were given a lashing, avoiding the death penalty because they were not implicated in events during which Spaniards had been killed. Sentences were carried out by Zabeleta in the native towns of those convicted.[97]

Cosío carried out his executions during the last week of March and the first week of April. Those condemned were taken to their native towns and drawn and quartered. Their limbs and heads were then prominently displayed in nearby parajes. At least nine were taken to different pueblos in the partido of Huehuetenango in Guatemala as Cosío's army made its way back to Santiago and were executed there. Clearly the audiencia wished to impress on the Maya throughout the highlands that any challenge to its authority would be punished with great severity.

After the executions, officials began an extensive review of the rebellion to inform the Crown of what had happened and to begin to examine its causes. As part of this process, Cosío issued seven ordinances intended to circumvent, for the short term, the likelihood of renewed violence.[98] He ordered that no native justicias were to allow talk of new miracles, nor were they to permit purchases of gunpowder in any quantity. Spaniards in Ciudad Real were forbidden to demand food and personal service of Indian pueblos as they traveled in the countryside. Landowners were ordered to inform the alcalde mayor whenever native workers were hired and to assure that the labor required was moderate and did not disrupt the pueblo's capacity to make tribute payments on time. Cattle ranchers who sold beef to Indians for the fiestas were told to charge fair prices. Finally, limits were placed on the labor drafts imposed on San Felipe, Chamula, and Zinacantán.

Before Cosío left the province, he also supervised the forced resettlement of the entire town of Cancuc. Townspeople were moved to a less remote site along a riverbank below the steep hill where the old village had been. He named the new town Nuestra Señora de la Presentación y Santo Toribio, commemorating the holy day on which Cancuc had been retaken and honoring his own namesake as well.

Cosío returned to Guatemala in early April, leaving fifty soldiers behind to enforce the peace. They continued to scout the countryside for any remnant rebel bands. In June, troops led by Juan de Quintanilla went to a small settlement near Ocosingo known as Coila.[99] Five rebel captains led by Gerónimo de Morales and Jacinto Gómez were rumored to have established a new shrine center there and were said to be calling the Maya back to defend the Virgin. When news of Quintanilla's approach reached them, they fled. The Virgin, the Spaniards were told, went back to Heaven.

Three years later, early in 1716, María's father and three other members of her family were brought to the Spanish authorities in Ciudad Real by the native justicias in Yajalón.[100] They were the last rebels to be tried and executed. During their trials, authorities learned that the indizuela had fled first to San Pedro Chenaló, accompanied by her father, husband, brother, and sister-in-law, as well as some twenty Indians from Oxchuc. They spent four weeks there, meeting with Sebastián Gómez de la Gloria and Nicolás Vásquez and living at a milpa where Gómez had built a shrine.[101] From San Pedro Chenaló, María's entourage struck out by themselves, passing near San Pablo and Hueytiupán and finally settling in a paraje known as Las Palmas outside of Yajalón. They would spend the next three years here, living in isolation and barely growing enough to feed themselves. Their only contacts were with three yajaloneros who occasionally brought them food and who kept their presence a secret. María spent each day in a small shrine built by her father, carrying on with her devotion to the Virgin. She died of complications during her first pregnancy. Fifteen days after her death, when a Maya from another paraje discovered who they were, her family was arrested by twenty armed men sent by the justicias in the town, who turned them over to the Spanish. Sebastián Gómez de la Gloria was luckier. He was never found.

THE AFTERMATH

Fray Francisco Ximénez wrote that the rebellion left the province of the Tzeltales "totally destroyed": "Many pueblos were burned and many houses; all the Indians robbed of mules, horses, axes, machetes, hoes, and much silver because the soldiers had looted from them like enemies. Many, many Indians were dead, some at the hands of other Indians, others at the hands of Spaniards in the skirmishes they fought with them, others executed, and there were many, for many were those who had excelled at their crimes."[102] The restoration of peace did not end the hardship. Between 1713 and 1716 the highlands were hit with the twin terrors of locusts and epidemic disease. Ximénez estimated that many pueblos lost half their population.[103] Chilón, he reported, was almost wiped out. Survivors fled their villages altogether to live and search for food in the monte serrado. The audiencia measured the costs of this period in another way. Twenty-five pueblos were unable to pay tribute for five years, a revenue loss that, when added to the expense of the pacification campaign, totaled 60,000 pesos.[104]

Communities in the highlands would not really begin to recover until the very end of the eighteenth century, and several factors combined to insure that conditions remained hard. Overall, the Indian population in Chiapas increased from about 50,000 inhabitants in 1725 to 75,000 in 1821.[105] But this slow growth was frequently interrupted by the periodic return of plagues and locusts.[106] A number of communities suffered extinction in this period and thus dropped off the tribute rolls altogether. Some towns still had smaller populations in 1778 than they had had in 1716. A particularly devastating plague struck in the early 1730s.[107] Entire parcialidades were wiped out in Tenango, Bachajón, and San Andrés, and a new padrón was ordered for Cancuc and Hueytiupán because of the losses. Infants and young children were said to be especially vulnerable to the virus. At this time the justicias in Cancuc requested that they be allowed to return to the site of their old pueblo.[108] Since Cosío had moved them sixteen years earlier, more than a thousand people had died, they said, because the new location had "bad air" and "bad land." By 1748 the pueblo had been resettled on higher ground, though not on its original site.[109]

Another factor was the renewal of the alcalde mayor's commercial activities after the rebellion and the persistence of the related practice of over-collecting tribute—this despite the fact that the president of the audiencia, the bishop, and the Dominican clergy all acknowledged that the repartimientos and tax frauds had contributed greatly to the outbreak of revolt. In July 1718, still another royal directive ordered that tribute be collected at fair prices, the Crown having recognized that overcollection had become routine.[110] Three years later the audiencia, chastened by events in the highlands and eager to avoid a new conflict, undertook another extensive judicial inquiry to document past wrongdoing by alcaldes mayores in Chiapas.[111] Their effort at reform had little effect. As Robert Wasserstrom has shown, the power of the alcalde mayor and the extent of his commercial enterprises were probably greater after 1712 than before.[112] In 1716 the bishop reported that the alcalde mayor continued to exercise a monopoly on the public auction of corn, beans, and chiles, and had recently expanded his estanco to include the city's marketing of beef. Then in 1732 a new alcalde mayor, Gabriel de Laguna, suppressed the cabildo of Ciudad Real by refusing to confirm the election of its officers.[113] He had silenced a major critic.

Under these conditions, ethnic tensions remained polarized, and provincial authorities were constantly alert for any sign of a new rebellion. In October 1722, for example, a curate in the Zoque community of Ocozocoautla was run out of town after several months of tension that began when he attempted to cut down a sacred ceiba tree whose roots were threatening the parish house.[114] There the matter ended. However, five years later, in June 1727, the fifteenth anniversary of the Virgin's appearance in Cancuc, a more serious incident took place. Andrés de Arze, the *teniente general* and *justicia mayor* of Tabasco, called out the militia when news reached him that Indians in at least three villages on the frontier had taken up arms, declaring their intention to kill all the Spaniards.[115] After making a show of force along the border with Chiapas, Arze established a camp at Jalapa and tried to find out what had been going on. His proceedings uncovered not one but two apparent conspiracies. The first was centered in the Zoque towns of Tecomaxiaca, Ixtapangajoya, and Solosuchiapa. Witnesses reported that Nicolás Castro, a *principal* from Tecomaxiaca, had met with Raymundo Palma, the Indian governor of the town, Pedro González, the fiscal, and other members of the local elite to raise an insurrection, hoping to carry the fight into Tehuantepec and Oaxaca, or "as far as it might reach."[116] Among their recruits was Diego Hernández, a Tzeltal from Chilón whose son Sebastián had married a Zoque woman from nearby Teapa. Diego Hernández was linked to a second revolt said to be brewing in Bachajón. Arze heard testimony from several witnesses who were workers on the estancia of Gaspar Sarmiento de Acosta. A foreman there, Antonio Vásquez, was from Cancuc. They reported that Vásquez, along with Marcos Velásquez from Bachajón, was fomenting rebellion. The Virgin of Cancuc had returned, they said. She had appeared in Bachajón, fulfilling a prophecy made fifteen years earlier. Vásquez and Velásquez were brought before Arze and claimed to have no knowledge of any of the accusations. They were tortured, and finally Vásquez admitted to having met with Velásquez after receiving a letter from Francisco Saroes, the fiscal in Bachajón. Saroes, who must certainly have been a kinsman of Gerónimo Saroes, had told Vásquez to come to Bachajón to see the Virgin. But Vásquez had not wanted to go, he told Arze, and neither had Marcos Velásquez. In the end, despite repeated torture, both denied any involvement in a rebellion.

Nonetheless, Arze was alarmed at the prospect of a coalition between rebellious Zoque principales and a revitalized Tzeltal conspiracy. He immediately wrote to the alcalde mayor of Chiapas, Martín Joseph de Bustamente, to report his findings and urge him to act quickly. Bustamente sent troops to Bachajón and wrote to local curates in Zoque and Tzeltal towns throughout the highlands, asking them to be especially alert for signs of rebellion and to send back news on conditions in their parishes. But no one reported anything unusual, including the curate in Cancuc, and Bustamente finally concluded that Arze had overreacted. His last report on the matter to the audiencia, as well as an addendum added by Luis Bucaro, the *abogado fiscal* to the court, were both highly critical of Arce's reliance on information obtained through torture. The incident highlights the fear and loathing with which Spaniards in these frontier provinces viewed the native majority. Moved by a deep race hatred and intense feelings of vulnerability because of their small numbers, they were easily aroused and were ready to react to the slightest rumor of trouble. Their combativeness assured that the potential for ethnic violence in Chiapas would remain high, and, indeed, it has never abated.

7

CONCLUSION

In "Landed Society in New Spain: A View from the South," William Taylor succinctly articulated the conventional wisdom about the social and political organization of native societies under Spanish rule:

> [T]he strength of the local community and what seems to have been a state of chronic warfare in the postclassic period of Indian prehistory promoted an exclusivist and suspicious posture toward the outside and a coherent and cohesive attitude within. Such a localized, enemy-oriented political and social system was both a weakness and a strength for the community. On the negative side, it prevented a united front against Spanish penetration, promoted discord among communities, and enabled the Spaniards to "divide and rule"; but the same values and cohesiveness also served well in resisting outside encroachments and in maintaining the lands that supported local society.[1]

The history of the highland Maya in seventeenth and early eighteenth century Chiapas sustains this view in its essentials but also suggests some cautions and modifications. The Tzeltal Revolt of 1712, as well as the existence of earlier cults in Zinacantán and Santa Marta, reveals that the Maya were capable of articulating and acting upon a broad ethnic consciousness. They recognized a common culture and a common historical experience even though their first loyalty was to their own community. News traveled fast among the villages, and there seems to have been considerable coming and going between them. Marriages across pueblo boundaries were not uncommon, nor were friendships between members of different communities. All of this conjures up images of a human landscape in which the range of social resources extended well beyond the bounds of the corporate town. Other evidence, however—like the election controversies in Guaguitepeque and

Cancuc in the 1680s and 1690s, and especially the raid on Chilón during the closing days of the rebellion—gives us a picture of pueblos riven by violent factional disputes, divided by loyalties to different calpules and rival groups of elites. This is hardly a picture of community solidarity.

Social dynamics among the Maya clearly were shaped by centrifugal as well as centripetal forces. Their political actions and political consciousness reflected the complex ways these forces interacted with one another. The ecology of milpa agriculture, the proximity of frontier zones, participation in city markets, informal trading between villages, and work on Spanish haciendas all tended to push Maya men and women into social relationships outside their communities. Simultaneously, origin myths, rules of marriage, the legal incorporation of the pueblo, parish organization, and tribute obligations pulled them together.

In the early eighteenth century, these factors combined to create at least three distinctive zones of the highland Maya. One, extending west of Ciudad Real along the road toward Chiapa de Indios, encompassed the tzotziles of Chamula, Zinacantán, and Ixtapa. Their political consciousness was shaped by their proximity to the capital, their participation in commerce along the Camino Real, and local economic specialization (craft production in Chamula and Zinacantán, and salt harvesting in Ixtapa). A second zone, reaching into the valley southeast of Ciudad Real toward Comitán, included the tzeltales of Amatenango, Aquacatenango, Teopisca, and Pinola. Their consciousness, too, was shaped by proximity to the commercial artery of the royal highway and to local Spanish and mestizo settlers, and by the relative fertility of their land, which made them the province's main source of raw cotton. The third zone was, of course, the eastern zone of the highlands, extending toward the frontiers of Tabasco and the Petén, the poorest and most isolated region in the province. Among all the native peoples of Chiapas, the tzeltales, tzotziles, and choles who lived in this third zone were least accustomed to the constant presence of Spaniards and least able to absorb the new financial demands placed on them at the end of the seventeenth century. The solidarity they displayed in 1712 built on that common experience.

María López's vision of the Virgin Mary, like the miracles and apparitions in Zinacantán, Santa Marta, and San Pedro Chenaló that preceded it, was an authentic manifestation of popular religious belief and also a revealing manifestation of the Maya's cultural disequilibrium. The Maya made few distinctions between the sacred and the profane. As their material conditions worsened at the end of the seventeenth century, and as they confronted an epidemic and the threat of famine in the years just prior to the rebellion, they recognized the developing crisis as spiritual in nature. They understood that the balance of supernatural forces had been upset. This belief was rooted in their indigenous worldview and was supported as well by Dominican preaching on sin and Christian obligation. The Virgin's appearance, first in Santa Marta and then in Cancuc, held the promise of returning the natural balance to equilibrium.

Initially, neither of these cults threatened armed rebellion. In both cases, tentative overtures were made to local church authorities in hopes that the shrine centers would be tolerated. A more artful response on the part of the provincial bishop might have enabled the Spanish to turn the cults to their own purposes. Instead, Bishop Toledo, with the cooperation of the Dominicans, rejected out of hand the authenticity of the miracles and condescendingly dismissed the sincerity of their adherents. As a result, the confrontation between popular faith and official orthodoxy grew more polarized, and the potential for violence escalated. Nevertheless, the Tzeltal Revolt was not a spontaneous popular uprising. Had the center held, had Maya alcaldes, fiscales, and other principales in the villages held true to their complicity with colonial authorities, a full-scale uprising likely would have been averted. But the center did not hold.

The rebellion was initiated by a small group of local Maya elites who articulated their own discontent in terms that revealed their self-interest. Mindful of the customary rights and privileges owed them as principales and disillusioned with the political and economic sacrifices forced upon them by Spanish alcaldes mayores and provincial bishops, they seized the opportunity presented to them by popular religious enthusiasm to organize a movement designed to preserve their legitimacy and reaffirm the social hierarchy. Ironically, in the end the cancuqueros' vision of a "new world" proved to be as oppressive to local interests as was Spanish colonialism. Ethnic solidarity among the Maya broke down as the rebel leaders enforced their supremacy within the new political order. When that happened, loyalist principales were ready to step forward to reassert local authority, reclaim their legitimacy, and renegotiate their relationship with the Spanish.

If the Tzeltal Revolt is understood as a defense of the Maya moral economy, it becomes clear why this revolt against colonial material exploitation took the form of a cultural revitalization movement. As outlined in the introduction, the concept of moral economy, by focusing on the construction of social norms, the development of a principle of reciprocity, and the symbolic expression of community values, offers important insights for linking the rebellion to Maya culture history. This approach is rooted in the work of Eric Wolf. Unlike William Taylor, I have emphasized conflict rather than cohesion in my reconstruction of Maya social and political relations. On a theoretical plane, this emphasis is consistent with recent critiques of earlier formulations of the moral economy of European peasants and speaks to broader issues concerning the conceptualization of culture among Mesoamerican ethnohistorians.

In "Crowds, Community, and Ritual in the Work of E. P. Thompson and Natalie Davis," Suzanne Desan argued that

> cultural systems may indeed reinforce the community, sustain "order," and endow various actions with legitimacy and meaning. But they can also become vehicles for creating power and sowing discord. Various members of the community have different attitudes toward symbolic systems and deliberately appropriate or manipulate symbols as part of a struggle for control. We must strive to construct as nuanced an analysis of dynamics within the community as the sources will permit. . . . We need now to ask how violence contributes not only to the definition of community and meaning, but also to the transformation of symbolic systems and the realignment of power, status, and roles within the community.[2]

The Tzeltal Revolt offers a case study of these dynamics at work. What began as a broad movement for cultural revitalization was transformed by its leaders into a campaign to realign the arrangements of power and hierarchy among the Maya themselves as well as between the Maya and the Spanish. For students of native peoples in colonial Mexico and Guatemala, Desan's critique is an ambitious charge to examine the dynamic between culture and society in all its complexities—to weigh the impact of "big" structures with an appreciation of human agency, to confront cultural disjunctions as well as cultural uniformities, and to rethink our idea of community. She echoes the prescription of Steve Stern to "treat peasant consciousness as problematical rather than predictable." Toward this end, Mesoamericanists will have to look beyond two familiar but constraining paradigms: acculturation and religious syncretism. The first, the child of modernization theory, promotes a unilineal and relatively static approach to culture change that draws attention away from the diverse and unexpected consequences of contact between Native Americans and Europeans. The second has focused attention on abstract structural and functional similarities between native religion and Christianity and has tended to divorce the analysis of culture from political, social, and economic contexts. Just as ethnographers have moved away from typologies and other schemes that reify culture as an inventory of particular traits, ethnohistorians need to study culture in terms of process and agency. Ultimately, this will lead us to new questions about how ethnic identities were reconstructed after the conquest and to a reevaluation of the very concept of "Indian-ness."

Studies of colonial rebellions and native revitalization movements ought to be a very vital part of this emerging historiography. In recent years, Frank Salomon, Jan Szeminski, and Alberto Flores Galindo for the Andes, and Serge Gruzinski, Grant Jones, and Eric Van Young for New Spain, have drawn our attention back to the religious dimension of native resistance.[3] They have identified new topics for study and have offered new conceptual approaches to the culture history of native peoples. Yet the field is still fresh and wide open. Among Mayanists, few have ventured into the Inquisition records housed in the Archivo de la Nación in Mexico City or searched for the diocesan *provisoratos* that Gruzinski identified and used so provocatively. We still lack comprehensive studies of two major Maya messianic movements, the Jacinto Canek rebellion in Yucatán in 1761 and the Atanasio Tzul uprising in Totonicapán, Guatemala, in 1820. The colonial ethnohistory of the Maya also ought to be enormously enriched by the provocative new work on Classic Maya history and political culture being done by archaeologists and art historians and by anthropologists' recent ethnographic studies on ethnic identity and contemporary strategies of resistance.[4] A strong tradition of interdisciplinary scholarship and the continued vitality of disciplines collateral to history promise to lead us in interesting new directions.

APPENDIX A

POPULATION OF FULL TRIBUTARIES, 1595–1778

	1595	1611	1684	1735	1778
PRIORATO DE CHIAPA					
Acalán	322	353			54
Chiapa	1,296	488			146
Chiapilla	52	88			24
Ostuta		131			
Pochuta	129	53			
Pueblo Nuevo		116			93
Suchiapa	176	164			100
Tuxtla	386	673			685
BARRIOS DE CIUDAD REAL					
Cuxtitali	28	15	25		36
Mexicanos	124	77	44		40
San Antonio					
San Diego					

SOURCES: AGI: AG, 161: Memoria de los pueblos y beneficios que hay de sus santo obispado de Chiapas, 1595; AGI: Mexico, 3102, 1611; AGCA: A3.2 15, 207 825: Padrón de los tributarios que estaban bajo la administración de religiosos de la provincia de San Vicente de Chiapa y Guatemala, 1684; AGI: AG, 375: Informe del alcalde mayor de la provincia de Chiapa y Guatemala haciendo remisión de las diligencias executadas en orden a siete curatos de los zendales, February 7, 1735; Trens, *Historia de Chiapas*, 182–187.

	1595	1611	1684	1735	1778
San Felipe					
Serillo	210	88	66		48
PRIORATO DE CIUDAD REAL					
Chamula	270	237	245		563
Ixtapa	286	292			82
San Gabriel		15			43
Soyaló		12			43
Zinacantán	422	211	294		434
CORONILLA Y GUARDIANÍA DE HUEYTIUPÁN					
Hueytiupán	308				118
Mitontic	21	30			120
San Andrés	140	45	37		260
San Bartolomé de los Platanos	25				52
San Pablo	52	46	27		134
San Pedro Chenaló	41	25	28		90
Santa Catarina	83	22	20		38
Santa María Magdalena	89	79	66		128
Santa Marta	104	80	61		70
Santiago	98	37	30		52
Simojovel	90	246			130
PROVINCIA DE LOS LLANOS					
Amatenango	233	123	167		185
Aquacatenango	194	142	189		87
Aquespala	119	140			
Chalchitán	150	26			
Chicomuselo	263	110			168
Coapa	322	60			
Comalapa	168	66			
Comitán		571	545		950

	1595	1611	1684	1735	1778
Coneta	145	188			10
Copanaguastla	290				
Esquintenango	350	309			29
Guitatán	144	57			
Istapilla	60	63			
Pinola	140	150			167
San Bartolomé	292	400			1,303
Socoltenango	350	313			118
Soyatitán	200	244			103
Teopisca	366	278	460		125
Totolapa	189	205			126
Yayaguita	294	156			
Zapaluta		195			316
PROVINCIA DE LOS ZENDALES					
Bachajón	476	427	424	110	176
Cancuc	151	240	306	71	432
Chilón	335	303	514		38
Guaguitepeque	158	324	375	96	87
Ocosingo	481	294	507		317
Oxchuc	168	185	374	618	530
Palenque	181	68		50	30
San Miguel Huistán	204	173	156		210
Sibacá	270	224	348		
Sitalá	164	229	377		102
Tenango	186	304	310	23	63
Tenejapa	117	140	171	119	88
Tila	266	268			452
Tumbalá	117	280			423
Yajalón	170	366	516	144	210

	1595	1611	1684	1735	1778
PROVINCIA DE LOS ZOQUES					
Amatán	90	35			
Chapultenango	299	285			69
Chicuacentepeque	107	108			33
Coapilla	80	44			36
Coapiltán	66	54			
Comeapa	56	57			
Comistahuacán	57	50			72
Copainalá	390	393			276
Ishuatán	72	94			132
Istapangajoya	66	41			50
Micapa		99			81
Ocotepeque	149	206			62
Ostuacán	99	85			100
Osumacinta	103	113			28
Pantepeque	151	117			80
Quechula	214	300			322
Sayula	198	68			84
Silosuchiapa	39	22			18
Sunuapa	63				41
Tapalapa	209	230			97
Tapilula	120	112			37
Tecpatlán	617	682			450
Xitoltepeque	220	75			42

APPENDIX B

MASSES, FIESTAS, AND CELEBRATIONS FOR WHICH A PRIEST WAS PAID TO ATTEND, 1690

BACHAJÓN
  monthly masses
  21 cofradía-sponsored fiestas
  titular saint's day
  5 alférez-sponsored fiestas

CANCUC
  monthly mass
  25 cofradía-sponsored fiestas
  titular saint's day
  la Semana Santa
  8 alférez-sponsored fiestas

CHILÓN
  monthly mass
  30 cofradía-sponsored fiestas
  titular saint's day
  12 alférez-sponsored fiestas

GUAGUITEPEQUE
  monthly masses
  8 cofradía-sponsored fiestas
  6 alférez-sponsored fiestas

HUISTÁN
  monthly masses (document illegible)
  17 cofradía-sponsored fiestas
  titular saint's day
  el Día de San Juan Apostol
  5 alférez-sponsored fiestas

MOYOS
  no monthly mass
  15 cofradía-sponsored fiestas
  la Semana Santa
  titular saint's day
  5 alférez-sponsored fiestas

OCOSINGO
  monthly masses (document illegible)
  17 cofradía-sponsored fiestas
  titular saint's day
  9 alférez-sponsored fiestas
  9 misas de Aguinaldos

OCOTITÁN
  monthly masses (document illegible)

SOURCE: AGI: AG, 215: Autos de la visita general, 1690.

19 cofradía-sponsored fiestas
el Día de Todos Santos
titular saint's day
5 alférez-sponsored fiestas
9 misas de Aguinaldos

OXCHUC

monthly masses
119 cofradía-sponsored fiestas
titular saint's day
la Semana Santa
6 alférez-sponsored fiestas

PALENQUE (no cofradías)

no monthly mass
el Día de Nuestra Virgen de la
    Concepción
el Día de Corpus Cristi
el Día de Santa Cruz
el Día de San Pedro Mártir
el Día de San Sebastián
el Día de San Miguel
el Día de Santa Anna
el Día de Santiago
el Día de Todos Santos

PETALSINGO

no monthly mass
14 cofradía-sponsored fiestas
titular saint's day
9 misas de Aguinaldos (Christmas)

SIMOJOVEL

mass per month
6 cofradía-sponsored fiestas
titular saint's day
el Día de Todos Santos
el Día de San Sebastián

SITALÁ

no monthly mass
16 cofradía-sponsored fiestas
la Semana Santa
5 alférez-sponsored fiestas

TENANGO

monthly masses (document illegible)
16 cofradía-sponsored fiestas
titular saint's day
4 alférez-sponsored fiestas

TENEJAPA

monthly mass
17 cofradía-sponsored fiestas
titular saint's day
4 alférez-sponsored fiestas

TILA

no monthly mass
8 cofradía-sponsored fiestas
titular saint's day
la Semana Santa

TUMBALÁ

monthly mass
14 cofradía-sponsored fiestas
titular saint's day
Pascua de Navidad
el Día de San Martín
el Día de San Cristóbal
la Semana Santa

YAJALÓN

monthly masses
9 cofradía-sponsored fiestas
titular saint's day
la Semana Santa
8 alférez-sponsored fiestas

NOTES

CHAPTER I. INTRODUCTION

1. The secondary literature on the Tzeltal Revolt includes the following works: Victoria Reifler Bricker, *The Indian Christ, the Indian King: The Historical Substrate of Maya Myth and Ritual*, chap. 5; Herbert S. Klein, "Peasant Communities in Revolt: The Tzeltal Republic of 1712"; Severo Martínez Peláez, *La sublevación de los zendales*; André Saint-Lu, "El poder colonial y la iglesia frente a la sublevación de los indígenas zendales de Chiapas en 1712"; Donald E. Thompson, *Maya Paganism and Christianity: A History of the Fusion of Two Religions*; and Robert Wasserstrom, "Ethnic Violence and Indigenous Protest: The Tzeltal (Maya) Rebellion of 1712."

2. William B. Taylor, *Drinking, Homicide, and Rebellion in Colonial Mexican Villages*, 115.

3. For recent work on colonial-period rebellions in New Spain see, for example, Brian R. Hamnett, *Roots of Insurgency: Mexican Regions, 1750–1824*; Friedrich Katz, ed., *Riots, Rebellion, and Revolution: Rural Social Conflict in Mexico*, esp. pt. 2; Severo Martínez Peláez, "Los motines de indios en el período colonial guatemalteco"; William B. Taylor, "La Indiada: Peasant Uprisings in Central Mexico and Oaxaca," and *Drinking, Homicide, and Rebellion*; John M. Tutino, "Peasant Rebellion at the Isthmus of Tehuantepec: A Socio-Historical Perspective," and *From Insurrection to Revolution in Mexico: The Social Bases of Agrarian Violence, 1750–1940*, esp. pt. 1. For the Andes, see Leon G. Campbell, "Recent Research on Andean Peasant Revolts, 1750–1820"; Oscar Cornbilt, "Society and Mass Rebellion in Eighteenth-Century Peru and Bolivia"; John R. Fisher, "Royalism, Regionalism, and Rebellion in Colonial Peru, 1808–1815"; Scarlett O'Phelan Godoy, *Rebellions and Revolts in Eighteenth Century Peru and Upper Bolivia*; and Steve J. Stern, ed., *Resistance, Rebellion, and Consciousness in the Andean Peasant World: 18th to 20th Centuries*, pts. 1 and 2. Recent review essays on colonial-period historiography include the following: Marcello Carmagnani, "The Inertia of Clio: The Social History of Colonial Mexico"; Benjamin Keen, "Main Currents in United States Writings on Colonial Spanish America,

1884–1984"; and William B. Taylor, "Between Global Process and Local Knowledge: An Inquiry into Early Latin American Social History, 1500–1900."

4. See, for example, David A. Brading, *Haciendas and Ranchos in the Mexican Bajío: Leon, 1700–1800*; Cheryl English Martin, *Rural Society in Colonial Morelos*; Claude Morin, *Michoacán en la Nueva España del siglo XVIII*; Hanns Prem, *Milpa y hacienda: Tendencia de la tierra indígena y española en la cuenca de Alto Atoyac, Puebla (1520–1650)*; William B. Taylor, *Landlord and Peasant in Colonial Oaxaca*; Eric Van Young, *Hacienda and Market in Eighteenth Century Mexico*; and the essays in *The Provinces of Early Mexico*, ed. Ida Altman and James Lockhart.

5. Steve J. Stern, "Approaches to the Study of Peasant Rebellions and Consciousness: Implications of the Andean Experience," 15.

6. Thompson, "The Moral Economy of the English Crowd," 78–79.

7. James C. Scott, *The Moral Economy of the Peasant: Subsistence and Rebellion in Southeast Asia*, 4.

8. Scott, "Protest and Profanation," 5.

9. Scott, *The Moral Economy of the Peasant*, 167.

10. Robert Redfield, *The Little Community* and *Peasant Society and Culture*; George M. Foster, "The Dyadic Contract: A Model of the Social Structure of a Mexican Peasant Village" and "Peasant Society and the Image of Limited Good"; and Eric R. Wolf, "Closed Corporate Peasant Communities in Mesoamerica and Java" and *Peasant Wars of the Twentieth Century*.

11. Eric R. Wolf, "The Vicissitudes of the Closed Corporate Peasant Community," 327.

12. Steve J. Stern, "The Struggle for Solidarity: Class, Culture, and Community in Highland Indian America."

13. Eric Van Young, "Conflict and Solidarity in Indian Village Life: The Guadalajara Region in the Late Colonial Period."

14. Lewis Coser, *The Function of Conflict*; Max Gluckman, *Custom and Conflict in Africa*. Van Young also cites Alan R. Beals and Bernard J. Siegel's book *Divisiveness and Social Conflict: An Anthropological Approach* as an important influence.

15. See Norman A. McQuown, *Report on the Man-in-Nature Project of the Department of Anthropology of the University of Chicago*, 3 vols.; Norman A. McQuown and Julian Pitt-Rivers, eds., *Ensayos de antropología en la Zona Central de Chiapas*; Evon Z. Vogt, *Bibliography of the Harvard Chiapas Project: The First Twenty Years, 1957–1977*; and Victoria R. Bricker and Gary H. Gossen, eds., *Ethnographic Encounters in Southern Mesoamerica: Essays in Honor of Evon Zartman Vogt, Jr.*

16. For an overview of postrevolutionary Chiapas and an introduction to the contemporary situation, see Thomas Benjamin, *A Rich Land, A Poor People: Politics and Society in Modern Chiapas*, esp. the epilogue.

17. See W. George Lovell, "Surviving Conquest: The Guatemalan Indian in Historical Perspective"; and Robert M. Carmack, ed., *The Harvest of Violence: The Maya Indians and the Guatemalan Crisis.*

CHAPTER 2. ENVIRONMENT AND EARLY HISTORY

1. John L. Stephens, *Incidents of Travel in Central America, Chiapas, and Yucatan,* 2:266–267.

2. Frans Blom and Oliver LaFarge, *Tribes and Temples,* 377.

3. General surveys of highland archaeology include Robert M. Adams, "Changing Patterns of Territorial Organization in the Central Highlands of Chiapas, Mexico"; T. Patrick Culbert, *The Ceramic History of the Central Highlands of Chiapas, Mexico*; Thomas A. Lee, Jr., "La arqueología de los Altos de Chiapas: Un estudio contextual"; and Gareth W. Lowe and J. Alden Mason, "Archaeological Survey of the Chiapas Coast, Highlands, and Upper Grijalva Basin."

4. José Luis Lorenzo, "Un buril de la cultura precerámica de Teopisca, Chiapas"; Arturo Guevara Sánchez, *Los talleres líticos de Aquacatenango, Chiapas.*

5. Lee, 272.

6. See Adams for a study of settlement patterns.

7. Lee, 278–279.

8. Culbert, 80.

9. See Terrence Kaufman, "Archaeological and Linguistic Correlations in Mayaland and Associated Areas of Mesoamerica"; and Norman A. McQuown, "The Classification of the Maya Languages."

10. Adams, 348.

11. Donald E. McVicker, "Prehispanic Trade in Central Chiapas, Mexico," 178.

12. See T. Patrick Culbert, ed., *The Classic Maya Collapse*; and Sylvanus G. Morley and George W. Brainerd, *The Ancient Maya,* revised by Robert J. Sharer, chap. 5.

13. Adams, 352–359.

14. Culbert, 86–87.

15. For a survey, see Morley and Brainerd, 157–186. For more specialized studies, see John W. Fox, *Maya Postclassic State Formation,* and J. Eric S. Thompson, "Putun (Chontal Maya) Expansion in Yucatan and the Pasión Drainage."

16. Mary Ellen Miller, *The Art of Mesoamerica from Olmec to Aztec,* 165–167, 170–179.

17. For an excellent introduction to the current debate, see Arlen F. Chase and Prudencia M. Rice, eds., *The Lowland Maya Postclassic: Questions and Answers.*

18. Donald McVickers, "The 'Mayanized' Mexicans."

19. Fox, *Maya Postclassic State Formation*, pt. 1.

20. John W. Fox, *Quiché Conquest*, 120.

21. For a survey of Maya texts, see Robert M. Carmack, *Quichean Civilization: The Ethnohistoric, Ethnographic, and Archaeological Sources*. For the Putun migration into the highlands see Carmack, "Toltec Influence on the Postclassic Culture History of Highland Guatemala," and *The Quiché Mayas of Utatlán*, chap. 3, as well as Fox, *Maya Postclassic State Formation*.

22. Edward E. Calnek, "Highland Chiapas Before the Spanish Conquest."

23. No original copy of the *Probranza* has ever been found, but the work was first summarized in 1702 by Bishop Francisco Núñez de la Vega in his *Constituciones diocesanas del obispado de Chiapas* and later in a second version by Ramón de Ordóñez y Aguiar in *Historia de la creación del Cielo y la Tierra*.

24. For a critique by an archaeologist of ethnohistorical reconstructions of early Quichean history, see Kenneth L. Brown, "Postclassic Relationships Between the Highland and Lowland Maya."

25. See Fox, *Maya Postclassic State Formation*, 86–100.

26. Calnek, p. 9 and chap. 15.

27. Cited in Peter Gerhard, *The Southeast Frontier of New Spain*, 158.

28. McVicker, "Prehispanic Trade in Central Chiapas, Mexico," 178, 185; Ulrich Kohler, "Reflections on Zinacantan's Role in Aztec Trade with Soconusco," 67.

29. Fray Bernardino de Sahagún, *Florentine Codex: General History of the Things of New Spain*, bk. 9, p. 21.

30. See Lowe and Mason, 208–230; Carlos Navarrete, *The Chiapanec History and Culture*.

31. Díaz del Castillo, 403.

32. Lowe, 232; Thomas A. Lee, Jr., "The Middle Grijalva Regional Chronology and Ceramic Relations: A Preliminary Report."

33. José M. Velasco Toro, "Perspectiva histórica," 53–56.

CHAPTER 3. SPANISH RULE IN THE HIGHLANDS

1. J. Eric S. Thompson, ed., *Thomas Gage's Travels in the New World*, 138.

2. Díaz del Castillo, 401–414; Fray Antonio de Remesal, *Historia general de las Indias Occidentales y particular de la gobernación de Chiapa y Guatemala*, 1:378–382; Manuel B. Trens, *Historia de Chiapas*, 67–74.

3. Díaz del Castillo, 405.

4. Manuel B. Trens, *Bosquejos Históricos de San Cristóbal de las Casas*, 11–37; Sidney David Markman, *Architecture and Urbanization in Colonial Chiapas, Mexico*, chap. 11; Jan de Vos, *San Cristóbal: Ciudad colonial*.

5. Remesal, 1:382–391; Robert S. Chamberlain, "The Governorship of the Adelantado Francisco de Montejo in Chiapas, 1539–1944," 163–207; Peter Gerhard, *The Southwest Frontier of New Spain*, 151–153.

6. Díaz del Castillo, 411–413; Trens, 95–96; Chamberlain, 180–182; Gerhard, 150–152.

7. Jan de Vos, *El Sumidero*; Eduardo Flores Ruíz, "Rebelión de los Chiapas."

8. See Jan de Vos, *La Paz de Dios y del Rey*, chap. 4.

9. William L. Sherman, *Forced Native Labor in Sixteenth Century Central America*, 60–63; Trens, 80–81.

10. Remesal, 2:68–73, 113–117, 240; Trens, 96–99, 100–101; Sherman, 144–147, 149–150, 169–170; Gerhard, 151.

11. Sherman, 93; Chamberlain, 181.

12. Trens, 100; Sherman, 144, 220–232.

13. Murdo J. MacLeod, *Spanish Central America*, 74, 81.

14. Remesal, 2:73–74, 113; Trens, 96–101; Chamberlain, 178–182.

15. Remesal, 2:73–74.

16. MacLeod, *Spanish Central America*, 77–78.

17. Remesal, 2:80–90, 91–92; Sherman, 129–132; MacLeod, *Spanish Central America*, 108. For a brief, concise overview of the New Laws, see C. H. Haring, *The Spanish Empire in America*, 51–52.

18. Remesal, 2:68–73, 113–117; Trens, 100–101; Sherman, 149–150, 169–170.

19. Sherman, chaps. 8–9; MacLeod, *Spanish Central America*, 108–119.

20. Remesal, 2:237–244; Trens, 100–101; Sherman, 149–150, 169–170.

21. Remesal, 2:143–168, 180–188, 211–217; Trens, chap. 6; Gerhard, 155–158.

22. Remesal, 2:242–249.

23. Remesal, 2:176–179; Trens, 95–96; Sherman, 291–292·

24. Sherman, 177.

25. A comprehensive study of colonial demography has yet to be written for Chiapas. For a good introduction, see Murdo J. MacLeod, "An Outline of Central American Colonial Demographics: Sources, Yields, and Possibilities," 7–9. Preliminary work can be found in Gerhard, 158–160; MacLeod, *Spanish Central America*, 98–99; Luis Reyes García, "Movimientos demograficos en la población indígena de Chiapas durante la poca colonial"; Aura Marina Arreola, "Población de

los altos de Chiapas durante el siglo XVII e incios del XVIII"; and Robert Wasserstrom, *Class and Society in Central Chiapas*, 73.

26. Gerhard, 158–160.

27. MacLeod, *Spanish Central America*, 204. For an overview, see MacLeod, chaps. 3– 5.

28. Gerhard, 151; AGI: AG, 44: Cabildo de Ciudad Real a Vuestra Magestad, Nov. 28, 1591.

29. AGI: AG, 161: Cartas del obispo de Chiapa a la Audiencia, Jan. 17, 1583; Nov. 30, 1595; Oct. 18, 1619.

30. AGI: AG, 44: Carta del obispo de Chiapa a la Audiencia, Oct. 19, 1619.

31. Gerhard, 160.

32. Huguette Chaunu and Pierre Chaunu, *Séville et l'Atlantique (1504–1650)*; François Chevalier, *Land and Society in Colonial Mexico*.

33. The following works provide a good introduction to the debate about the seventeenth century: Lesley B. Simpson, "Mexico's Forgotten Century"; John Lynch, *Spain Under the Habsburgs*, 2:219–231; J. I. Israel, "Mexico and the General Crisis of the Seventeenth Century"; Richard Boyer, "Mexico City in the Seventeenth Century: Transition of a Colonial Society," John Tepaske and Herbert Klein, "The Seventeenth Century Crisis in New Spain: Myth or Reality."

34. John C. Super, "The Agricultural Near North: Querétaro in the Seventeenth Century"; William B. Taylor, "Town and Country in the Valley of Oaxaca, 1750–1812"; Marta Espejo-Ponce Hunt, "The Processes of the Development of Yucatán, 1600–1700."

35. Peter Bakewell, *Silver Mining and Society in Colonial Mexico: Zacatecas, 1546–1700*; TePaske and Klein, "The Seventeenth Century Crisis in New Spain: Myth or Reality."

36. MacLeod, *Spanish Central America*, pt. 3.

37. MacLeod, *Spanish Central America*, 218; Gerhard, 161.

38. AGI: AG, 375: Informe del alcalde mayor de la provincia de Chiapa hacienda remisión de la diligencias executadas en orden a siete curatos, Point 6, 1735.

39. AGCA: A1.23 (I) 1521, folio 223: Doctrinas, 1679; AGA: AG, 215: Carta del fiscal Joseph de Escals a la Audiencia, July 3, 1697.

40. AGCA: A1.57 (I) 2256 315: Juzgado de tierras, 1701; AGCA: A1.57 (I) 2266 316: Juzgado de tierras, 1709; AGCA: A1.24 (I) 10203 1559, folio 188: Carta de Diego Manrique y Sebastián Luis, alcaldes de Ocosingo, May 5, 1636; AGCA: A1.24 (I) 10216 1572: Confirmaciones de titulos, 1701.

41. Gage, 146.

42. Gage, 146.

43. Markman, pt. 5.

44. Trens, 182–187; Gerhard, 161; AGI: AG, 375: Informe del alcalde mayor, nomina de todos los curatos de seculares, 1735.

45. MacLeod, *Spanish Central America*, 324–329.

46. Charles Gibson, *Aztecs Under Spanish Rule*, 249, 252–256; Magnus Morner, "The Spanish American Hacienda: A Survey of Recent Research and Debate"; William B. Taylor, "Landed Society in New Spain: A View from the South"; Eric Van Young, "Mexican Rural History Since Chevalier."

47. Richard Salvucci, *Textiles and Capitalism in Mexico*, chap. 4.

48. Taylor, "Town and Country"; Espejo-Ponce Hunt.

49. This perspective was best articulated by Stanley and Barbara Stein in their classic book *The Colonial Heritage of Latin America*.

50. For a comprehensive review of the literature, see Steve J. Stern, "Feudalism, Capitalism, and the World-System in the Perspective of Latin America and the Caribbean." William Taylor includes an admirably lucid, jargon-free discussion of dependency and world-systems theory in "Between Global Process and Local Knowledge," 123–140.

51. Carol A. Smith, "Local History in a Global Context," 86–89.

52. AGI: México, 3102, Oct. 1, 1611.

53. Eric R. Wolf, *Europe and the People Without History*, 79–88.

54. Farriss, "Indians in Colonial Yucatan: Three Perspectives," 8–9.

55. MacLeod, *Spanish Central America*, 343.

56. Wortman, *Government and Society in Central America, 1680–1840*, 93.

57. MacLeod, "Ethnic Relations and Indian Society in the Province of Guatemala, ca. 1620–ca. 1800," 207–208; Wortman, 96.

58. Lynch, *Spain Under the Habsburgs*, 2:283–289.

59. Wortman, 95–96.

60. Wortman, 104.

61. Wortman, 100.

62. Wortman, 96.

63. Wortman, 97–98.

64. AGI: AG, 33: Cartas de Guatemala sobre la reforma que hizo en aquella audiencia a Don Joseph de Escals; Las ordenanzas hechas por Escals y publicadas en la provincia de Chiapa; Carta de la Audiencia a Vuestra Magestad, July 5, 1697.

65. Wortman, 99.

66. AGCA: A3.16 (I) 4753 367: Carta del justicia mayor a Vuestra Magestad, 1705.

67. Trens, 126–132.

68. See Gerhard, 153–154.

69. AGI: Contaduria, 971: De los cargos que se sacaron contra Don Diego de las Bavillas del tiempo que fue juez de milpa de la provincia de los zendales, 1622.

70. AGI: AG, 45: Testimonio de los autos fechos entre el alcalde mayor de la provincia de Chiapa y oficiales reales de la ciudad de Guatemala y su teniente en dicha provincia sobre la cobranza y administración de los reales tributos, 1651.

71. AGI: AG, 35: Testimonios y autos hecho del fiscal Don Pedro de Barreda, 1690; Carta del Rey al Audiencia, June 22, 1691.

72. See, for example, AGCA: A1.30 20 (I): Autos de la visita general, 1690; AGCA: A3.16 (I) 4554 257: Tasaciones, 1693.

73. AGI: AG, 312, quaderno 3: Autos fechos en virtud de real cédula de Vuestra Magestad sobre extirpar los fraudes por los alcaldes mayores, 1721. Folios 14–20 provide a complete account of how tributes were dispersed.

74. AGI: AG, 97: Confirmaciones de encomiendas, 1619; AGI: AG, 418: Cédulas de concesiones, confirmaciones, perogaciones, mercedes, y pensiones, 1602–1679; AGCA: A3.16 (I) 2554 257: Tasaciones, 1693.

75. Gibson, 202.

76. MacLeod, "Ethnic Relations," 190–191.

77. AGCA: A3.16 (I) 37, 648 2566: Padrones, 1665.

78. AGI: AG, 29: Fiscal a Vuestra Magestad, May 12, 1679.

79. See tasaciones for various years in AGCA: A3.16 (I).

80. AGCA: A3.16 (I) 358 4603: Padrón de la parcialidad nombrada Amatlán incluisa en el pueblo de Santo Domingo Tecpatlán, 1711.

81. AGI: AG, 221: Testimonio del escrito presentado por Don Clemente de Ochoa Velasco y Don Manuel de Morales, 1708; AGI: AG, 312: Autos contra Don Pedro de Zabaleta, 1720–1721.

82. AGI: AG, 35: Testimonio y autos contra el alcalde mayor Don Manuel de Maisterra y Atocha, 1690; AGI: AG, 221: Testimonio del escrito presentado por Don Clemente de Ochoa y Velasco y Don Manuel de Morales, 1708; AGI: AG, 312: Expediente sobre la averiguación de los fraudes por los alcaldes mayores, 1718–1729; Ximénez, 3:257–259 (unless otherwise noted, references to Ximénez are to the 1929–31 edition); MacLeod, *Spanish Central America*, 316; Brooke Larson and Robert Wasserstrom, "Coerced Consumption in Colonial Bolivia and Guatemala."

83. Gage, 142.

84. AGCA: A1.51 (I) 2049 297: Testimonio del cabildo real a la Audiencia, 1675.

85. AGI: AG, 221: Testimonio del escrito presentado por Don Clemente de Ochoa y Velasco y Don Manuel de Morales, 1708. The alcalde mayor, Martín González de Vergara was the subject of an extensive investigation after he left office. The

records include hundreds of pages of documents in AGCA: A1.30, legajos 184, 185, 186, for 1709.

86. AGCA: A1.30.1 184–186: La residencia del alcalde mayor de Chiapa, Martín de Vergara, 1716; AGI: AG, 312: Expediente sobre la averiguación de los fraudes cometidos por los alcaldes mayores, 1717–1718.

87. AGI: AG, 215: Carta del fiscal Joseph de Escals a la Audiencia, July 3, 1697; AGI: AG, 33: Las ordenanzas hechas por Joseph de Escals, 1697.

88. Wasserstrom, *Class and Society*, chaps. 3–4.

89. AGCA: A1.11.13 (I) 707 72: Testimonio de Fray Ambrosio de Solorcano, Feb. 9, 1644.

90. AGCA: A1.30.20 1473 191: Autos de la visita general, Chilón, April 1690.

91. AGI: AG, 295: Las ordenanzas de Toribio de Cosío, March 15, 1713.

92. AGCA: A3.2 (I) 15, 207 825: Tributos, 1684. This document includes a complete list of Dominican parishes and the number of priests in each priory. See also Remesal, 2:611; Trens, 117–118; and Gerhard, 157.

93. Ximénez, 2:286–312; Trens, 124. The increase in the number of parishes in the 1660s temporarily resolved the conflict between the Dominicans and Bishop Mauro de Tovar y Valle, a Benedictine who had tried to secularize many of the order's parishes.

94. AGCA: A1.30.20 (I): Autos de la visita general, 1690; AGI: AG, 215: Autos de la visita general, 1690.

95. AGCA: A1.23 (I) 1521, folio 217: Doctrinas, 1679; Trens, 117–118; Ximénez, 2:288, 305, 311.

96. AGI: AG, 215: Autos de la visita general, 1690; AGI: AG, 29: Testimonio de los autos fechos por informe del obispo de Chiapa contra el alcalde mayor, 1686.

97. AGI: AG, 7: Peticiones de los indios encomendados de Don Andrés de Castilla, 1631; AGI: AG, 962: Memoria sobre los abusos de los curas regulares del obispado de Guatemala, 1722 (this *memoria* does specifically concern the conduct of Dominicans in Chiapas, but the charges are similar to those voiced by secular bishops and civil officials in Ciudad Real).

98. Robert Ricard, *The Spiritual Conquest*, 1–8, 239–252; Haring, 168–175.

99. Ximénez, 2:286–312; Trens, 123–126.

100. Ximénez, 3:411–413, 454–458; Trens, 123–126, 135–136; AGI: AG, 375: Expediente sobre que se mantenga a la religión de Santo Domingo en las siete curatos que administren en la provincia de los zendales de Chiapas, 1689–1740; AGI: AG, 179: Peticiones, 1683; AGI: AG, 370: Vicario general a Vuestra Magestad, Sept. 5, 1748; Wasserstrom, *Class and Society*, chap. 3; Wortman, *Government and Society*, 132–135.

101. AGI: AG, 375: Informe del alcalde mayor de la provincia de Chiapa haciendo remisión de las diligencias executadas en orden a siete curatos de los zendales, Feb. 7, 1735, esp. point 1.

102. AGI: AG, 215: Autos de la visita general, 1690.

103. AGI: AG, 215: Carta del fiscal Joseph de Escals a la Audiencia, July 3, 1697.

104. AGI: AG, 33: Las ordenanzas hechas por Joseph de Escals, 1697; AGI: AG, 370: Vicario general a Vuestra Magestad, Sept. 5, 1748.

105. For the Dominican defense of *cofradías*, see Ximénez, bk. 7 (1971 edition), 157–159.

106. AGCA: A1.24 (I) 10216 1572, folios 410, 412, 427, 430: Confirmaciones de titulos, Nov. 10, 1701; García de León, 1:51; Wasserstrom, *Class and Society*, 26–27, 37, 41.

107. Wortman, 53–57; Wasserstrom, *Class and Society*, chap. 3.

108. AHDSC: Libros de cofradías for Chilón, Yajalón, and Sibacá, 1677–1709.

109. Ximénez, 3:257.

110. AHDSC: Libros de Cofradía for Chilón, Yajalón, and Sibacá, 1709.

111. Ximénez, 3:258.

112. Fray Francisco Núñez de la Vega, *Constituciones diocesanas del obispado de Chiapa*, 756.

113. Eric R. Wolf, *Peasants*, 1–17; James Scott, *The Moral Economy of the Peasant*; John Tutino, *From Insurrection to Revolution*, chap. 1.

114. Tutino, *From Insurrection to Revolution*, 31.

115. The phrase is from Charles Tilly's book of the same name, *Big Structures, Large Processes, and Huge Comparisons*.

116. Wasserstrom, *Class and Society*, 35.

117. Ximénez, 3:258.

CHAPTER 4. NATIVE SOCIETIES AFTER THE CONQUEST

1. Fray Francisco Ximénez, 3:257–258.

2. Linda Newsom, "Indian Population Patterns in Colonial Spanish America."

3. John Super, *Food, Conquest and Colonization in Sixteenth-Century Spanish America*; Sherburne F. Cook and Woodrow Borah, "Indian Food Production and Consumption in Central Mexico Before and After the Conquest (1500–1650)."

4. Peter Gerhard, *The Southeast Frontier of New Spain*, 158–160.

5. Gerhard, 160.

6. Murdo J. MacLeod, "An Outline of Central American Colonial Demographics: Sources, Yields, and Possibilities," 8.

7. AGI: AG, 312: Expediente sobre la averiguación de los fraudes por los alcaldes mayores, cuaderno 3, March 30, 1721; AGCA: A3.16 4635 359: Padrones informe de la extinción de varios pueblos, 1731–1732.

8. Murdo J. MacLeod, *Spanish Central America*, 231, 341.

9. William L. Sherman, *Forced Native Labor in Sixteenth Century Central America*, 280.

10. Sherman, 60–63.

11. Fray Antonio Remesal, *Historia general de las Indias occidentales y particular de la gobernación de Chiapas y Guatemala*, 1:465–501; Manuel B. Trens, *Historia de Chiapas*, 95–96; Sherman, 291–292.

12. Remesal, 1:119–120.

13. AGCA: A1.24 10216 1572, folio 85: Titulo de gobernador del pueblo de Chiapa y sus anexos a Don Cristóbal Morales, March 6, 1701.

14. Charles Gibson, *The Aztecs Under Spanish Rule*, chap. 7.

15. AGCA: A1.24 10216 1572, folio 100: Titulo de gobernador de los pueblos de Istapa, Zinacantán, San Gabriel, y Soyaló a Don Cristóbal Sanchez, March 16, 1701.

16. Karen Spalding, "Social Climbers: Changing Patterns of Mobility Among the Indians of Colonial Peru"; and "*Kurakas* and Commerce: A Chapter in the Evolution of Andean Society."

17. William B. Taylor, *Landlord and Peasant in Colonial Oaxaca*; John Tutino, "Provincial Spaniards, Indian Towns, and Haciendas: Interrelated Agrarian Sectors in the Valleys of Mexico and Toluca, 1750–1810," 182–187; S. L. Cline, *Colonial Culhuacan, 1580–1600*; Robert S. Haskett, "Indian Town Government in Colonial Cuernavaca: Persistence, Adaptation, and Change."

18. AGCA: A1.57 2263 316: Don Agustín de Aquino, indio principal y cacique del pueblo de San Marcos Tuxtla, pide la aprobación del titulo de la medida de unas tierras, 1706; Thomas Gage, *Thomas Gage's Travels in the New World*, 146.

19. AHDSC: Testimony of Don Mateo Castro, cacique and gobernador of the barrio de los mexicanos, Nov. 16, 1787; and Election of Jorge Franco, gobernador of the barrio de Tlaxcala y mexicano, Feb. 23, 1793.

20. Gage, 146.

21. Fray Francisco Ximénez, *Historia de la Provincia de San Vicente de Chiapa y Guatemala*, 3:290, 295; AGCA: A1.11 707 72: Información de la manera en que los frailes dominicos administren las doctrinas de los zendales, 1642.

22. Ximénez, 3:295; AGCA: A1.24 10223 1579, folio 286: Carta de Don Juan Agustín Ximénez, cacique y gobernador de Chiapa de Indios, Sept. 6, 1712

(notes cooperation of Don Juan Agustín Ximénez, *cacique* and *gobernador* of Chiapa de Indios).

23. AGCA: A1.24 10216 1572, folio 100: Título de gobernador de los pueblos de Istapa, Zinacantán, San Gabriel, y Soyaló a Don Cristóbal Sanchez, March 16, 1701.

24. AGCA: A3.16 4516 355: Tributos, 1601; Edward E. Calnek, "Highland Chiapas Before the Spanish Conquest," 93–94.

25. AGI: AG, 312: Autos fechos . . . sobre los recaudimientos de maíz, chile, frijole de la provincia de Chiapa, 1716.

26. AGCA: A3.16 4642 359: Padrones, Carta de Don Joseph Domingo Telasque por los indios justicias del pueblo de Ocosingo, 1743.

27. Ximénez, 1:340. For example, Ximénez reported that when the Dominicans arrived in Ciudad Real in 1545, "No pueblo or Indian *principal* remained who did not bring us gifts, and many poor *macehuales* came to see us, as well" (1:340).

28. Fray Domingo de Ara, *Vocabulario en lengua tzeldal según el orden de Copanabastla*; Calnek, "Highland Chiapas," chap. 9; Mario Humberto Ruz, *Copanaguastla en un espejo*, 190–191. Calnek and Ruz each examined the Tzeltal words that Ara translated as *principal*, and each concluded that Ara, who had lived and preached in the highlands for more than a decade, understood the term to refer to inherited status. The Tzeltal referent *aghau* was an element in a number of words that the friar equated with Spanish terms concerning inherited nobility:

aghau: señorrey	aghavetic: hidalgo
aghauetic: señores	aghuaynon: ennoblecerse
aghaulel teepanil: nobleza	aghaueticon: principal

Both Calnek and Ruz argue that Ara would not have applied *principal* in this context unless it was consistent with contemporary Spanish notions of birthright and *hidalguía*.

29. Fray Francisco Núñez de la Vega, *Constituciones diocesanas del obispado de Chiapa*, preamble. Edward Calnek has linked these myths to an invasion of Mexicanized Chontal Maya in the fourteenth century, and he has argued that, at contact, highland rulers claimed descent from Toltec lineages (Calnek, "Highland Chiapas," chap. 3).

30. AGI: AG, 33: Las ordenanzas hechas por Don José de Escals, 1697; AGCA: A3.16 4607 358: Padrón de Yajalón, 1715.

31. AGCA: A3.16 4516 355, 1607: Tributos; this is a petition asking for exemption from tribute payments by sons of the cacique in Chamula. Don Martín Gómez had served as regidor and alcalde. "Probanza de Magdalenas, 1560," cited by Wasserstrom, reveals that caciques and principales were instructed to organize

cabildos in Santa Marta and Santa Magdalena (Wasserstrom, *Class and Society*, 272n31).

32. AHDSC: Libro de elecciones y juramentos del pueblo de San Gabriel, Confirmación de elección, Jan. 13, 1734. This document outlines the *justicias'* duties in detail.

33. AGI: AG, 215: Autos de la visita general, 1690.

34. AGCA: A3.16 4547 357: Tributo exoneración, Palenque, 1684 (notes payment of two *reales* by "indios casados"); AGCA: A3.16 4607 358: Padrones, 1758 (notes payments of one manta per year for the *bienes de comunidad*, or community fund).

35. AGCA: A1.20.20 1473 191: Autos de la visita general, 1690.

36. Gibson, 156, 163–165; Taylor, 49–52.

37. Taylor, 45–48.

38. Robert M. Carmack, *The Quiché Mayas of Utatlán*, 324; Klein, "Peasant Communities in Revolt: The Tzeltal Republic of 1712," 247–248.

39. Alfonso Villa Rojas, "The Tzeltal," 220.

40. Eric R. Wolf, "Closed Corporate Peasant Communities in Mesoamerica and Java," 12–14; and *Sons of the Shaking Earth*, 213–215.

41. For an example of this approach, see Carmack, *The Quiché Mayas*, 324: "It is clear that by the middle of the colonial era the Quichés had developed a civil-religious hierarchy similar to the organizations found in modern times by anthropologists. . . . It signaled the replacement of the native aristocracy with a more egalitarian and collective form of leadership, as surely did the elimination of chiefly rights. The descendants of Utatlán could no longer support the luxury of a native aristocracy, dividing their limited resources and political power. The civil-religious hierarchy leveled their differences in wealth and permitted the natives of each community to present a common front to their colonial exploiters."

42. AGCA: A1.30 1423 183: Autos de la visita general, Guaguitepeque, 1690.

43. AGCA: A1.14.21 908 119: Auto sobre una elección en Ocotenango [Cancuc], April 9, 1675, and Petición de las justicias del pueblo de San Juan Evangelista Ocotenango [Cancuc], piden aprobación de elecciones, Jan. 1, 1677.

44. AGCA: A1.15 559 49: Autos sobre la motin habido en Tuxtla fue asesinado el alcalde mayor, 1693.

45. *Recopilación de leyes de los reynos de las Indias*, bk. 6, title 3, law 6, cited in Anne C. Collins, "The *Maestros Cantores* of Yucatan," 240; Robert Ricard, *The Spiritual Conquest of Mexico*, 96–101.

46. Collins, 240–241; Nancy M. Farriss, *Maya Society Under Colonial Rule*, 233.

47. AGI: AG, 293: Testimonio de los autos fechos contra diferentes indios de diversos pueblos por haber administrado los Santos Sacramentos, October 1713. Following the end of the Tzeltal Revolt, eighteen fiscales from rebel towns were held for trial. The document cited here is the record of that proceeding.

48. AGI: AG, 375: Informe del alcalde mayor de la provincia de Chiapa hacienda remición de los diligencias ejecutadad en orden a siete curatos de los zendales, point 6, 1735.

49. AHDSC: Autos sobre excesos cometidos por Nicolas Martín, fiscal del pueblo de Tenejapa, Oct. 1673. Martínez was accused by a former fiscal and other witnesses of having baptized a young boy, heard confession, and said mass in the streets of the pueblo. Among the charges was the accusation that he wore priestly vestments. Martín defended himself, claiming that his dress was the traditional ceremonial costume for a fiesta that preceded Ash Wednesday (*carenestolendas*), and objected that he was the victim of a vendetta by enemies in the pueblo. The tribunal apparently believed him, for he was exonerated on January 5, 1674, after nearly three months of investigations.

50. Ricard, *The Spiritual Conquest*, 181–182; see also Gibson, 127–135.

51. Juan de Pineada, "Descripción de la provincia de Guatemala, año 1594," 442–444, cited in Wasserstrom, *Class and Society*, 23–24; AHDSC: Libro de la Cofradía de San Sebastián, Chilón (the book begins with a series of *ordenanzas* written on June 17, 1613); Murdo J. MacLeod, "The Social and Economic Roles of Indian Cofradías in Colonial Chiapas," 76.

52. MacLeod, "Social and Economic Roles," 7.

53. Francisco Orozco y Jiménez, ed., *Colección de documentos inéditos relativos a la iglesia de Chiapas*, 1:145. A Dominican defense of the cofradías is found in AGI: AG, 370: El Vicario General a Vuestra Magestad, Sept. 5, 1748.

54. AHDSC: Libros de cofradías, Chilón. In January 1677, Bishop Marcos Bravo de la Serna found that most cofradías had allowed their record keeping to lapse. For subsequent history, see AHDSC: Libros de la Cofradía de Santa Cruz, Sibacá (Ocotitán), 1677–1716, 1719–1783; Libro de la Cofradía de San Sebastián, Chilón, 1613–1827; Libro de la Cofradía del Santissimo Sacramento, Chilón, 1677–1827; Libro de la Cofradía de la Parroquia de Santo Domingo, Chilón, 1677–1827; Libro de la Cofradía del Nombre de Jesús, Yajalón, 1713–1781; Libro de la Cofradía de Jesús Nazareño, Yajalón, 1713–1799.

55. For comparisons, see John K. Chance and William B. Taylor, "Cofradías and Cargos: An Historical Perspective on the Mesoamerican Civil-Religious Hierarchy"; Ernesto de la Torre Villar, "Algunos aspectos acerca de las cofradías y la propiedad territorial en Michoacán"; Gibson, 127–132; and Farriss, 361–365.

56. MacLeod, "Social and Economic Roles," 86.

57. Wasserstrom, 40–41.

58. Adriaan C. Van Oss, *Catholic Colonialism: A Parish History of Guatemala, 1524–1821*, 112.

59. Farriss, 269–270.

60. AGI: AG, 215: Autos de la visita general, 1690; Trens, 138; Wasserstrom, 29.

61. Ximénez, 2:194–200.

62. AGI: AG, 215: Autos de la visita general, 1690.

63. AHDSC: Libro de la Cofradía de San Sebastián, Chilón, 1613–1827.

64. AHDSC: Libro de la Cofradía de la Parroquia de Santo Domingo, Chilón, 1677–1827.

65. AHDSC: Libro de la Cofradía del Nombre de Jesús, Yajalón, 1713–1781; Libro de la Cofradía de Jesús Nazareno, Yajalón, 1713–1799; Libro de la Cofradía de Santa María Rosario, Yajalón, 1713–1716.

66. See, for example, Fernando Cámara, "Religious and Political Organization"; Frank Cancian, "Political and Religious Organizations" and *Economics and Prestige in a Maya Community: The Religious Cargo System of Zinacantan*; Pedro Carrasco, "The Civil Religious Hierarchy in Mesoamerican Communities: Pre-Spanish Background and Colonial Development"; Billie R. DeWalt, "Changes in the Cargo Systems of Mesoamerica"; Waldemar R. Smith, *The Fiesta System and Economic Change*; and James B. Greenberg, *Santiago's Sword: Chatino Peasant Religion and Economics*.

67. Eric R. Wolf, "Closed Corporate Peasant Communities"; Manning Nash, "Political Relations in Guatemala," 69.

68. See Cámara's contrast of centripetal vs. centrifugal organization in "Religious and Political Organization," 279–280; Oliver LaFarge, "Maya Ethnology: The Sequence of Cultures"; Richard N. Adams, *Political Changes in Guatemalan Indian Communities: A Symposium*, 48.

69. Cancian, *Economics and Prestige*, 137–138.

70. Cancian, *Economics and Prestige*, 140.

71. James Dow, "Religion in the Organization of a Mexican Peasant Economy."

72. Dow, 219–222.

73. Marvin Harris, *Patterns of Race in the Americas*, 30–32.

74. Harris, 29.

75. John K. Chance and William B. Taylor, "Cofradías and Cargos: An Historical Perspective on the Mesoamerican Civil-Religious Hierarchy."

76. Chance and Taylor, 7–12.

77. Chance and Taylor, 14–20.

78. Jan Rus and Robert Wasserstrom, "Civil-Religious Hierarchies in Central Chiapas."

79. AHDSC: Libro de la Cofradía de Santa Cruz, Sibacá, 1719–1783.

80. See especially Victoria Reifler Bricker, *Ritual Humor in Highland Chiapas* and *The Indian Christ, the Indian King: The Historical Substrate of Maya Myth and Ritual*, pt. 5; and Gary H. Gossen, "The Chamula Festival of Games: Native Macroanalysis and Social Commentary in a Maya Carnival."

81. Kazuyasu Ochiai, *Cuando los santos vienen marchando*; Vogt, 362–365; Ruben E. Reina, "Annual Cycle and Fiesta Cycle," 322–323.

82. Ximénez, 2:194–200.

83. Eric R. Wolf, "Closed Corporate Peasant Communities," 2.

84. Eric R. Wolf, "Types of Latin-American Peasantry: A Preliminary Discussion" and "Closed Corporate Peasant Communities."

85. Robert Redfield, *Peasant Society and Culture*, 23–39.

86. Nancy M. Farriss, "Nucleation vs. Dispersal: The Dynamics of Population Movement in Colonial Yucatan" and *Maya Society*, chap. 7.

87. David J. Robinson and Carolyn McGovern, "Population Change in the Yucatán, 1700–1820: Uman Parish in Its Regional Context"; and David J. Robinson, "Indian Migration in Eighteenth Century Yucatán: The Open Nature of the Closed Corporate Community." See also Kevin Gosner, "Umán Parish: Open, Corporate Communities in Eighteenth Century Yucatán."

88. W. George Lovell, "Surviving Conquest: The Maya of Guatemala in Historical Perspective," 32–35.

89. MacLeod, "Central American Colonial Demographics," 8; Rodney C. Watson, "La dinámica espacial de los cambios de población en un pueblo colonial mexicano: Tila, Chiapas, 1595–1794," 106; Luis Reyes García, "Movimientos demográficos en la población indígena de Chiapas durante la epoca colonial," 42–43; AGI: AG, 294: Autos sobre la sublevación, folio 752: Petición de los alcaldes, regidores, y principales de Palenque.

90. AHDSC: Libro de la Cofradía del Nombre de Jesús, Yajalón, Jan. 1, 1716.

91. Remesal, 2:247; MacLeod, *Spanish Central America*, 328.

92. AGI: AG, 7: Peticiones de indios encomendados de Don Andrés de Castilla, Jan. 23, 1631. This document contains a complaint from a priest that because Indians were living in isolated homesteads, they were difficult to minister to. References to tzeltales near Yajalón living near their milpas can be found in AGI: Guatemala, 296: Testimonio de Agustín López, 1716; and AGI: AG, 294: Autos sobre la sublevación, folios 714–715.

93. AGCA: A3.16 3951 293: Tributos, 1715.

94. MacLeod, "Central American Colonial Demographics," 5.

95. These earlier figures represent marriages between men and women from different pueblos prior to 1715 and prior to the rebellion. The counts for Sitalá and

Ocosingo in the following table are partial counts based on available censuses for the subdivisions (*parcialidades*) of Ozelotepeque and Chilajón, respectively. The counts for Chilón and Tumbalá are for the entire pueblo.

Pueblo	"indios casados"	"indios casados en pueblos"	"indias casadas en otros pueblos"
Sitalá	32%	60%	8%
Ocosingo	53	34	13
Chilón	61	15	19
Tumbalá	81	6	14

SOURCE: Parcialidad Ozelotepeque, AGCA: A3.16 4547 357: Padrón, 1681; parcialidad Chilajón, AGCA: A3.16 4554 357: Padrón, 1693; AGCA: A3.16 4567 357: Padrón, 1703; AGCA: A3.16 4550 357: Padrón, 1690.

96. William B. Taylor, *Drinking, Homicide, and Rebellion in Colonial Mexican Villages*, 24.

97. Farriss, "Nucleation vs. Dispersal," 203–204.

98. Taylor, *Drinking, Homicide, and Rebellion*, 148.

99. Brian Hamnett, *The Roots of Insurrection*; John Tutino, *From Insurrection to Revolution in Mexico*, chap. 4.

100. Villa Rojas, "The Tzeltal"; Henri Favre, *Cambio y continuidad entre los Mayas de México*, pt. 2; Evon Vogt, *Zinacantan*, chap. 7.

101. Villa Rojas, 213; Favre, 189–199.

102. Eva Hunt and June Nash, "Local and Territorial Units," 262–264.

103. Hunt and Nash, 257; Villa Rojas, 220.

104. Favre, 179.

105. AHDSC: Libro de elecciones y juramentos del pueblo de San Gabriel; Confirmación de elección, Jan. 13, 1734.

106. Hunt and Nash, 260.

107. Wasserstrom, 94.

108. Edward E. Calnek, "Los pueblos indígenas de las tierras altas."

109. Carmack, 324.

110. Robert M. Hill II and John Monaghan, *Continuities in Highland Maya Social Organization*, chap. 5.

111. Hill and Monaghan, chap. 7.

112. Sandra Orellana, *The Tzutujil Mayas*, 230.

113. AGCA: A3.16 357: Tributos.

114. AGI: AG, 295, cuaderno 5, Jan. 18, 1713. In this document, alcaldes from Yajalón report their rank. Another document refers to an alcalde associated with a specific calpul; AGI: AG, 295, Dec. 22, 1712: Testimonio de Dominica López.

115. Calnek, "Los pueblos indígenas," 108–109, 120–121.

116. AGCA: A3.16 3951 293: Padrones, San Miguel Huistán, Dec. 10, 1715.

117. AGCA: A3.16 3951 293: Padrones, Ocosingo, Dec. 3, 1715.

118. Hunt and Nash, 261; Favre, 175–182.

119. See, for example, Hill and Monaghan, chap. 5.

120. Anthony F. C. Wallace, "Revitalization Movements," 265–275.

CHAPTER 5. RELIGION AND THE MORAL ECONOMY
OF MAYA POLITICS

1. Evon Z. Vogt, *The Zinacantecos of Mexico*, 81.

2. My account of the Atonal conspiracy is drawn entirely from "Relación que hace el obispo de Chiapas, Fray Pedro de Feria, sobre la reincidencia en sus idolatrias de los indios de aquel país despues de treinta años de cristianos," *Colección de documentos inéditos relativos a la iglesia de Chiapas*, vol. 2, ed. Francisco Orozco y Jiménez, no pagination.

3. For a recent account of the Landa trials, see Inga Clendinnen, *Ambivalent Conquests: Maya and Spaniards in Yucatan, 1517–1570*.

4. For an excellent overview of Maya concepts of kingship, see Linda Schele and Mary Ellen Miller, *The Blood of Kings: Dynasty and Ritual in Maya Art*, chap. 2.

5. Thompson, *Maya History and Religion*, 170.

6. The best analysis of the religious consequences of the Spanish conquest for native elites is found in Nancy M. Farriss, *Maya Society Under Colonial Rule*, chaps. 10 and 11.

7. Fray Antonio de Remesal, *Historia general de las Indias Occidentales y particular de la gobernación de Chiapa y Guatemala*, 1:536–538; Fray Francisco Ximénez, *Historia de la Provincia de San Vicente de Chiapa y Guatemala*, 1:476–479.

8. See Farriss, chap. 11.

9. William A. Christian, Jr., *Apparitions in Late Medieval and Renaissance Spain*, 14.

10. Evon Vogt, *Zinacantan: A Maya Community in the Highlands of Chiapas*, chap. 17; Garrett Cook, "Quichean Folk Theology and Southern Maya Supernaturalism."

11. For an excellent overview of the scholarship on nagualism, including an extensive bibliography, see Alfredo López Austin, *The Human Body and Ideology: Concepts of the Ancient Nahuas*, 1:362–375, 2:283–284.

12. Fray Francisco Núñez de la Vega, *Constituciones diocesanas del obispado de Chiapa*, Ninth Pastoral Letter, 752–760; Alan Watters Payne, ed. and trans., "Calendar and Nagualism of the Tzeltals." For an overview of nagualism in prehispanic Chiapas, see Edward E. Calnek, "Highland Chiapas Before the Spanish Conquest," chap. 7.

13. AGI: AG, 295, quaderno 3: Testimonio de Sebastiana González, folio 149, Jan. 1713.

14. Payne, 60.

15. Payne, 65; AGI: AG, 295, quaderno 3: Testimonio de Sebastiana González, folio 149, Jan. 1713.

16. Maud Oakes, *The Two Crosses of Todos Santos*, 19, 58–59.

17. Alfonso Villa Rojas, "Kinship and Nagualism in a Tzeltal Community, Southeastern Mexico," 583.

18. Eva Hunt, *The Transformation of the Hummingbird*, chap. 3.

19. Hunt, chap. 4; Evon Z. Vogt, "Some Aspects of the Sacred Geography of Highland Chiapas."

20. Robert M. Laughlin and Carol Karasik, *The People of the Bat*.

21. Laughlin and Karasik, 4–11; Susan Tax Freeman, "Notes from the Chiapas Project: Zinacantán, Summer 1959," 92.

22. Laughlin and Karasik, 65.

23. Christian, chap. 1.

24. Christian, 4.

25. Jacques Lafaye, *Quetzalcóatl and Guadalupe*, 224–230.

26. Fray Luis G. Alonso Getino, *Origen el rosario y leyendas castellanas del siglo XIII sobre Sto. Domingo de Guzmán*.

27. Núñez de la Vega, 732–733, 749.

28. Lafaye, chaps. 12–14; William B. Taylor, "The Virgin of Guadalupe in New Spain: An Inquiry into the Social History of Marian Devotion."

29. See Lafaye, chap. 13.

30. Taylor, 10–15.

31. Ximénez, 3:262–264; Klein, "Peasant Communities in Revolt: The Tzeltal Republic of 1712," 232; Bricker, *Indian Christ, Indian King*, 55–56.

32. Ximénez, 3:263.

33. MacLeod, 345.

34. Ximénez, 3:264.

35. AGI: AG, 293: Testimonio de los autos fechos sobre decirse que hace aparecido la Virgen Santísima Nuestra Señora a una india del pueblo Santa Marta, May 13, 1712; Ximénez, 3:265; Klein, 252–253; Bricker, *Indian Christ, Indian King*, 65–69.

36. AGI: AG, 293: Testimonio de Dominica López, May 30, 1712.

37. AGI: AG, 293: Testimonio de Juan Gómez, May 30, 1712.

38. AGI: AG, 293: Declaración de Manuel Ruíz, April 3, 1712; Declaración de Lorenzo Yanez, April 17, 1712; Declaración de Joseph Antonio de Zavaleta, May 23, 1712.

39. Ximénez, 3, 267–268; Klein, 252; Bricker, *Indian Christ, Indian King*, 59.

CHAPTER 6. THE HIGHLANDS IN REVOLT

1. AGI: AG, 296, quaderno 6: Testimonio de Francisco de Torre y Tobilla, folio 12, Feb. 19, 1713.

2. AGI: AG, 296: Testimonio de los autos y causas criminales en razón de haber parecido difunta la mala india María de la Candelaria (hereafter cited as Testimonio de los autos): Testimonio de Agustín López, folio 60, 1716.

3. Ximénez, 3:268–269.

4. Ximénez, 3:269.

5. AGI: AG, 296: Testimonio de los autos: Testimonio de Agustín López, folio 59, 1716; Testimonio de María Hernández, folio 16, 1716.

6. AGI: AG, 296: Testimonio de los autos: Testimonio de Agustín López, 1716.

7. AGI: AG, 296: Testimonio de los autos: Testimonio de Agustín López, folio 88, 1716.

8. AGI: AG, 296: Testimonio de los autos: Testimonio de María Hernández, folio 18, 1716.

9. AGI: AG, 296: Testimonio de los autos: Testimonio de Agustín López, folio 64, 1716.

10. AGI: AG, 295, quarderno 5: Testimonio de Gerónimo Saroes, folios 294–295.

11. Ximénez, 3:281; AGI: AG, 295, quaderno 5: Testimonio de Gerónimo Saroes, folio 294, March 1713; Testimonio de Nicolás Vásquez, folio 201, March 1713.

12. Ximénez, 3:269–270.

13. AGI: AG, 295, quaderno 5: Testimonio de Gerónimo Saroes, folio 294, March 1713; AGI: AG, 296, quaderno 6: Testimonio de Francisco de Torre y Tobilla, folios 10–11, Feb. 19, 1713.

14. AGI: AG, 296, quaderno 6: Testimonio de Francisco de Torre y Tobilla, folio 10, Feb. 19, 1713, translation from Bricker, *Indian Christ, Indian King*, 61.

15. AGI: AG, 293: Testimonios de 1713: Testimonio de Domingo Méndez, folio 52, Feb. 15, 1713.

16. Ximénez, 3:271.

17. Ximénez, 3:271.

18. Klein, 254; Wasserstrom, "Ethnic Violence and Indigenous Protest," 12.

19. Ximénez, 3:260–261.

20. AGI: AG, 296: Testimonio de los autos: Testimonio de Agustín López, folio 62, 1716; AGI: AG, 295, quaderno 5: Testimonio de Gerónimo Saroes, folio 294, March 1713.

21. AGI: AG, 295, quaderno 5: Testimonio de Nicolás Vásquez, folio 202, March 1713; Testimonio de Gerónimo Saroes, folio 294, March 1713.

22. AGI: AG, 294: Memoria de los indios brujos y cabesillas del pueblo de Bachajón, folios 500–501.

23. Calnek, "Highland Chiapas," 68.

24. AGI: AG, 296, quaderno 6: Testimonio de Jacinto Domínguez, folio 4, Feb. 1713.

25. AGI: AG, 296, quaderno 6: Testimonios de Andrés Sánchez y Miguel Martínez, folios 14–69, Feb. 1713.

26. Herbert Klein reached a different conclusion, writing that "[t]he rebel leaders were, in fact, the elders of the community, the traditional principales, fiscales, and other officeholders who governed their communities under the Spanish superstructure in time of peace, and who led them in time of revolt into war and independence" (p. 263). In contrast, Robert Wasserstrom argued that "Gómez and his confederates did not allow local councils of this sort to assume more than a minor role in the uprising" ("Ethnic Violence and Indigenous Protest," 16). Though I disagree with Wasserstrom's view of Sebastián Gómez de la Gloria's authority, his view of the role of the traditional hierarchy is correct.

27. AGI: AG, 295, quaderno 5: Testimonio de Nicolás Vásquez, folio 201, March 1713; AGI: AG, 296: Testimonio de los autos: Testimonio de Agustín López, folio 62, 1716; Ximénez, 3:272.

28. Ximénez, 3:273–274.

29. Ximénez, 3:288–289; AGI: AG, 294: Carta de Toribio de Cosío al Consejo, Sept. 12, 1712.

30. Ximénez, 3:272–273, 278–279; AGI: AG, 294: Carta del Virrey al Consejo, Dec. 15, 1712.

31. AGI: AG, 295, quaderno 5: Testimonio de Nicolás Vásquez, folio 206, March 1713.

32. Ximénez, 3:279–280; AGI: AG, 296, quaderno 6: Testimonio de Francisco de Torre y Tobilla, folios 11–12, Feb. 19, 1713; AGI: AG, 295, quaderno 5: Testimonio de Gerónimo Saroes, folios 297–298, March 1713.

33. AGI: AG, 293: Testimonios de los autos fechos contra diferentes indios de

diversos pueblos por haber administrado los santos sacramentos durante el tiempo de la sublevación de la provincia de los zendales por Don Fray Juan Bauptista Alvarez de Toledo, Feb. 1713 (hereafter cited as Los autos por Toledo). Testimony by the women is reprinted in the *Boletín del Archivo General de la Nación* 19 (1948): 503–535. The quotation is from Testimonio de Anna Torres in Klein, 259.

34. AGI: AG, 293: Autos por Toledo: Testimonio de Juana Bárbara Gutiérrez, April 1713.

35. Ximénez, 3:326; AGI: AG, 295, quaderno 5: Testimonio de Nicolás Vásquez, folio 205, March 1713; AGI: AG, 296: Testimonio de los autos: Testimonio de Agustín López, folio 68, 1716.

36. Ximénez, 3:324–326; AGI: AG, 294, quaderno 4 (proceso 1 includes testimony on the murders of Colindres and Mariscal; proceso 2, on the killing of Gómez); AGI: AG, 295, quaderno 5: Testimonio de Nicolás Vásquez, folios 204–205, March 1713.

37. Ximénez, 3:286–287.

38. Bricker, *Indian Christ, Indian King*, 64; AGI: AG, 295, quaderno 5: Testimonio de Nicolás Vásquez, folio 208, March 1713. A *cédula* of April 15, 1715, granted Simojovel a two-year exemption from tribute payments in compensation for damage inflicted by the Cancuc rebels (AGI: AG, 743).

39. AGI: AG, 294: Petition from *principales* of Palenque, folio 752.

40. Ximénez, 3:288–289; AGI: AG, 294: Carta de Toribio de Cosío al Consejo, Sept. 12, 1712.

41. AGI: AG, 296: Testimonio de los autos: Testimonio de Agustín López, folio 69, 1716.

42. Ximénez, 3:290.

43. Ximénez, 3:291; AGI: AG, 294: Carta del Virrey al Consejo, Dec. 15, 1712. Among the dead was Bartolomé Tercero de Rosas, the alcalde mayor of Soconusco.

44. Ximénez, 3:292.

45. Ximénez, 3:294–295; AGI: AG, 294: Carta de Toribio de Cosío al Consejo, Oct. 18, 1712.

46. Ximénez, 3:296–297; AGI: AG, 293, quaderno 2, 1712 (includes a list of names for all the foot soldiers in the Spanish army and letters that include firsthand accounts of the campaign); AGI: AG, 294 (several letters included in this long *legajo* describe the organization of the Spanish counteroffensive, in particular "Los autos hechos sobre la sublevación," folios 1–40, Sept. 1712 to Nov. 1713).

47. Ximénez, 3:297–298.

48. Ximénez, 3:299.

49. Ximénez, 3:285.

50. Ximénez, 3:285; AGI: AG, 296: Testimonio de los autos: Testimonio de María Hernández, folio 19, 1716, quaderno 6; Testimonio de Jacinto Domínguez, folio 2, Feb. 1713; AGI: AG, 294, Dec. 1712, quaderno 1 (includes a complete inventory of religious paraphernalia found in the Cancuc shrine and the town church).

51. Ximénez, 3:285.

52. AGI: AG, 293: Autos por Toledo (includes the testimony of all those who were ordained in September).

53. See, for example, AGI: AG, 293: Autos por Toledo: Testimonio de Miguel Hernández, folio 41, Feb. 1713.

54. Ximénez, 3:281–284; Klein, 256; Wasserstrom, "Ethnic Violence and Indigenous Protest," 12–16.

55. AGI: AG, 295, quaderno 5: Testimonio de Gerónimo Saroes, folio 296, March 1713.

56. AGI: AG, 296, quaderno 6: Testimonio de Jacinto Domínguez, folio 3, Feb. 1713.

57. AGI: AG, 295, quaderno 5: Testimonio de Nicolás Vásquez, folio 202, March 1713.

58. AGI: AG, 296, quaderno 6: Testimonio de Francisco de Torre y Tobilla, folio 12, Feb. 19, 1713; Testimonio de Jacinto Domínguez, folio 3, Feb. 1713. Wasserstrom, citing Hermilio López Sánchez, indicates that Juan García of Cancuc was also to be named king. While the sources I have examined show that García was a capitán general and one of the first captains chosen, I have not seen him referred to as a future king.

59. Klein disagrees: "After the first several weeks of organization, three full-time captains general were appointed to lead the armies, and it seems these war leaders implicitly accepted the leadership of the Virgin and were selected for their military ability only" (p. 259).

60. AGI: AG, 295, quaderno 3: Testimonio de Felipe Pérez, folios 10–11, Jan. 1713.

61. Wasserstrom, "Ethnic Violence and Indigenous Protest," 14; Bricker, *Indian Christ*, 68–69.

62. Ximénez, 3:283.

63. Ximénez, 3:283.

64. Ximénez, 3:309; AGI: AG, 294: Autos sobre la sublevación, folios 181–183, Dec. 1712.

65. AGI: AG, 294: Autos sobre la sublevación, folio 207, 1712.

66. Calnek, "Highland Chiapas Before the Spanish Conquest," 68.

67. See Alfredo López-Austin, *Hombre-Dios: Religión y política en el mundo nahuatl*, and Serge Gruzinski, *Man-Gods of the Mexican Highlands*.

68. AGI: AG, 296: Testimonio de los autos: Testimonio de María Hernández, folio 16, 1716.

69. Vogt, *Zinacantán*, 365–366; Duane Metzger and Gerald Williams, "Tenejapa Medicine, I: The Curer," 400.

70. Thompson, *Maya History and Religion*, 189.

71. Nelson Reed, *The Caste War of Yucatan*; Bricker, *The Indian Christ*, 87–118.

72. Thompson, *Maya History and Religion*, 162.

73. AGI: AG, 293: Autos por Toledo, Dec. 1712. The evidence against various native priests included entries in the parish registers of marriages and baptisms made during the rebellion.

74. Ximénez, 3:310–311.

75. AGI: México, 485: Sublevación y sometiento de los pueblos zendales en 1712–1713, reprinted in María Angeles Eugenio Martínez, *La defensa de Tabasco, 1600–1717*.

76. Ximénez, 3:296–301.

77. Ximénez, 3:303.

78. Ximénez, 3:304.

79. AGI: AG, 296: Testimonio de los autos: Testimonio de Agustín López, folios 71–77, 1716; Testimonio de María Hernández, folios 21–23, 1716.

80. Ximénez, 3:304–305.

81. Ximénez, 3:308; AGI: AG, 294: Autos sobre la sublevación, folios 181–183, 203–240, Dec. 1712 (includes Cosío's report on the response to the offer of amnesty).

82. Ximénez, 3:308.

83. Ximénez, 3:309.

84. Ximénez, 3:313; AGI: AG, 294: Autos sobre la sublevación, Cartas de Toribio de Cosío al Consejo, Dec. 4, 6, 1712; AGI: AG, 295, quaderno 3: Testimonio de Mateo Hernández, folio 130, Jan. 1713.

85. AGI: AG, 295, quaderno 3: Testimonio de Sebastiana González, Jan. 1713; AGI: AG, 294: Memoria de los indios brujos y cabesillas del Bachajón, 1713.

86. AGI: AG, 295, quaderno 3. This entire *legajo* is devoted to the raid on Chilón and the trials of its participants in January 1713.

87. AGI: AG, 295, quaderno 3: Testimonio de Bernabe Júarez, folio 34, Jan. 1713; AGI: AG, 296, quaderno 3: Testimonio de Sebastián Gómez, folio 205, Jan. 1713.

88. AGI: AG, 294: Autos de la sublevación, folios 128–130, Jan. 1713.

89. AGI: AG, 295, quaderno 3, Jan. 1713.

90. Ximénez, 3:310–311, 316; AGI: México, 485.

91. Ximénez, 3:316–317, 329; AGI: AG, 296: Autos por Zabeleta, Jan. 1713.

92. Ximénez, 3:317–323; AGI: AG, 369: Relación de meritos de Fray Joseph Monroy (includes letters from Cosío dated Dec. 17, 1712, and March 12, 1713, on the search for María de la Candelaria).

93. Ximénez, 3:315–317.

94. AGI: AG, 295, quaderno 5, 1713.

95. AGI: AG, 295, quaderno 5, 1713.

96. AGI: AG, 293: Autos por Toledo, 1713.

97. AGI: AG, 296: Autos por Zabeleta, 1713.

98. AGI: AG, 295: Las ordenanzas de Toribio de Cosío, March 15, 1713.

99. AGI: AG, 369: Relación de meritos de Fray Joseph Monroy y Calzadilla, Carta de Don Juan de Santander al Catedral, July 11, 1713; Bricker, *Indian Christ, Indian King*, 66.

100. AGI: AG, 296: Testimonio de los autos, 1716.

101. AGI: AG, 296: Testimonio de los autos: Testimonio de Agustín López, 1716. López's account of the actions of the *indizuela* and her entourage after the fall of Cancuc is the most complete.

102. Ximénez, 1971 ed., bk. 6, p. 354.

103. Ximénez, 1971 ed., bk. 6, p. 354.

104. Ximénez, 1971 ed., bk. 6, p. 357; Trens, 158.

105. Murdo J. MacLeod, "An Outline of Central American Colonial Demographics: Sources, Yields, and Possibilities," 8.

106. For an overview of plagues, locust infestations, and famine in the eighteenth century, see Gerhard, 160, and Wasserstrom, *Class and Society*, 72.

107. AGCA: A1.1 3 1, 1734: Diligencias hechas sobre la extinción de varios pueblos de la provincia de Chiapas por Gabriel de la Laguna; reprinted as "Despoblación de Xiquipilas, Tacoasintepec, Las Pitas, Coneta, Suchiltepeque, Popocatepeque, Ecatepec, Bachajón, San Andrés, Ixtapilla, y Sacualpa, 1733–1734," in *Boletín del Archivo General de Chiapas* [Tuxtla Gutiérrez, Chiapas] 3 (1955): 27–68.

108. AGCA: A1.10 646 61, 1730: Orden que se da al alcalde mayor del la provincia de Chiapas para que poble en en lugar que destine a los indios del pueblo de la Presentación Cancuc dandoles sementeras.

109. Eduardo Flores Ruíz, "Secuela parroquial de Chiapas: Un documento inédito," 30.

110. AGI: AG, 312: Expediente sobre la averiguación de los fraudes de los alcaldes mayores, cédula, July 17, 1718.

111. AGI: AG, 312, quaderno 1: Expediente sobre la averiguación de los fraudes de los alcaldes mayores, 1717–1718.

112. Wasserstrom, *Class and Society*, chap. 3

113. Wasserstrom, *Class and Society*, 45; Gerhard, 154.

114. "Motín indígena de Ocozocoautla, 1722," *Boletín del Archivo General de Chiapas* [Tuxtla Gutiérrez, Chiapas] 2 (1953): 55–66.

115. AGCA: A1.15 176 13, 1727: Autos fechos sobre las noticias dadas por el alcalde mayor de la provincia de Chiapa a su Señoría el Señor Presidente Gobernor y Capitán General de este reyno.

116. AGCA: A1.15 176 13, 1727: Autos fechos sobre las noticias dadas por el alcalde mayor de la provincia de Chiapa a su Señoría el Señor Presidente Gobernador y Capitán General de este reyno: Testimonio de Diego Ximénez, folio 34.

CHAPTER 7. CONCLUSION

1. William B. Taylor, "Landed Society in New Spain: A View from the South," 407.

2. Suzanne Desean, "Crowds, Community, and Ritual in the Work of E. P. Thompson and Natalie Davis," 71. In a similar vein, Eric Wolf recently criticized unifying theories of culture and argued: "What Levi-Strauss called the 'surplus of signifiers' must be subjected to parsimonious selection before the logic of cultural integration can be actualized. This indexing, as some have called it, is no automatic process, but passes through power and through contentions over power, with all sorts of consequences for signification." ("Distinquished Lecture: Facing Power— Old Insights, New Questions," 592).

3. See Frank Salomon, "Ancestor Cults and Resistance to the State in Arequipa, ca. 1748–1754," and "Shamanism and Politics in Late Colonial Ecuador"; Jan Szeminski, "Why Kill the Spaniard? New Perspectives on Andean Insurrectionary Ideology in the 18th Century"; Alberto Flores Galindo, "In Search of an Inca"; Serge Gruzinski, *Man-Gods in the Mexican Highlands: Indian Power and Colonial Society, 1520–1800*; Grant Jones, *Maya Resistance to Spanish Rule*; and Eric Van Young, "Millennium on the Northern Marches: The Mad Messiah of Durango and Popular Rebellion in Mexico, 1800–1815."

4. See Linda Schele and David Freidel, *A Forest of Kings: The Untold Story of the Maya*; Kay Warren, *The Symbols of Subordination*; and Sheldon Annis, *Gods and Production in a Guatemalan Town*.

GLOSSARY

alcalde. Town councilman above the rank of regidor; member of cabildo.

alcalde mayor. Spanish regional governor.

alférez. Sponsor of religious rite; literally, a standard-bearer.

almud. Unit of dry measure; about one-half peck.

arroba. Unit of measure; twenty-five pounds.

audiencia. Political and judicial jurisdiction below viceroyalty.

barrio. Town subdivision.

brujo. Witch.

cabecera. Parish seat.

cabildo. Municipal council.

cacicazgo. Political jurisdiction ruled by a cacique; the rights and privileges inherited by a cacique.

cacique. Native lord.

caja. Treasury; literally, a strongbox.

calpul. Subdivision of an Indian town.

cofradía. Confraternity; parish sodality.

congregación. Resettlement of dispersed populations into villages.

cuadra. Unit of linear measure; a city block; approximately 400 yards.

derechos por la visita. Fees collected during diocesan tours of inspection.

encomendero. Titleholder of an encomienda.

encomienda. Grant of Indians for tribute.

ermita. Chapel; shrine; hermitage.

estancia. Cattle ranch.

fanega.   Unit of dry measure; about one and a half bushels.

fiscal.   Lay assistant to a parish priest.

justicia.   Cabildo officeholder.

macehual.   Indian commoner.

maestro de coro.   Choirmaster.

manojo.   Unit of measure for tobacco; literally, a handful.

manta.   Bolt of cloth.

milpa.   Cornfield.

monte.   Scrubland; forest.

nagual.   Spirit familiar.

nagualista.   Indian shaman.

oidor.   Judge on an audiencia.

padrón.   Tribute census.

paraje.   Subdivision of an Indian town; hamlet.

parcialidad.   Subdivision of an Indian town.

peso.   Monetary unit; eight reales.

pierna.   Unit of linear measure; about thirty-three inches.

principal.   Member of the lesser Indian nobility; high-ranking Indian.

prioste.   Holder of the highest office in a cofradía.

real.   Monetary unit; one-eighth of a peso.

regidor.   Town councilman below the rank of alcalde.

repartimiento.   Labor draft.

repartimiento de mercancías.   System of forced sales imposed on Indians by Spanish officials.

servicio del tostón.   Tax of two reales per full Indian tributary.

tostón.   Monetary unit; four reales, or one-half peso.

tributario entero.   Full tributary; married male.

visita.   Tour of inspection.

zonte.   Unit of measure for cacao; 400 cacao beans.

BIBLIOGRAPHY

ABBREVIATIONS

AGI   Archivo de las Indias
AG   Audiencia de Guatemala
AGCA   Archivo General de Centroamérica
AHDSC   Archivo Histórico Diocesano, San Cristóbal de las Casas
CEDAL   Congreso Centroamericano de Historia, Demográfica, Económica y Social

MANUSCRIPTS

ARCHIVO DE LAS INDIAS, SEVILLE (AGI)

Audiencia de Guatemala
Contaduria
México

ARCHIVO GENERAL DE CENTROAMÉRICA, GUATEMALA (AGCA)

Asuntos generales
Juicios de residencia
Juros, pensiones, sueldos, ayudas de costa, castillos, ayudas de Montepío
Juzgado de tierras
Reales cédulas y decretos
Reales tributos y encomiendas
Real patronato
Registro de la real cancilleria

ARCHIVO HISTÓRICO DIOCESANO, SAN CRISTÓBAL DE LAS CASAS, MEXICO (AHDSC)

PUBLISHED WORKS

Adams, Richard N. "Ethnohistorical Research Methods: Some Latin American Features." *Ethnohistory* 9 (1962): 179–205.

———. *Political Changes in Guatemalan Indian Communities: A Symposium*. New Orleans: Middle American Research Institute, 1974.

Adams, Robert M. "Changing Patterns of Territorial Organization in the Central Highlands of Chiapas, Mexico." *American Antiquity* 26 (1961): 341–360.

Altman, Ida, and James Lockhart, eds. *The Provinces of Early Mexico*. UCLA Latin American Center Publications. Los Angeles: The Center, 1976.

Annis, Sheldon. *God and Production in a Guatemalan Town*. Austin: University of Texas Press, 1987.

Arreola, Aura Marina. "Población de los altos de Chiapas durante el siglo xvii e inicios de xviii." In *VIII Mesa Redonda: Los mayas del sur y sus relaciones con los nahuas meridionales*. Mexico City: Sociedad Mexicana de Antropología, 1961.

Bakewell, Peter J. *Silver Mining and Society in Colonial Mexico*. Cambridge: Cambridge University Press, 1971.

Beals, Alan R., and Bernard J. Siegel. *Divisiveness and Social Conflict: An Anthropological Approach*. Stanford, Calif.: Stanford University Press, 1966.

Benjamin, Thomas. *A Rich Land, a Poor People: Politics and Society in Modern Chiapas*. Albuquerque: University of New Mexico Press, 1989.

Blom, Frans, and Oliver LaFarge. *Tribes and Temples*. New Orleans: Middle American Research Institute, Tulane University, 1926.

Borah, Woodrow. *New Spain's Century of Depression*. Ibero-Americana, vol. 35. Berkeley: University of California Press, 1951.

Boyer, Richard. "Mexico in the Seventeenth Century: Transition of a Colonial Society." *Hispanic American Historical Review* 57 (1977): 455–478.

Brading, David A. *Haciendas and Ranchos in the Mexican Bajío: Leon, 1700–1800*. Cambridge: Cambridge University Press, 1978.

Bricker, Victoria Reifler. *The Indian Christ, the Indian King: The Historical Substrate of Maya Myth and Ritual*. Austin: University of Texas Press, 1981.

———. *Ritual Humor in Highland Chiapas*. Austin: University of Texas Press, 1973.

Bricker, Victoria Reifler, and Gary H. Gossen, eds. *Ethnographic Encounters in Southern Mesoamerica: Essays in Honor of Evon Zartman Vogt, Jr*. Albany, N.Y.: Institute for Mesoamerican Studies, 1989.

Brown, Kenneth L. "Postclassic Relationships Between the Highland and Lowland Maya." In *The Lowland Maya Postclassic: Questions and Answers*, Arlen F. Chase and Prudencia M. Rice. Austin: University of Texas Press, 1985.

Calnek, Edward E. "Highland Chiapas Before the Spanish Conquest." Ph.D. diss., University of Chicago, 1962.

―――. "Los pueblos indígenas de las tierras altas." In *Ensayos de Antropología en la zona central de Chiapas*, ed. Norman A. McQuown and Julian Pitt-Rivers. Mexico City: Instituto Nacional Indigenista, 1970.

Cámara, Fernando. "Religious and Political Organization." In *Heritage of Conquest*, ed. Sol Tax. New York: Macmillan, 1952.

Campbell, Leon G. "Recent Research on Andean Peasant Revolts, 1750–1820." *Latin American Research Review* 14 (1979): 3–49.

Cancian, Frank. *Economics and Prestige in a Maya Community: The Religious Cargo System in Zinacantan*. Stanford, Calif.: Stanford University Press, 1965.

―――. "Political and Religious Organization." In *Handbook of Middle American Indians*, vol. 6, ed. Robert Wauchope. Austin: University of Texas Press, 1967.

Carmack, Robert M. "Ethnography and Ethnohistory: Their Application in Middle American Studies." *Ethnohistory* 18 (1971): 127–143.

―――. *Quichean Civilization: The Ethnohistoric, Ethnographic, and Archaeological Sources*. Berkeley: University of California Press, 1973.

―――. *The Quiché Maya of Utatlán: The Evolution of a Highland Guatemala Kingdom*. Norman: University of Oklahoma Press, 1981.

―――, ed. *Harvest of Violence: The Maya Indians and the Guatemalan Crisis*. Norman: University of Oklahoma Press, 1988.

Carmack, Robert M., John Early, and Christopher Lutz, eds. *The Historical Demography of Highland Guatemala*. Albany, N.Y.: Institute for Mesoamerican Studies, 1982.

Carmagnani, Marcello. "The Inertia of Clio: The Social History of Colonial Mexico." *Latin American Research Review* 20 (1985): 149–165.

Carr, Raymond, ed. *Latin American Affairs*. St Anthony's Papers, no. 2. Oxford, 1970.

Carrasco, Pedro. "The Civil-Religious Hierarchy in Mesoamerican Communities: Pre-Spanish Background and Colonial Development." *American Anthropologist* 63 (1961): 483–497.

Casarrubias, Vicente. *Rebeliones indígenas en la Nueva España*. Biblioteca de Cultura Popular, vol. 18. Guatemala City: Biblioteca de Cultura Popular, 1951.

Chamberlain, Robert S. "The Governorship of the Adelantado Francisco de Montejo in Chiapas, 1539–1544." In *Contributions to American Anthropology and History*, vol. 9. Carnegie Institute of Washington, Publication 574. Washington, D.C., 1948.

Chance, John, and William B. Taylor. "Cofradías and Cargos: An Historical Perspective on the Mesoamerican Civil-Religious Hierarchy." *American Ethnologist* 12 (1985): 1–26.

Chase, Arlen F., and Prudencia M. Rice, eds. *The Lowland Maya Postclassic: Questions and Answers*. Austin: University of Texas Press, 1985.

Chaunu, Pierre, and Huguette Chaunu. *Séville et l'Atlantique*. 8 vols. Paris: Colin, 1955–59.

Chevalier, François. *Land and Society in Colonial Mexico*. Berkeley: University of California Press, 1970.

Christian, William A., Jr. *Apparitions in Late Medieval and Renaissance Spain*. Princeton, N.J.: Princeton University Press, 1981.

Clendinnen, Inga. *Ambivalent Conquests: Maya and Spaniard in Yucatan, 1517–1570*. Cambridge: Cambridge University Press, 1987.

Cline, S. L. *Colonial Culhuacan, 1580–1600*. Albuquerque: University of New Mexico Press, 1986.

Collier, George A. *Fields of the Tzotzil: The Ecological Bases of Tradition in Highland Chiapas*. Austin: University of Texas Press, 1975.

Collins, Anne C. "The Maestros Cantores in Yucatan." In *Anthropology and History in Yucatan*, ed. Grant D. Jones. Austin: University of Texas Press, 1977.

Cook, Garrett. "Quichean Folk Theology and Southern Maya Supernaturalism." In *Symbol and Meaning Beyond the Closed Community: Essays in Mesoamerican Ideas*, ed. Gary H. Gossen. Albany, N.Y.: Institute for Mesoamerican Studies, 1986.

Cook, Sherburne F., and Woodrow Borah. "Indian Food Production and Consumption in Central Mexico Before and After the Conquest (1500–1650)." In *Essays in Population History: Mexico and California*, vol. 3, ed. Sherburne F. Cook and Woodrow Borah. Berkeley: University of California Press, 1979.

Cornbilt, Oscar. "Society and Mass Rebellion in Eighteenth-Century Peru and Bolivia." In *Latin American Affairs*, ed. Raymond Carr. St Anthony's Papers, no. 2. Oxford, 1970.

Coser, Lewis. *The Functions of Social Conflict*. New York: Free Press, 1956.

Culbert, T. Patrick. *The Ceramic History of the Central Highlands of Chiapas, Mexico*. Provo, Utah: New World Archaeological Foundation, Brigham Young University, 1965.

Desan, Suzanne. "Crowds, Community, and Ritual in the Work of E. P. Thompson and Natalie Davis." In *The New Cultural History*, ed. Lynn Hunt. Berkeley: University of California Press, 1989.

"Despoblación de Xiquipilas, Tacoasintepec, Las Pitas, Coneta, Suchiltepeque, Popocatepeque, Ecatepec, Bachajón, San Andrés, Ixtapilla y Sacualpa, 1733–1734." *Boletín del Archivo General de Chiapas* [Tuxtla Gutiérrez, Chiapas] 3 (1955): 26–66.

de Vos, Jan. *La Paz de Dios y del Rey: La conquista de la selva Lacandona, 1525–1821.* Chiapas: Colección Ceiba, 1980.

―――. *San Cristóbal: Ciudad colonial.* Mexico City: Instituto Nacional de Antropología e Historia, 1986.

―――. *El Sumidero.* Published by the author.

DeWalt, Billie R. "Changes in the Cargo Systems of Mesoamerica." *Anthropological Quarterly* 48 (1975): 87–105.

Díaz del Castillo, Bernal. *The True History of the Conquest of Mexico.* New York: Robert M. McBride and Company, 1927.

Dow, James. "Religion in the Organization of a Mexican Peasant Economy." In *Peasant Livelihood: Studies in Economic Anthropology and Cultural Ecology,* ed. Rhoda Halperin and James Dow. New York: St. Martin's, 1977.

Edmunson, Munro S. *Nativism, Syncretism, and Anthropological Science.* Middle American Research Institute Publication 19. New Orleans, 1960.

Espejo-Ponce Hunt, Marta. "The Processes of the Development of Yucatan, 1600–1700." In *The Provinces of Early Mexico*, ed. Ida Altman and James Lockhart. UCLA Latin American Center Publications. Los Angeles: The Center, 1976.

Eugenio Martínez, María Angeles. *La defensa de Tabasco, 1600–1717.* Seville: Escuela de Estudios Hispano-Americanos, 1971.

Farriss, Nancy M. "Landed Estates in Colonial Yucatan: Some Observations on Spanish Poverty and Indian Autonomy." Paper presented to the 43rd International Congress of Americanists, Vancouver, 1979.

―――. *Maya Society Under Colonial Rule: The Collective Enterprise of Survival.* Princeton, N.J.: Princeton University Press, 1984.

―――. "Nucleation versus Dispersal: Population Movements in Colonial Yucatan." *Hispanic American Historical Review* 58 (1978): 178–216.

―――. "Sacred Power in Early Colonial Yucatan." Paper presented to the American Anthropological Association, Washington, D.C., December 1982.

Favre, Henri. *Cambio y continuidad entre los Mayas de México.* Mexico City: Instituto Nacional Indigenista, 1973.

Feria, Fray Pedro de. "Relación que hace el obispo de Chiapas sobre la reincidencia en sus idolatrias de los indios de aquel país despues de treinta años de cristianos." In *Colección de documentos inéditos relativos a la iglesia de Chiapas*, vol. 2, ed. Francisco Orozco y Jiménez. San Cristóbal de las Casas, Mex.: Imprenta de la Sociedad Católica, 1911.

Fisher, John R. "Royalism, Regionalism, and Rebellion in Colonial Peru, 1808–1815." *Hispanic American Historical Review* 59 (1979): 232–257.

Flores Galindo, Alberto. "In Search of an Inca." In *Resistance, Rebellion, and Consciousness in the Andean Peasant World: 18th to 20th Centuries*, ed. Steve J. Stern. Madison: University of Wisconsin Press, 1987.

Flores Ruíz, Eduardo. "Rebelión de los Chiapas." In *Rebeliones de la época colonial*, ed. Maria Teresa Huerta and Patricia Palacios. Mexico City: Instituto Nacional de Antropología e Historia, 1976.

———. "Secuela parroquial de Chiapas: Un documento inédito." *Boletín del Archivo Historico Diocesano* 2 (1985): 2–119.

Foster, George M. "Cofradía and Compadrazgo in Spain and Spanish America." *Southeastern Journal of Anthropology* 9 (1953): 1–28.

———. "The Dyadic Contract: A Model of the Social Structure of a Mexican Peasant Village." *American Anthropologist* 63 (1961): 1173–1192.

———. "Peasant Society and the Image of Limited Good." *American Anthropologist* 67 (1965): 293–315.

Fox, John W. *Maya Postclassic State Formation: Segmentary Lineage Migration in Advancing Frontiers*. Cambridge: Cambridge University Press, 1987.

———. *Quiché Conquest: Centralism and Regionalism in Highland Guatemalan State Development*. Albuquerque: University of New Mexico Press, 1978.

Frank, Andre Gunder. *Capitalism and Underdevelopment in Latin America: Historical Studies of Chile and Brazil*. New York: Monthly Review Press, 1969.

Freeman, Susan Tax. "Notes from the Chiapas Project: Zinacantán, Summer 1959." In *Ethnographic Encounters in Southern Mesoamerica: Essays in Honor of Evon Zartman Vogt, Jr.*, ed. Victoria R. Bricker and Gary H. Gossen. Albany, N.Y.: Institute for Mesoamerican Studies, 1989.

Gage, Thomas. *Thomas Gage's Travels in the New World*. Ed. J. Eric S. Thompson. Norman: University of Oklahoma Press, 1969.

García de León, Antonio. *Resistencia y Utopía*. 2 vols. Mexico City: Ediciones Era, 1985.

Geertz, Clifford. *The Interpretation of Cultures*. New York: Basic Books, 1973.

Gerhard, Peter. *The Southeast Frontier of New Spain*. Princeton, N.J.: Princeton University Press, 1979.

Getino, Luis G. Alonso. *Origen del rosario y leyendas castellanas del siglo XIII sobre Santo Domingo de Guzmán*. Madrid: Tipografía de "El Santisima Rosario," 1925.

Gibson, Charles. *The Aztecs Under Spanish Rule*. Stanford, Calif.: Stanford University Press, 1964.

———. *Spain in America*. New York: Harper and Row, 1966.

Gluckman, Max. *Custom and Conflict in Africa*. Oxford: Oxford University Press, 1966.

Gosner, Kevin. "Uman Parish: Open, Corporate Communities in Eighteenth Century Yucatan." Paper presented to the Seventy-fifth Annual Meeting of the Association of American Geographers, Philadelphia, 1979.

Gossen, Gary H. "The Chamula Festival of Games: Native Macroanalysis and Social Commentary in a Maya Carnival." In *Symbol and Meaning Beyond the Closed Community: Essays in Mesoamerican Ideas*, ed. Gary H. Gossen. Albany, N.Y.: Institute for Mesoamerican Studies, 1986.

———, ed. *Symbol and Meaning Beyond the Closed Community: Essays in Mesoamerican Ideas*. Albany, N.Y.: Institute for Mesoamerican Studies, 1986.

Greenberg, James B. *Santiago's Sword: Chatino Peasant Religion and Economics*. Berkeley: University of California Press, 1981.

Greene, Graham. *Another Mexico*. New York: Viking Press, 1939.

Gruzinski, Serge. *Man-Gods in the Mexican Highlands: Indian Power and Colonial Society, 1520–1800*. Stanford, Calif.: Stanford University Press, 1989.

Guevara Sánchez, Arturo. *Los talleres líticos de Aquacatenango, Chiapas*. Colección Científica 95. Mexico City: Instituto de Antropología e História, 1981.

Halperin, Rhoda, and James Dow. *Peasant Livelihood: Studies in Economic Anthropology and Cultural Ecology*. New York: St. Martin's Press, 1977.

Hammond, Norman, ed. *Mesoamerican Archaeology: New Approaches*. Austin: University of Texas Press, 1974.

Hamnett, Brian R. *Roots of Insurgency: Mexican Regions, 1750–1824*. Cambridge: Cambridge University Press, 1986.

Haring, C. H. *The Spanish Empire in America*. New York: Harcourt, Brace, and World, 1947.

Harris, Marvin. *Patterns of Race in the Americas*. New York: W. W. Norton and Co., 1964.

Haskett, Robert S. "Indian Town Government in Colonial Cuernavaca: Persistence, Adaptation, and Change." *Hispanic American Historical Review* 67 (1987): 203–231.

Hill, Robert M., and John Monaghan. *Continuities in Highland Maya Social Organization: Ethnohistory in Sacapulas, Guatemala.* Philadelphia: University of Pennsylvania Press, 1987.

Homenaje a Pablo Martínez del Río. Mexico City: Instituto Nacional de Antropología e História, 1961.

Huerta, María Teresa, and Patricia Palacios, eds. *Rebeliones indígenas de la época colonial.* Mexico City: Instituto Nacional de Antropología e Historia, 1976.

Hunt, Eva. *The Transformation of the Hummingbird: Cultural Roots of a Zinacantecan Mythical Poem.* Ithaca, N.Y.: Cornell University Press, 1977.

Hunt, Eva, and June Nash. "Local and Territorial Units." In *Handbook of Middle American Indians*, vol. 6, ed. Robert Wachope. Austin: University of Texas Press, 1967.

Hunt, Lynn, ed. *The New Cultural History.* Berkeley: University of California Press, 1989.

Israel, J. I. "Mexico and the General Crisis of the Seventeenth Century." *Past and Present* 63 (1974): 33–57.

Jones, Grant D. *Maya Resistance to Spanish Rule: Time and History on a Colonial Frontier.* Albuquerque: University of New Mexico Press, 1989.

———, ed. *Anthropology and History in Yucatan.* Austin: University of Texas Press, 1977.

Katz, Friedrich, ed. *Riot, Rebellion, and Revolution: Rural Social Conflict in Mexico.* Princeton, N.J.: Princeton University Press, 1988.

Kaufman, Terence. "Archaeological and Linguistic Correlations in Mayaland and Associated Areas of Mesoamerica." *World Archaeology* 8 (1976): 101–118.

Keen, Benjamin. "Main Currents in United States Writings on Colonial Spanish America, 1884–1984." *Hispanic American Historical Review* 65 (1985): 657–682.

Klein, Herbert S. "Peasant Communities in Revolt: The Tzeltal Republic of 1712." *Pacific Historical Review* 35 (1966): 247–263.

Kohler, Ulrich. "Reflections on Zinacantan's Role in Aztec Trade with Soconusco." In *Mesoamerican Communication Routes and Cultural Contacts*, ed. Thomas A. Lee, Jr., and Carlos Navarrete. Provo, Utah: New World Archaeological Foundation, Brigham Young University, 1978.

LaFarge, Oliver. "Maya Ethnology: The Sequence of Cultures." In *The Maya and Their Neighbors*, ed. C. J. Hays, S. K. Lothrop, and H. L. Shapiro. New York: Appleton-Century, 1940.

Lafaye, Jacques. *Quetzalcóatl and Guadalupe: The Formation of Mexican National Consciousness, 1531–1813*. Chicago: University of Chicago Press, 1976.

Landa, Diego de. *Landa's* Relación de las cosas de Yucatán. Trans. and ed. Alfred M. Tozzer. Papers of the Peabody Museum, Harvard University, vol. 18. Cambridge, Mass., 1941.

Larson, Brooke, and Robert Wasserstrom. "Coerced Consumption in Colonial Bolivia and Guatemala." *Radical History Review* 27 (1983): 49–78.

Laughlin, Robert M., and Carol Karasik. *The People of the Bat: Mayan Tales and Dreams from Zinacantán*. Washington, D.C.: Smithsonian Institution Press, 1988.

Lee, Thomas A., Jr. "La arqueología de los Altos de Chiapas: Un estudio contextual." *Mesoamérica* 18 (1989): 257–294.

———. "Coapa, Chiapas: A Sixteenth Century Coxoh Maya Village on the Camino Real." In *Mesoamerican Archaeology: New Approaches*, ed. Norman Hammond. Austin: University of Texas Press, 1974.

———. "The Middle Grijalva Regional Chronology and Ceramic Relations: A Preliminary Report." In *Maya Archaeology and Ethnohistory*, ed. Norman Hammond and Gordon R. Willey. Austin: University of Texas Press, 1979.

Lee, Thomas A., Jr., and Carlos Navarrete, eds. *Mesoamerican Communication Routes and Cultural Contacts*. Provo, Utah: New World Archaeological Foundation, Brigham Young University, 1978.

Lessa, William A., and Evon Z. Vogt. *Reader in Comparative Religion: An Anthropological Approach*. New York: Harper and Row, 1965.

Lewis, Leslie. "In Mexico City's Shadow: Some Aspects of Economic Activity and Social Processes in Texcoco, 1570–1620." In *The Provinces of Early Mexico*, ed. Ida Altman and James Lockhart. UCLA Latin American Center Publications. Los Angeles: The Center, 1976.

López Austin, Alfredo. *Hombre-Dios: Religión y política en el mundo nahuatl*. Mexico City: Universidad Nacional Autónoma de México, 1973.

———. *The Human Body and Ideology: Concepts of the Ancient Nahuas*. 2 vols. Salt Lake City: University of Utah Press, 1988.

Lorenzo, José Luis. "Un buril de la cultura precerámica de Teopisca, Chiapas." In *Homenaje a Pablo Martínez del Río*. Mexico City: Instituto Nacional de Antropología e História, 1961.

Lovell, W. George. "Surviving Conquest: The Maya of Guatemala in Historical Perspective." *Latin American Research Review* 23 (1988): 25–57.

Lowe, Gareth W., and J. Alden Mason. "Archaeological Survey of the Chiapas Coast, Highlands, and Upper Grijalva Basin." In *Handbook of Middle American Indians*, vol. 2, ed. Robert Wauchope. Austin: University of Texas Press, 1965.

Lynch, John. *Spain Under the Habsburgs.* 2 vols. New York: Oxford University Press, 1964–69.

MacLeod, Murdo J. "Ethnic Relations and Indian Society in the Province of Guatemala, ca. 1620–ca. 1800." In *Spaniards and Indians in Southeastern Mesoamerica: Essays on the History of Ethnic Relations*, ed. Murdo J. MacLeod and Robert Wasserstrom. Lincoln: University of Nebraska Press, 1983.

————. "An Outline of Central American Colonial Demographics: Sources, Yields, and Possibilities." In *The Historical Demography of Highland Guatemala*, ed. Robert M. Carmack, John Early, and Christopher Lutz. Albany, N.Y.: Institute for Mesoamerican Studies, 1982.

————. "Papel social y económico de las cofradías indígenas de la colonia en Chiapas." *Mesoamérica* 5 (1983): 64–86.

————. *Spanish Central America: A Socioeconomic History, 1520–1720.* Berkeley: University of California Press, 1973.

MacLeod, Murdo J., and Robert Wasserstrom. *Spaniards and Indians in Southeastern Mesoamerica: Essays on the History of Ethnic Relations.* Lincoln: University of Nebraska Press, 1983.

McQuown, Norman A. "The Classification of the Maya Languages." *International Journal of American Linguistics* 22 (1956): 191–195.

————, ed. *Report on the 'Man-in-Nature' Project of the Department of Anthropology of the University of Chicago.* 3 vols. Chicago: Department of Anthropology, University of Chicago, 1959.

McQuown, Norman A., and Julian Pitt-Rivers, eds. *Ensayos de antropología en la zona central de Chiapas.* Mexico City: Instituto Nacional Indigenista, 1970.

McVickers, Donald. "The Mayanized Mexicans." *American Antiquity* 50 (1985): 82–101.

————. "Prehispanic Trade in Central Chiapas, Mexico." In *Mesoamerican Communication Routes and Cultural Contacts*, ed. Thomas A. Lee, Jr., and Carlos Navarrete. Provo, Utah: New World Archaeological Foundation, Brigham Young University, 1978.

Markman, Sidney David. *Architecture and Urbanization in Colonial Chiapas, Mexico.* Philadelphia: American Philosophical Society, 1984.

Martin, Cheryl English. *Rural Society in Colonial Morelos.* Albuquerque: University of New Mexico Press, 1985.

Martínez Peláez, Severo. "Los motines de indios en el período colonial guatemalteco." In *Ensayos de historia centroamericana*, German Romero Vargas et al. San José, Costa Rica: CEDAL, 1974.

————. *La sublevación de los zendales.* Tuxtla Gutiérrez, Mexico: Publicación Cultural de la Universidad Autónoma de Chiapas, 1977.

Metzger, Duane, and Gerald Williams. "Tenejapa Medicine, I: The Curer." In *Reader in Comparative Religion: An Anthropological Approach*, ed. William A. Lessa and Evon Z. Vogt. New York: Harper and Row, 1965.

Miller, Mary Ellen. *The Art of Mesoamerica from Olmec to Aztec.* London: Thames and Hudson, 1986.

Molina, Cristóbal. *War of the Castes: Indian Uprising in Chiapas, 1867–70.* Middle American Research Institute Publication 5, no. 8. New Orleans, 1934.

Morin, Claude. *Michoacán en la Nueva España del siglo XVIII: Crecimiento y desigualdad en una economía colonial.* Mexico City: Fondo de Cultura Económica, 1979.

Morley, Sylvanus G., and George W. Brainerd. *The Ancient Maya.* Revised by Robert J. Sharer. Stanford, Calif.: Stanford University Press, 1983.

Morner, Magnus. "The Spanish American Hacienda: A Survey of Recent Research and Debate." *Hispanic American Historical Review* 53 (1973): 183–214.

"Motín indígena de Ocozocoautla, 1722." *Boletín del Archivo General de Chiapas* [Tuxtla Gutiérrez, Chiapas] 2 (1953): 54–66.

Murra, John V. "Social Structural and Economic Themes in Andean Ethnohistory." *Anthropological Quarterly* 34 (1961): 47–59.

Nash, June. *In the Eyes of the Ancestors.* New Haven: Yale University Press, 1970.

Navarrete, Carlos. *The Chiapanec History and Culture.* Provo, Utah: New World Archaeological Foundation, Brigham Young University, 1966.

Newsom, Linda A. "Indian Population Patterns in Colonial Spanish America." *Latin American Research Review* 20 (1985): 41–74.

Nicholson, H. B. "Ethnohistory: Mesoamerica." *Handbook of Latin American Studies*, no. 23 (1961): 57–70.

Núñez de la Vega, Fray Francisco. *Constituciones diocesanas del obispado de Chiapa.* Ed. María del Carmen León Cázares and Mario Humberto Ruz. Mexico City: Universidad Nacional Autónoma de México, 1988.

Oakes, Maud. *The Two Crosses of Todos Santos: Survivals of Mayan Religious Ritual*. New York: Pantheon Books, 1951.

Ochiai, Kazuyasu. *Cuando los santos vienem marchando: Rituales públicos intercomunitarios Tzotziles*. San Cristóbal, Mex.: Centro de Estudios Indígenas, Universidad Autónoma de Chiapas, 1985.

O'Phelan Godoy, Scarlett. *Rebellions and Revolts in Eighteenth Century Peru and Upper Bolivia*. Cologne: Bohlau Verlag, 1985.

Ordóñez y Aguiar, Ramón. *Historia de la creación del Cielo y la Tierra, conforme al sistema de la gentilidad mexicana*. Mexico City, 1907.

Orellana, Sandra L. *The Tzutujil Mayas*. Norman: University of Oklahoma Press, 1984.

Orozco y Jiménez, Francisco, ed. *Colección de documentos inéditos relativos a la iglesia de Chiapas*, 2 vols. San Cristóbal de las Casas, Mex.: Imprenta de la Sociedad Católica, 1911.

Padden, R. C. *The Hummingbird and the Hawk: Conquest and Sovereignty in the Valley of Mexico, 1503–1541*. Columbus: Ohio State University Press, 1966.

Paniagua, Flavio Antonio, ed. *Documentos y datos para un diccionario etimológico, histórico, y geográfico de Chiapas*. Vol. 1. San Cristóbal de las Casas, México: Tipografía de Manuel Bermúdez R., 1908.

Payne, Alan Watters, ed. and trans. "Calendar and Nagualism of the Tzeltals." *Maya Society Quarterly* 2 (1932): 56–64.

Pineda, Vicente. *Historia de las sublevaciones indígenas habidas en el estado de Chiapas*. San Cristóbal de las Casas, Mex.: Tipografía de Gobierno, 1888.

Prem, Hans J. *Milpa y hacienda: Tenencia de la tierra indígena y española en la cuenca del Alto Atoyac, Pueblo, México, 1520–1650*. Wiesbaden, Ger.: Steiner, 1978.

Price, Barbara J. "The Burden of the Cargo: Ethnographical Models and Archaeological Inference." In *Mesoamerican Archaeology: New Approaches*, ed. Norman Hammond. Austin: University of Texas Press, 1974.

Proskouriakoff, Tatiana. *A Study of Classic Maya Sculpture*. Carnegie Institute of Washington, Publication 593. Washington, D.C., 1950.

Redfield, Robert. *Peasant Society and Culture*. Chicago: University of Chicago Press, 1969.

Reed, Nelson. *The Caste War of Yucatan*. Stanford, Calif.: Stanford University Press, 1964.

Remesal, Fray Antonio. *Historia general de las Indias occidentales y particular de la gobernación de Chiapas y Guatemala*. 2 vols. Guatemala City: Biblioteca Goathemala, 1932.

Reyes García, Luis. "Movimientos demográficos en la población indígena de Chiapas durante la época colonial." *La Palabra y el Hombre: Revista de la Universidad Veracruzana* 21 (1962): 25–48.

Ricard, Robert. *The Spiritual Conquest of Mexico*. Berkeley: University of California Press, 1966.

Robinson, David J. *Research Inventory of the Mexican Collection of Colonial Parish Registers*. Salt Lake City: University of Utah Press, 1980.

Robinson, David J., and Carolyn McGovern. "Population Change in the Yucatan, 1700–1820: Uman Parish in Its Regional Context." Paper presented to the Seventy-fifth Annual Meeting of the Association of American Geographers, Philadelphia, 1979.

Romero Vargas, German, Severo Martínez Peláez, Omar Jaen Suárez, Oscar R. Aquilar Bulgarelli, José Luís Vega Carballo, Vilma Lainez, and Victor Meza. *Ensayos de historia centroamericana*. San José, Costa Rica: CEDAL, 1974.

Roys, Ralph L. *Ritual of the Batabs*. Norman: University of Oklahoma Press, 1965.

———. *The Titles of Ebtun*. Carnegie Institute of Washington, Publication 505, Washington, D.C., 1939.

Rus, Jan. "Post-Colonial Society in the Chiapas Highlands and the 'Caste War' of 1869." In *Spaniards and Indians in Southern Mesoamerica*, ed. Murdo J. MacLeod and Robert Wasserstrom. Lincoln: University of Nebraska Press, 1983.

Rus, Jan, and Robert Wasserstrom. "Civil-Religious Hierarchies in Central Chiapas: A Critical Perspective." *American Ethnologist* 7 (1980): 466–478.

Ruz, Mario Humberto. *Copanaguastla en un espejo: Un pueblo tzeltal en el Virreinato*. San Cristóbal de las Casas, Mex.: Universidad Autónoma de Chiapas, Centro de Estudios Indígenas, 1985.

Sahagún, Fray Bernardino de. *Florentine Codex: General History of the Things of New Spain*. Ed. and trans. Arthur J. O. Anderson and Charles E. Dibble. 12 vols. Santa Fe: School of American Research and University of Utah, 1952–82.

Saint-Lu, André, "El poder colonial y la Iglesia frente a la sublevación de los indígenas zendales de Chiapas en 1712." *Mesomamérica* 11 (1986): 23–33.

Salamon, Frank. "Ancestor Cults and Resistance to the State in Arequipa, ca. 1748–1754." In *Resistance, Rebellion, and Consciousness in the Andean Peasant*

World: 18th to 20th Centuries, ed. Steve J. Stern. Madison: University of Wisconsin Press, 1987.

———. "Shamanism and Politics in Late-Colonial Ecuador." *American Ethnologist* 10 (1977): 413–428.

Salvucci, Richard J. *Textiles and Capitalism in Mexico.* Princeton, N.J.: Princeton University Press, 1987.

Schele, Linda, and David Freidel. *A Forest of Kings: The Untold Story of the Maya.* New York: Morrow, 1990.

Schele, Linda, and Mary Ellen Miller. *Blood of the Kings: Dynasty and Ritual in Maya Art.* Fort Worth, Tex.: Kimball Art Museum, 1986.

Scholes, France V., and Ralph L. Roys. *The Maya Chontal Indians of Acalan-Tixchel.* Carnegie Institute of Washington, Publication 560. Washington, D.C., 1948.

Scholes, France V., Ralph L. Roys, and Eleanor B. Adams. *Report and Census of the Indians of Cozumel.* Carnegie Institute of Washington, Publication 523. Washington, D.C., 1940.

Scott, James C. *The Moral Economy of the Peasant: Subsistence and Rebellion in Southeast Asia.* New Haven, Conn.: Yale University Press, 1976.

———. "Protest and Profanation: Agrarian Revolt and the Little Tradition." *Theory and Society* 4 (1): 1–38.

Sherman, William L. *Forced Labor in Sixteenth Century Central America.* Lincoln: University of Nebraska Press, 1979.

Simpson, Lesley Byrd. "Mexico's Forgotten Century." *Pacific Historical Review* 22 (1953): 113–121.

Smith, Carol A. "Local History in Global Context: Social and Economic Transitions in Western Guatemala." *Comparative Studies in Society and History* 26 (1984): 193–228.

Smith, Waldemar R. *The Fiesta System and Economic Change.* New York: Columbia University Press, 1977.

Solano, Francisco de. *Los Mayas del siglo XVIII.* Madrid: Ediciones Cultura Hispanica, 1974.

Spalding, Karen. "The Colonial Indian: Past and Future Research Perspectives." *Latin American Research Review* 7 (1972): 47–76.

———. "*Kurakas* and Commerce: A Chapter in the Evolution of Andean Society." *Hispanic American Historical Review* 53 (1973): 581–599.

———. "Social Climbers: Changing Patterns of Mobility Among the Indians of Colonial Peru." *Hispanic American Historical Review* 50 (1970): 645–664.

Stavig, Ward. "Ethnic Conflict, Moral Economy, and Population in Rural Cuzco on the Eve of the Thupa Amaro II Rebellion." *Hispanic American Historical Review* 68 (1988): 737–770.

Stein, Stanley, and Barbara Stein. *The Colonial Heritage of Latin America.* New York: Oxford University Press, 1970.

Stephens, John L. *Incidents of Travel in Central America, Chiapas, and Yucatan.* Vol. 2. New York: Dover Publications, 1969.

Stern, Steve J. "Approaches to the Study of Peasant Rebellions and Consciousness: The Implications of the Andean Experience." In *Resistance, Rebellion, and Consciousness in the Andean Peasant World: 18th to 20th Centuries,* ed. Steve J. Stern. Madison: University of Wisconsin Press, 1987.

———. "Feudalism, Capitalism, and the World-System in the Perspective of Latin America and the Caribbean." *American Historical Review* 93 (1988): 829–872.

———. "The Struggle for Solidarity: Class, Culture, and Community in Highland Indian America." *Radical History Review* 27 (1981): 461–491.

———, ed. *Resistance, Rebellion, and Consciousness in the Andean Peasant World: 18th to 20th Centuries.* Madison: University of Wisconsin Press, 1987.

"Sublevación de los indios tzendales, Año de 1713." *Boletín del Archivo General de la Nación* [Mexico City] 19 (1948): 503–535.

Super, John C. "The Agricultural Near North: Querétaro in the Seventeenth Century." In *The Provinces of Early Mexico,* ed. Ida Altman and James Lockhart. UCLA Latin American Center Publications. Los Angeles: The Center, 1976.

———. *Food, Conquest, and Colonization in Sixteenth Century Spanish America.* Albuquerque: University of New Mexico Press, 1988.

Szeminski, Jan. "Why Kill the Spaniard? New Perspectives on Andean Insurrectionary Ideology in the 18th Century." In *Resistance, Rebellion, and Consciousness in the Andean Peasant World: 18th to 20th Centuries,* ed. Steve J. Stern. Madison: University of Wisconsin Press, 1987.

Szewczyk, David M. "New Elements in the Society of Tlaxcala, 1519–1618." *In The Provinces of Early Mexico,* ed. Ida Altman and James Lockhart. UCLA Latin American Center Publications. Los Angeles: The Center, 1976.

Tax, Sol, ed. *Heritage of Conquest.* New York: Macmillan, 1952.

Taylor, William B. "Between Global Process and Local Knowledge: An Inquiry into Early Latin American Social History, 1500–1900." In *The World of Social History,* ed. Oliver Zunz. Chapel Hill: University of North Carolina Press, 1985.

————. *Drinking, Homicide and Rebellion in Colonial Mexican Villages*. Stanford: Stanford University Press, 1979.

————. "La Indiada: Peasant Uprisings in Central Mexico and Oaxaca, 1700–1810." Paper presented to the Symposium Interdisciplinaire sur les Insurrections Indiennes Paysannes. 42d International Congress of Americanists. Paris, 1976.

————. "Landed Society in New Spain: A View from the South." *Hispanic American Historical Review* 54 (1974): 387–413.

————. *Landlord and Peasant in Colonial Oaxaca*. Stanford, Calif.: Stanford University Press, 1972.

————. "Town and Country in the Valley of Oaxaca, 1750–1812." In *The Provinces of Early Mexico*, ed. Ida Altman and James Lockhart. UCLA Latin American Center Publications. Los Angeles: The Center, 1976.

————. "The Virgin of Guadalupe in New Spain: An Inquiry Into the Social History of Marian Devotion." *American Ethnologist* 14 (1987): 9–33.

TePaske, John, and Herbert Klein. "The Seventeenth Century Crisis in New Spain: Myth or Reality?" *Past and Present* 90 (1981): 116–135.

Thompson, Donald. *Maya Paganism and Christianity: A History of the Fusion of Two Religions*. Middle American Research Institute, Publication 19. New Orleans: The Institute, 1954.

Thompson, E. P. "The Moral Economy of the English Crowd in the Eighteenth Century." *Past and Present* 50 (1971): 76–136.

Thompson, J. Eric S. *Maya History and Religion*. Norman: University of Oklahoma Press, 1970.

Tilly, Charles. *Big Structures, Large Processes, Huge Comparisons*. New York: Russell Sage Foundation, 1984.

Torre Villar, Ernesto de la. "Algunos aspectos de las cofradías y la propriedad territorial en Michoacán." *Jahrbuch für Geschichte von Staat, Wirtschaft, und Gesellschaft LateinoAmerikas* 4 (1967): 410–439.

Trens, Manuel B. *Historia de Chiapas*. Mexico City: "La Impresora," 1942.

Tutino, John M. *From Insurrection to Revolution in Mexico: Social Bases of Agrarian Violence, 1750–1940*. Princeton, N.J.: Princeton University Press, 1986.

————. "Peasant Rebellion at the Isthmus of Tehuantepec: A Socio-Historical Perspective." Paper presented to the Symposium Interdisciplinaire sur les Insurrections Indiennes Paysannes. 42d International Congress of Americanists. Paris, 1976.

————. "Provincial Spaniards, Indian Towns, and Haciendas: Interrelated Agrarian Sectors in the Valleys of Mexico and Toluca, 1750–1810." In *Provinces of Early Mexico*, ed. Ida Altman and James Lockhart. UCLA Latin American Center Publications. Los Angeles: The Center, 1976.

Van Oss, Adriaan C. *Catholic Colonialism: A Parish History of Guatemala, 1524–1821*. Cambridge: Cambridge University Press, 1986.

Van Young, Eric. *Hacienda and Market in Eighteenth Century Mexico: The Rural Economy of the Guadalajara Region, 1675–1820*. Berkeley: University of California Press, 1981.

————. "Mexican Rural History Since Chevalier: The Historiography of the Colonial Hacienda." *Latin American Research Review* 18 (1983): 5–61.

————. "Millennium on the Northern Marches: The Mad Messiah of Durango and Popular Rebellion in Mexico, 1800–1815." *Comparative Studies in Society and History* 28 (1986): 385–413.

Velasco Toro, José M. "Perspectiva histórica." In *Los Zoques de Chiapas*, ed. Alfonso Villa Rojas et al. Mexico City: Instituto Nacional Indigenista, 1975.

Villa Rojas, Alfonso. "Kinship and Nagualism in a Tzeltal Community, Southeastern Mexico." *American Anthropologist* 49 (1947): 578–587.

Villa Rojas, Alfonso, José M. Velasco Toro, Félix Báez-Jorge, Francisco Córdoba, and Norman Dwight Thomas, eds. *Los Zoques de Chiapas*. Mexico City: Instituto Nacional Indigenista, 1975.

Vogt, Evon Z. *Bibliography of the Harvard Chiapas Project: The First Twenty Years, 1957–1977*. Cambridge, Mass.: Harvard University Press, 1978.

————. "Chiapas Highlands." In *Handbook of Middle American Indians*, vol. 7, ed. Robert Wauchope. Austin: University of Texas Press, 1969.

————. *Zinacantan: A Maya Community in the Highlands of Chiapas*. Cambridge, Mass.: Belknap Press/Harvard University Press, 1969.

————. *The Zinacantecos of Mexico: A Modern Maya Way of Life*. New York: Holt, Rinehart and Winston, 1970.

Wallace, Anthony F. C. *Culture and Personality*. New York: Random House, 1970.

————. "Revitalization Movements." *American Anthropologist* 58 (1956): 264–281.

Wallerstein, Immanuel. *The Modern World-System II: Mercantilism and the Consolidation of the European World Economy, 1600–1750*. New York: Academic Press, 1980.

Warren, Kay B. *The Symbols of Subordination: Indian Identity in a Guatemalan Town*. Austin: University of Texas Press, 1989.

Wasserstrom, Robert. *Class and Society in Central Chiapas*. Berkeley: University of California Press, 1983.

―――. "Colonial Society in Chiapas, 1680–1790." Paper presented to the 43rd International Congress of Americanists, Vancouver, 1979.

―――. "Ethnic Violence and Indigenous Protest: The Tzeltal (Maya) Rebellion of 1712." *Journal of Latin American Studies* 12 (1980): 1–19.

―――. "Land and Labour in Central Chiapas: A Regional Analysis." *Development and Change* 8 (1977): 441–463.

―――. "Population Growth and Economic Development in Chiapas." *Human Ecology* 6 (1978): 127–143.

Watson, Rodney C. "La dinámica espacial de los cambios de población en un pueblo colonial mexicano." *Mesoamérica* 5 (1983): 87–108.

Wauchope, Robert, ed. *Handbook of Middle American Indians*. Vol. 6. Austin: University of Texas Press, 1967.

Willey, Gordon R. *An Introduction to American Archaeology*. Vol. 1. Englewood Cliffs, N.J.: Prentice-Hall, 1966.

Wolf, Eric R. "Closed Corporate Peasant Communities in Mesoamerica and Java." *Southwestern Journal of Anthropology* 13 (1957): 1–18.

―――. "Distinguished Lecture: Facing Power—Old Insights, New Questions." *American Anthropologist* 92 (1990): 586–596.

―――. *Europe and the People Without History*. Berkeley: University of California Press, 1982.

―――. *Peasants*. Englewood Cliffs, N.J.: Prentice-Hall, 1966.

―――. *Peasant Wars of the Twentieth Century*. New York: Harper and Row, 1969.

―――. *Sons of the Shaking Earth*. Chicago: University of Chicago Press, 1959.

―――. "Types of Latin-American Peasantry: A Preliminary Discussion." *American Anthropologist* 57 (1955): 1–27.

―――. "The Vicissitudes of the Closed Corporate Peasant Community." *American Ethnologist* 13 (1986): 325–329.

Wortman, Miles L. *Government and Society in Central America, 1680–1840*. New York: Columbia University Press, 1982.

Ximénez, Fray Francisco. *Historia de la provincia de San Vicente de Chiapa y Guatemala*. 3 vols. Guatemala City: Biblioteca Goathemala, 1929–31.

―――. *Historia de la provincia de San Vicente de Chiapa y Guatemala*. Books 5–7. Guatemala City: Biblioteca Goathemala, 1971.

Zunz, Oliver, ed. *The World of Social History*. Chapel Hill: University of North Carolina Press, 1985.

INDEX

ABOUT THE AUTHOR

KEVIN GOSNER is an assistant professor of history at the University of Arizona. He studied history and anthropology at the University of Pennsylvania, where he received his doctorate in 1984. His interests include historical demography, ethnohistory, culture theory, and colonial labor history. He has conducted research in archives in Guatemala, Spain, and Mexico, and he is currently working on a study of shamanism and ethnic consciousness in sixteenth- and seventeenth-century Central America.